The Big Walk

A 73-year-old man's incredible
3,200km solo walk around England

David Wilson
SECOND EDITION

http://www.fast-print.net/bookshop

THE BIG WALK:
A 73-Year-Old Man's Incredible 3,200km Solo Walk Around England

A catalogue record for this book is available from the British Library

ISBN 978-178456-313-4

First published 2012 by Indepenpress

Second edition published 2016 by
FASTPRINT PUBLISHING
Peterborough, England.

Written in memory of a wonderful woman –
my mother

Contents

I have only been able to include a few images within this book.
To view the complete set of images taken throughout the walk, please visit: *www.davesbigwalk.com/photo-gallery*

Author's comments regarding the 'Notes of Interest'

These sections have been written with the intention of providing information about the places visited along the walk and to connect them to the past in a lively and engaging manner, rather than resorting to a dry history lesson. The material has been gathered from various sources and researched to the best of my ability, but despite good intentions, I cannot guarantee the authenticity of all the material.

Most ancient historical data, although academically researched, is likely to be heavily biased or distorted in one way or another. For example, the recording of key events of the day will always be slanted in favour of the victor of the battle, never the vanquished. Important happenings will typically be expressed from the point of view of the ruler or occupier, never the subjugated. You only have to imagine how history would have viewed the events of WWI and WWII had the Allies been defeated!

In relating what I see as being of potential interest to the reader, I always bore brevity in mind, in attempting to keep the total work to a proportionate size. This was also uppermost in my thoughts when transcribing the 140 diary extracts.

Preface

Before you join me on my walk around England, I think it appropriate to provide a brief insight into my brush with prostate cancer. It was at the age of seventy, while still running my boat tour business, that I was diagnosed with the disease. The revelation came as quite a shock as I had experienced no symptoms whatsoever; it was only coercion from my kids that had induced me to visit my GP. After undergoing a complete medical check-up I returned to Brighton Marina later that day to continue running my business. I was convinced that I would hear nothing more on the matter so I was quite surprised when, days later, a message came through from my doctor requesting my presence to discuss the results from the blood tests.

I had always thought I was one of the healthiest senior citizens on the planet; I was soon to be sadly disillusioned. At the surgery my doctor explained that all results were normal apart from the PSA blood test, which had recorded a high level of 26.6. He then quickly assured me that the PSA reading was just an indicator and that the result might be due to some other abnormality, so he arranged for me to have a biopsy.

Days later, I was given the news that the biopsy had shown positive and I suddenly realised that I had prostate cancer. Although the news came as a bit of a shock, I soon became resigned to the situation and began to regard it with a philosophical frame of mind. A bone scan was then arranged to detect 'hot spots'. It would indicate whether cancer cells from the prostate gland had spread elsewhere in the body. Fortunately none were found. My oncologist recommended a course of radiation and hormone therapy. The treatment weakened me for some time and for a while I had problems with my water works. If the urge to pass water came over me it was crucial to empty my bladder almost immediately. This resulted in a few embarrassing occasions that I'll not enlarge upon!

During a series of quarterly, then half-yearly blood tests, my PSA level was seen to drop satisfactorily. I had returned to the gym and was starting to slowly regain my strength. I had also put myself on a walking programme as, apart from swimming, it was the least stressful way to get fit.

About two years from the start of my treatment I had my last consultation with my oncologist. My PSA level had dropped to 0.22, a huge difference from that first reading of 26.6! My oncologist said that it seemed they might have caught the disease in its early stage. He then ended the interview by saying that he didn't want to see me again. Sweet words! I felt I was walking on air as I left his consulting room.

It was about two to three weeks later that the idea came to me of the possibility of walking around England. I'd do this to raise awareness of the importance of early diagnosis and at the same time raise funds for Cancer Research.

But there was more to it than this. I viewed this venture as a challenge to myself; to test not just my physical ability but also the psychological pressures that would undoubtedly arise during the walk.

During the UK winter of 2008/9 I went over to New Zealand and Australia to visit friends and family, but also to develop walking strength and stamina. The last few weeks in Australia I intensified my walking programme by walking about 450 kilometres in 20 days, sometimes accompanied by my daughter, Carolyn. Rob, my son, has offered to be the support driver on my walk around England, a great sacrifice from him for which I was extremely grateful.

I returned to England mid-February and immediately continued with gym and road work. By mid-March a website had been created for me and donations in support of my walk started to roll in.

I was now committed; there was no going back.

Introduction

This book I hope will appeal to a wide variety of readers.

To begin with, it might bring encouragement to those individuals affected in some way by prostate cancer or other forms of the disease, that there can be a good life after treatment.

For those wishing to take up walking seriously, a section at the back of the book is aimed at achieving fitness through a walking activity programme entitled 'Step by Step'; a formula based on my own walking experiences. It may also provide inspiration to the many senior citizens among us who would like to improve their fitness levels and, in consequence, their lifestyles.

When walking long distance, thoughts slide surreptitiously into the conscious mind, some to be mulled over while others come and go in rapid succession. Occasionally a random thought will find its way into a day's diary entry. Memories of the distant past emerge; events and days long forgotten; the war years, a father killed, a mother's grief, evacuation, impoverished times; a parallel journey that becomes sporadically interwoven within the diary pages.

The book will enlighten many on various geographical aspects of England; for instance I didn't know that there was a town in England called Boston; I was unsure where places like Lowestoft, Maryport or Chelmsford were located on the map; I'd never heard of places with intriguing names like Garstang or Seahouses and I used to think that Skegness was in Scotland!

Those of you interested in history will gather significant information in the 'Notes of Interest' sections about the town or area where we stop after each day's walk.

So why not accompany me through some of the most beautiful parts of England.

You'll become aware of the remoteness of the northern Pennines and reflect upon the dramatic and rugged coastlines of Northumberland and those breathtaking coastal stretches seen from the South West Coast Path, where you might also ponder over the geological wonders of the Jurassic coast.

Follow me along sealed pathways that were once the route of steam trains from days gone by; routes that will take you through parts of the Tarka Trail, the lovely Wirral Way or through Yorkshire's scenic countryside and spectacular coastal region.

We'll follow dykes made by a self-imposed king of the sixth century and discover places like the charismatic Welsh border village of Tintern and the evocative and dramatic ruins of Tintern Abbey in the River Wye valley. While turning the pages you might visualise the grandeur of the Lake District or imagine the tranquillity of walking along a towpath on a Lancashire canal...and maybe glimpse a scene or two from yesteryear!

So wander with me around this land and I'll lead you along delightful coastal paths and through charming villages but also through unsightly industrial regions and uninspiring urban areas. We'll walk through verdant, canopied byways and leafy, overgrown bridle tracks; paths unfrequented and places that busy lives have long forgotten.

Discover an England that many have never seen.

This is the first of four map sections of my Around England Walk

This section took 6½ weeks to walk a distance of around 555 pedometer miles (893km). I walked through six counties before reaching **Humberside** in preparation for crossing the **Humber Bridge**.

As early as **Hastings** a nagging knee pain begins to worry me. After leaving **Deal** I get into trouble in uncharted territory. A strange coincidental happening unfolds on my walk from **Tilbury** to **Brentwood**. A confrontation with an angry bull occurs while walking to **Southwold**. Friends from Brighton pay a visit at **Well-next-the-Sea**. I kill an injured badger on the **Peddars Way**. A wrong track is taken near **Tetney Lock** and we enjoy a celebratory evening in **Great Limber**.

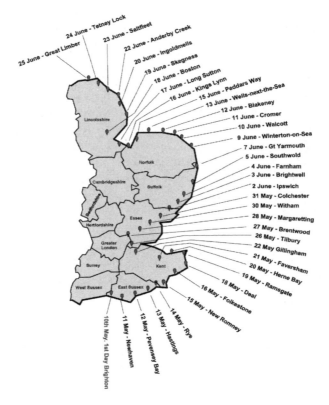

CHAPTER 1
SUSSEX

The first of May came tumbling in. I was already weeks behind schedule as I had fully intended to start the walk around mid-April, but I hadn't anticipated the amount of things that had to be done.

I had purchased a camper van to be used as my support vehicle; it was, I thought, the only sensible way at my age to maintain an intensive regime and still have some degree of comfort after a hard day's walk. My son Robert had already agreed to be my support driver over the period and was about to arrive from Melbourne, Australia. The van had yet to be sign-written. I also needed more tuition on how to update my daily diary entries and progress maps on the website.

There were still a number of items to purchase such as an extra pair of walking boots , a GPS navigator for the van, more bedding, an additional Calor gas container, a TV, a microwave oven, books, sun cream, a couple of chairs and a table for outside use and so on. I had yet to buy survey maps of Kent, which was to be my first county on this anti-clockwise walk around England.

My new start date was to be Sunday, 10th May and I was determined not to let anything stand in my way from being ready by that deadline.

Throughout my preparation I was beset by a number of negative thoughts. Was I really able to accomplish this venture that I was about to embark upon? Was I kidding myself? Was I being naive in thinking that a man of 73 years could possibly maintain a walking schedule of about 16 miles (25.6km) a day, six days a week for months on end? I knew I was fit enough with regard to stamina as I had tested myself on a number of occasions, but I just couldn't rid myself of the thought that some physical injury might force me to abort the walk. Things like a sprained ankle, twisted knee, groin injury or even torn hamstrings; legs can be so vulnerable, especially when you're walking on 'em six to seven hours a day. Worse still, will it happen in the very early stages of the walk? My overriding worry was the thought of letting my supporters down.

There was a battle going on inside my head; I had to maintain a positive outlook, but it was difficult keeping those worrying thoughts at bay.

Thoughts

If you have ever done any lengthy lone walking you will be aware that as you walk, you think. It is an involuntary and unrestrained natural process and you cannot escape from it. As you walk, thoughts emerge into your conscious mind to be analysed or mulled over. Sometimes negative thoughts arise and when they do you must eliminate them and focus instead on positive thinking, for then the physical being will respond in kind. Thoughts have a powerful influence over the body; they are subtle forces that constantly shape our lives according to the way we think. Think old and you'll age faster than someone who possesses a young mind. Dwell constantly on personal ailments and sickness will surely find you. Convince yourself that you are healthy and a state of well-being will often preside over you. Some lines in an old song by Bing Crosby and the Andrew Sisters simplify the message:

You've got to accentuate the positive, and eliminate the negative.

And *...don't mess with Mr In-between!*

SUNDAY, 10TH MAY 2009
BRIGHTON – NEWHAVEN

At last! The day has arrived!

It is Sunday, the weather is great and my supporters are eager and ready to accompany me on my first leg to Newhaven. We all meet up at Brighton pier at the pre-arranged time of 10.30am where an *Argus* newspaper photographer is waiting to take a photo session of the event. As soon as the photographer has finished with us we start heading eastward toward the marina. Once there, others begin to join us as we stroll through to the boat yard and onto the under-cliff walk. The sun is shining and the waters of the English Channel are a sparkling blue as we make our way to the Saltdean Lido.

It's up onto the clifftop and then onto the coastal road that takes us through Peacehaven before returning to the clifftop track again. This coastal path takes us in leisurely style along the cliffs toward our destination and we finally descend onto Fort Road in the port town of Newhaven. It's now 2.45pm.

We have completed the 9½-mile walk from Brighton Pier in 4¼ hours. A brief mental calculation makes me realise that I will need to vastly improve that hourly walking rate if I want to complete my trek around England before the onset of winter.

Once on the Fort Road we make our way to the Ark hotel. It's a session of carefree drinking, eating and laughter that my support group are interested in and I am keen to be a part of it; yet at the back of my mind lurks the thought of the task that lies ahead of me. Nevertheless, I enjoy this celebratory time with my friends and although it's meant to be a sort of valedictory occasion, I can't help the feeling that it's something of an anti-climax as unfortunately, I still have unfinished business to attend to back in Brighton. I need to go to A to Z's in Worthing to collect my hi-vis sign-written jacket; it is an essential piece of clothing and I cannot leave without it.

Today we walked: 15.5km (9.62 miles).

Notes of Interest: Newhaven

The expansive south coast of England has throughout the ages always attracted invaders due to its handy proximity to Europe; especially the area around Seaford Bay and Newhaven. There is evidence of defensive activity in the region that probably dates back to the Bronze Age when a large enclosed fort was built on the clifftop.

During their occupation the Romans also built fortifications on the site and since that period defence structures have been rebuilt over the years culminating in the Newhaven Fort structure that's there today.

War has primarily been the reason for improving coastal defence buildings, but in peacetime these structures were often left to the ravages of nature.

The current Newhaven fortification was built around the mid-nineteenth century and was the largest defence structure ever built in the county at that time. Since WWII, the building has again suffered years of neglect, but in recent times has been restored to become a popular visitor attraction.

MONDAY, 11TH MAY 2009
SEAFORD

A chilly south-easterly wind is blowing as we leave the Sheepcote Valley Caravan Club site. Its 9am and we are about to drive to Worthing to pick up my hi-vis jacket from Mark of A to Z Signs. Afterwards, we'll tie up a few other loose ends before heading back to the marina.

Its late afternoon now and we head east once more, but this time I'm enjoying the luxury of being a passenger in our campervan support vehicle driven by my son Rob.

We drive to the nearest available caravan camping site, which is located on the outskirts of Seaford and in the evening we walk along the beach front to Seaford town. After buying a couple of grocery items, we wander through this attractive seaside resort, but the wind is pretty cold and it's not long before we return to the warmth of the camper van.

No real walking is done today, but tomorrow Rob will drive me back to The Ark Hotel in Newhaven to start my day's walk; and tomorrow is when the serious stuff begins!

Notes of Interest: Seaford

During the Middle Ages, Seaford was regarded as a major port in southern England.

From the beginning of the thirteenth century, Seaford became a limb of the Cinque Ports Confederation, probably linked to the Cinque Port of Hastings.

During the fourteenth and fifteenth centuries, the town was burned down several times by pirating invaders; but its main enemy was coastal sedimentation caused by longshore drift for this was slowly but inexorably silting up its harbour.

It is said that in later years the people of Seaford became known as 'shags' due to their practice of looting ships wrecked in the bay and exploiting their rights under the 'flotsam and jetsam' laws of the day.

However, history suggests that this practice was common in many coastal areas around England. People would cause ships to run aground by placing fake harbour lights on the cliffs or lighting fires on the beach. It is likely that the Seaford Shags did the same by luring vessels into unsafe waters, then stripping the helpless vessels of their cargoes.

In the nineteenth century, Seaford was to become popular as a seaside resort when the railway system arrived, for with its new rail link to Lewes and London it made the town more accessible to the public.

TUESDAY, 12TH MAY 2009
NEWHAVEN – SEAFORD – PEVENSEY BAY

It's almost 7.30am and we leave Seaford campsite after having a good breakfast. Rob drives me back to The Ark Hotel in Newhaven where we had finished the walk on Sunday. The wind is a strong easterly – just my luck! Over the last few weeks the weather has been coming from the prevailing south-west direction, which is why I chose to go eastward and have the wind at my back along the south coast but today it'll be against me.

I begin my journey from Newhaven at 8.15am with a strange mixture of emotions. There is the exhilarating thought that I am finally on my way; a sense of freedom, but also one of apprehension about what might lie ahead.

The wind is freshening all the time often making it difficult to make headway. Soon I am once again walking along Seaford's attractive seafront listening to the surf pounding on the pebbled beach. At the eastern end I find a track that allows me to divert inland over the Cuckmere River toward the A259. I meet up with Rob at the Seven Sisters parking site where I stop to stretch and eat before tackling the steep Cuckmere Hill.

The hill is busy with traffic and I notice that there is very little room for a walker on this uphill stretch. I see what look like walking tracks in the fields on the right side of the road so I climb over a fence and walk upward over the grassy hills. The strong south-easterly wind makes this uphill climb both strenuous and tiring.

Once at the top I rejoin the A259 and continue along the winding road to East Dean where more hills await me. I pass the turn-off to

Beachy Head and soon find myself on a path that leads me down to Eastbourne's elegant seafront.

I battle against the strong headwind as I walk along the attractive promenade towards Eastbourne Pier; yet despite the wind there are many people strolling along the promenade enjoying the midday sunshine. Unfortunately, I haven't the time to stop and look around this lovely city with its Regency architecture and genteel atmosphere.

I reluctantly make my way out of Eastbourne via King William Parade and walk along Pevensey Bay Road and onto the coast road that leads to Pevensey Bay. Although I still have the headwind to contend with, I am enjoying the walk, listening to the pounding surf that spills from the turbulent foam-flecked sea and having the green undulating fields of the Sussex countryside displayed around me.

I finally arrive at the Pevensey campsite. I look at my watch; it's 3.35pm. I have been walking for almost seven hours. We soon have the van connected to the power and I immediately take off my walking gear and shoes and go for a shower. Once back in the van, I find I am just too weary to fire up my laptop; instead I sit back to watch TV and soon begin to nod off.

The extreme tiredness and aching legs are obviously due to walking a long, unaccustomed distance, much of it on hilly terrain while battling against strong headwinds all day; yet this is just the start! I try to stifle doubts that are once again beginning to creep inside my head.

Today's pedometer reading: 27.5km (17 miles).

Notes of Interest: Pevensey Bay

There on a ridge of land, which juts out onto marshland, sits the small village of Pevensey. Up until around the thirteenth century there might easily have been access to the sea through the marshes. However, over the centuries longshore drift has gradually cut the area off from the sea and the result is the lovely Pevensey Marshes we see today.

Since before the fifth century, Pevensey and much of the south and east coasts of Britain had been under frequent attack from marauding barbarian tribes like the Saxons and Vikings. To counter these attacks the Romans built a total of eleven forts between Essex and the Isle of Wight. This coastal defence area became known as the Saxon Shore.

When the Roman army departed from Britain, the land was even more vulnerable to attack. The Romanised native Britons (Romano-Britons) now found it difficult to defend their island from the aggressive tribes arriving from across the channel.

The Saxons were the most dominant and by the end of the fifth century they began to colonise much of the south coast. This part of the conquered coastal area became known as the Kingdom of the South Saxons; part of that area we know as Sussex.

It is believed that male Britons, if caught would often be shipped back to the enemy's homeland to become slaves, while those that had managed to evade capture fled north into the forests or westward toward Wales, or even by boat taking them over the channel to what is now Brittany.

WEDNESDAY, 13TH MAY 2009
PEVENSEY BAY – HASTINGS

It's almost 10am as we leave the Pevensey caravan site and 10.20am before I start walking from yesterday's pick-up point. I am very disappointed and angry with myself for having started at such a late hour. I planned to be up very early each morning and be walking by 7.00am at the latest, yet here I was on only the third day out and already almost four hours behind my start schedule. Things will have to change.

It's quite misty today and there's a dampness in the air as I make my way eastwards, but thankfully the easterly wind has disappeared.

I walk on the coastal road, then on the Herbrand Walk with its lovely uninterrupted view of the English Channel, while all around me lay the green fields and hedgerows of the Sussex countryside.

As I pass the Cooden Beach golf course, distant memories of my early teenage years return for, oddly enough, my first real job after leaving school was as a catering assistant at the Cooden Beach Golf Club.

Clear images begin to emerge despite having lain dormant in my consciousness for nearly 60 years and I feel compelled to visit the place once more.

An odd feeling comes over me as I approach the club premises for the exterior of the building, apart from one extension, appears to have remained as I remembered it all those years ago. I leave the place with thoughts of those years still lingering in my mind.

As a 15 year old at Cooden Beach Golf Club - I'm the one in the middle!

Soon I am walking along the lovely seafront promenade of Hastings. As it was with Eastbourne, I would again have to pass through this historical town without stopping to experience its unique charm and character.

Some will say it is sacrilege to visit Hastings and not take what is reputed to be the UK's steepest funicular railway to view the surrounding areas. From the West Hill section there are spectacular vantage points with stunning views stretching across to Beachy Head and out over one of the busiest sea lanes in the world, the English Channel. But I have a daily schedule to maintain and so continue my walk along Carlisle and Marine Parade and out of the town.

I have walked about 11½ miles at this stage and I am a little worried as the outer side of my left knee is hurting. I'm wondering how it's going to affect my ability to make the huge climb up the hill to connect with the clifftop coastal walk. A fog descends as I trudge up the long hill, becoming denser the higher I climb. It is now almost 4.30pm. I would have finished this walk at least three hours ago if I hadn't started so late this morning!

11

The walk takes me through to Fairlight Road where I think Rob will be waiting for me, but after walking another mile or so I finally realise he is waiting on a different road from the one I am walking on. However, thanks to that modern invention, the mobile phone, we eventually meet up.

Once at the Fairlight Wood caravan camping site I enjoy having a great shower and a good pasta meal before we settle down to watch a video. I am tired, but apart from the ache in my left knee I feel okay. But the knee is beginning to worry me.

Today pedometer reading: 25.9km (16.1miles).

Notes of Interest: Hastings

I suppose the most famous historic event connected to this town is the Battle of Hastings. The conflict was created when Edward the Confessor supposedly handed the throne of England over to the Saxon leader, Harold, while on his deathbed.

The trouble arose because Duke William of Normandy believed that he should be the legitimate heir to the throne because it had been promised to him by Edward, the English King (who had strong ties with the Normans). William also claimed that Harold Godwinson had, in the past, also made a sacred oath to relinquish his rights to the throne in his (William's) favour.

Duke William duly declared his succession to the throne of the now dead King, but his proclamation was ignored by Harold and his court. Angry at this injustice, William prepared for war and with his invasion fleet he crossed the English Channel.

It is said that Harold, who had recently returned from a victorious conflict at the Battle of Stamford Bridge, had little time to savour his victory as a message reporting William's landing on the south coast arrived soon after.

Harold began marching his war-weary veterans from York to Sussex, and you can bet there would have been a lot of grumbling among the ranks! But he recruited fresh troops from the surrounding populace on the way and arrived in Sussex on October 13th, where he immediately prepared to face the Normans. (It is thought by many historians that if Harold had waited two or three days to rest his men and gather further manpower from the area, the outcome might well have been different.)

The Battle of Hastings began the very next day on October 14th, 1066. It was to become probably one of the greatest historical events in English history.

The Saxons established their base at Caldbec Hill; then under Harold's command they took up a defensive position on a high ridge known as Senlac. It was probably the only clear ground in what would have been a heavily forested area.

The Norman infantry and the cavalry found it difficult breaking through the Saxon lines due possibly to the enclosed space of the battle field. It was only after a tactical error by the Saxons that the situation changed in William's favour. By late afternoon the now weakened Saxon lines began wavering under continued Norman attacks

Then, the most famous arrow in English history was released from a Norman archer's bow, and (it is said) pierced King Harold in the eye. From then on the invaders took control and the now leaderless Saxons had no choice but to turn and run from the conflict. It is thought that a Norman who had hacked Harold's lifeless body with his sword during the final onslaught was severely reprimanded by William.

Duke William of Normandy had won the day and his victory would dramatically create a major political and cultural change in the island's future and he would become known as William the Conqueror.

The body of King Harold was eventually buried in Waltham Abbey in Essex.

THURSDAY, 14TH MAY 2009
HASTINGS – RYE

The alarm goes off at 5.30am. I lie there feeling pretty wretched. Suddenly it's 6.30am – boy, that hour has flown by! I struggle out of bed to face a grey and overcast day. I still feel tired – it's as if I haven't slept at all. I go to the ablutions to shower hoping it will enliven me. The shower block is some distance away so it gives me a chance to test out my left knee. I return to the van feeling refreshed but miserable because the pain in the knee is still there.

I have no desire to start walking and after breakfast I get down to updating my diary on Word Document. I tell myself it is essential to do this but another voice says, "Hey, you can do that at the end of the day; you're using this as an excuse to keep from walking".

I ignore the voice and carry on completing my updates and answering emails.

During lunch, self-discipline kicks in and I mentally prepare myself to walk on to Rye. It's about a 9-mile walk from yesterday's finishing point so it will be a good distance to really test my knee. I return to the Fairlight Road and I'm soon walking along the Pett Level coastal path. I keep to a slower rhythmic pace and begin to enjoy the Sussex countryside and the lovely coastal views despite the heavy grey skies. From Cliff End I make my way through to Winchelsea Beach and then turn toward the A259 that will take me on to Rye.

As I walk this section I begin worrying unduly about my left knee. The pain was bearable, but my concern is that it might get worse.

The dilemma precipitates some rash thoughts: what if it got so bad that I have to give up? Cripes, I'm only a few miles out of Hastings! I'm dreading the thought of having to abort at this early stage. I imagine a few heads nodding sagely back at the marina with comments like, "I could have told him he was barmy taking it on". Or hear condescending remarks on my return such as, "Never mind Dave, you gave it your best shot".

If the worst came to the worst I'd just have to swallow my pride and face the music. But then I say to myself, "Look, if the pain gets so bad that you can't carry on, you can always get a room somewhere back in Hastings and just make out to everyone that you are still walking around England. Then, after 5 months you could suddenly appear, say in Worthing, and just walk the 12-odd miles back to Brighton. It would be a doddle Dave!"

I was being facetious, but even fanciful thoughts can keep your mind off a worrisome knee ache so I play with the idea a little longer.

If I was holed up in a room somewhere I wouldn't be able to get out much just in case anybody recognised me so I'd have to get all my meals delivered. Now if you're sitting around doing nothing apart from making fictitious entries into your web diary or emailing friends telling them how lovely the Yorkshire countryside is or extolling the beauty of Northumberland's coastline, you're eventually going to get bored stiff and the main thing on your mind will be food.

I began thinking about what I would look like after five months of eating lots of food (and possibly consuming too many beers) without any physical activity whatsoever. I reckon I'd be fat, or in reality, at least quite porky!

Now if it's known that you've been walking around England averaging around 16-odd miles a day for a period of five months, the last thing onlookers will expect to see is some overweight character waddling along the promenade towards Brighton Pier. Such a scenario would, I suppose, arouse suspicion among many and then it would only be a matter of time before my fraudulent act would be finally exposed to everyone.

The thought reminded me of the sad story of Donald Crowhurst, the lone yachtsman, who, on the 31st October, 1968, set sail in the *Sunday Times* Golden Globe non-stop, around-the-world yacht race.

In past years, global circumnavigation had seen the demise of many an accomplished seaman and even today it's a feat regarded by many as the yachtsman's Holy Grail.

Donald Crowhurst was to embark upon this formidable venture, although neither he nor his boat was equipped to seriously take on this challenge. However, big prize money and other lucrative returns plus celebrity status were the things that probably drove Donald Crowhurst on. The trophy was to go to the first man to circumnavigate the earth non-stop using the old tea-clipper route that runs south through the Atlantic, around the Cape of Good Hope, east across the Indian and Pacific Oceans, skirting Australia and New Zealand then heading eastward to round Cape Horn before the final northerly stretch back to the home port in Britain; a distance of some 25,000 miles or more.

The Golden Globe trophy would go to the first single-handed yachtsman home, but the prize money of £5,000 would go to the yachtsman whose vessel recorded the fastest time. Each vessel was allowed to embark on any date within a certain period and start at any chosen port on the British mainland but was to finish at the same port without touching land or receiving physical assistance at sea.

Once into the race, Donald Crowhurst soon realised that he and his vessel, the Teignmouth Electron, were not capable of competing in such a venture; but he thought of the ignominy of returning home without even crossing the Atlantic. Not only was his pride at stake, but he was also unwilling to risk losing his house that had been heavily mortgaged on the venture; so Crowhurst decided to sever

15

all contact with his support team as a desperate scheme began to formulate in his brain.

It had dawned on him that it would be possible to just drift around the Atlantic while at the same time falsifying log entries about his progress. His plan was to 'reappear' toward the last stage of the voyage claiming to have rounded the Horn and be on his way home. So for the next few months he cleverly devised on-going fictitious locations and recording them into his log book. (With modern satellite tracking systems, such erroneous information would simply not be credible today.)

As time went on, he began to get increasingly worried about the likelihood of exposure, so as he began his homeward run his plans took a different turn; his idea was now to come in last. That way he would still receive the accolade attributed to all who completed the voyage but not be subject to official scrutiny of his log book.

Unfortunately fate was to conspire against him. He received news from his excited wife who pointed out that he stood every chance of winning because although Robin Knox-Johnston was already nearing his home port, he had started months earlier, so in his present position he (Crowhurst) could certainly win the £5,000 prize for the fastest boat.

But what really concerned the man was the news that Nigel Tetley's Trimaran had capsized and that he, Crowhurst, and Robin Knox-Johnston were now the only competitors left in the race. This meant that whatever time it took to reach his home port he would still be deemed to have come second, therefore his log entries would automatically be scrutinised by a group of marine experts headed by an already suspicious Sir Francis Chichester.

Donald Crowhurst realised that all the lies he had told about his 'incredible exploits' would finally be exposed to a waiting world bringing public humiliation for himself and upon the family he loved so instead of heading toward home, he turned away and continued to wander around in the South Atlantic.

This poor man, alone on his yacht, in a sea that offered no solace, began to behave irrationally. Some of his final log entries on July 1st, 1969 gave an indication of his growing introspective and deranged mental condition: 'It is finished,' he had scrawled – before repeating the words to emphasise the finality of it all; and then, as the irrevocable comprehension dawned, he wrote: 'It is the end of my game. The truth has been revealed'.

It is assumed that Donald Crowhurst must have jumped or had accidentally fallen into the sea soon after those entries had been logged. His abandoned yacht was found some time later by a Royal Mail ship, 600 miles off the Azores. His body was never found. Less than three years later, Nigel Tetley, the last competitor to capitulate when his vessel capsized in the Atlantic while on his homeward run, was found hanging from a tree. The coroner's inquest recorded the death as suicide.

Although the pain in my knee persists it is no worse than when I started out, so that is a good sign I think.

It is almost 4pm before I meet up with Rob in Rye. We return to the Fairlight Wood Caravan Club Site where I have a wonderfully refreshing shower and then nurse my knee for the rest of the day. Robert cooks up another pasta meal this evening. It is very tasty; it needs to be because I am going to have to get used to them over the next few months!

Today's pedometer reading: 15.62km (9.7 miles).

Notes of Interest: Rye

It is possible that the name of Rye derives from the Norman French 'La Rie' meaning a bank, although this is no more than an assumption.

It was once a harbour that provided safe anchorage for vessels plying the south coast, probably as early as 500 AD; but continual longshore drift was a problem. Then violent storms, particularly those of 1250 and 1287, silted up the harbour completely cutting Rye off from the sea.

It is likely that during this period the town would have been subject to raids from foreign pirates, especially the French, for the town was sacked and burnt on a number of occasions.

By the end of the seventeenth century, smuggling had become widespread throughout the southern coastal regions. It was eventually made a criminal offence and those found guilty would be subsequently hanged. Such was the fate of the Hawkhurst Gang who, it is said, spent time in the Mermaid Inn in Rye.

In 1928 the town experienced its worst disaster in history when the 17-man crew on board the Mary Stanford Lifeboat perished when the vessel sank in the harbour.

An old folk-song that relates to this unfortunate incident is known as 'The Mary Stanford of Rye'.

FRI, 15TH MAY 2009
RYE – NEW ROMNEY

We leave Fairlight Wood fairly late as we needed to catch up on washing clothes etc. The caravan site is well run and is set in idyllic surroundings.

Rain begins to fall as I start walking from the outskirts of Rye, but the south-west wind is nudging me along so I am more than happy. An hour into the walk and the initial concerns about my left knee begin to dissipate along with the showers for the pain is now no more than a dull ache.

As I walk, my thoughts return to the Cooden Beach Golf Club that I'd passed just two days before. It's funny how we can evoke memories from the distant past yet sometimes find it difficult to recall a name or a place that had been made known to us only weeks or even days before.

Almost six decades had slid into the past since my employment at the golf club, yet I still remembered that the Club Secretary was a Major Weekes. I also recalled the name of the working manager of the club; his name was Vic and his wife was named Pat. There was also a young blonde lady, a waitress, who was also called Pat.

I can also recall the person who was to lead me on the road to Merchant Navy life; his name was Mr Kincaid, a regular patron of the club and a keen golfer. He was a marine architect and ship designer for The Blue Funnel Line owned by Alfred Holt & Company, one of the finest cargo shipping lines of its time with most of the fleet sailing out of Liverpool.

I got to know Mr Kincaid reasonably well and one day he asked me to consider going to a sea training school for a career in the Merchant Navy and offered to arrange it for me. I said I'd give it some thought and that I'd also need to ask my mother, but I think my mind was already made up to go. Within weeks I was on the train heading for the Outward Bound Sea Training School at Aberdovy on the Welsh coast.

I am welcomed into the county of Kent by a sign on the side of the road; hopefully this sign would be one of many! I walk on through the lovely Kent countryside, finally ending the day's walk 2½ miles this side of New Romney. Rob drives us down the road where we find a lovely small campsite called Romney Farm and we are settled in by 3.30pm.

Today's pedometer reading: 18.9km (11.73 miles).

Notes of Interest: New Romney

The earliest record of Romney dates from 791 AD. The name was once thought to derive from the word 'Roman-ney', but more up-to-date evidence suggests that the word might come from the Saxon term meaning marsh water.

It is said that by 1140 New Romney was a flourishing port and its harbour extended along the north bank of the River Rother.

In 1250 a severe storm hit the Channel. As with other areas along this part of the coast, New Romney harbour was vulnerable to the effects from longshore drift. The area was later hit by another severe storm creating huge islands of shingle and mud that devastated the harbour. The prosperity of the village gradually declined after this period.

The Marshes, however, date back thousands of years. There are signs of human activity dating back to the Bronze Age and it is also thought that the Romans made their first landfall in the area. It's been the fierce storms and continual longshore drift over the years that have gradually added to the marshland area creating a natural habitat of world renown; a naturalist's wonderland populated with rare flora and fauna.

Wool smuggling during the sixteenth century was rife throughout the coastal regions, but excise taxes were being imposed on other goods and by the end of the seventeenth century the smuggling of these commodities became more profitable. But by the mid-1800s excise men had become more proactive in the prevention of smuggling, so much so that the illicit trade almost became a thing of the past.

A local legend has it that in the late 1700s a young girl was found hanged in a room of the New Inn. If you happen to stay there, be careful, for it is said that her ghostly form still walks around the rooms and passageways.

CHAPTER 2
KENT

SATURDAY, 16TH MAY 2009
NEW ROMNEY – FOLKESTONE

It is 5.20am when I finally clamber out of bed. Just a single glance out of the window is enough to tell me that the morning's weather is lousy. Rob is up and already has the kettle on. I feel very weary, but I force myself out of bed and get dressed. After a breakfast of toast and marmalade washed down with two cups of black coffee I feel better and ready to tackle another day.

We leave Romney Farm campsite at 7am. Rob drives me back at the place where I had stopped my walk yesterday. With my wet weather gear on I reluctantly step out of the van to start the day's walk. It is cold and a steady drizzle is falling from leaden skies. The only good thing is the wind; being a south-westerly it's at my back helping me travel at a faster pace.

I walk the 2½ miles to New Romney then travel through St Mary's Bay to get onto the delightful coastal path route past the Dymchurch Rotunda and into the pretty town of Hythe. Half an hour later and with the sun breaking out, I start out on the five-mile walk to Folkestone by way of the delightful Princes Parade seafront route. I thoroughly enjoy the sparkling sea views to my right as I walk past Sandgate and into Folkestone.

During this stretch of the walk my thoughts, for some obscure reason, turn to my mother.

I begin thinking about all the hardships she must have gone through during the early dark years of the war. She loved us kids; we all knew that, so it must have been so much harder for her to have parted with us, especially after the recent loss of her husband. Her troubles started with our father being killed in France a month or so before the Dunkirk evacuation and then being coerced by government bulletins and by persistently persuasive elderly parents to evacuate her children out of the London area. So Mick, my elder brother and I were sent away to Norfolk and my two sisters sent up north, whilst my mother was evacuated elsewhere with Carol, a babe in arms. Although we all would have loved nothing more than being back home, I think as kids we adapted more easily to our situation for we had been led to believe that within a few weeks we'd all be back home again. Our mother would have known different and because of that I reckon she would have suffered the most.

I was 4½ going into Dr Barnado's and aged 11 when I came back home. Then, before reaching 16, I was at the sea school in Aberdovey, Wales, preparing for a life in the merchant navy; only to migrate to New Zealand about 18 months later. So, apart from being at home for the first four years of my life, I would spend no more than a further five years back home with my mother.

And yet those years after evacuation were the happiest of years for me and my siblings. We were impoverished in the way of material things but were replenished ten-fold with the love and care our mother gave us. There was no such thing as pocket money nor was there any electricity or running hot water in the house, but we were never without a warm bed, good food and the constant feeling of security.

Being in receipt of nothing more than a war widow's pension (paltry in those days) meant that our mother had to go out to work much of the time, but when she was home her total preoccupation was her concern for her family.

I remember feeling sorry for some of the kids we played with for apart from Moe, my mate who had a good home life, many of the others were at best neglected, at worst physically and verbally abused by a drunken father or mother.

I suppose it's because our mother is no longer with us that I have this sense of guilt about being away from her for most of my adult life. I always had the feeling that she wanted more time with me. It was as if, being the only sibling hardly ever at home, she could never fully make amends (as she could with the others) for sending me away during the war years.

I often recall my mother's plea before I left to go to New Zealand. She was standing on the platform at Euston Station as the train to Glasgow steamed and hissed nearby. She was holding me tightly and through her tears she pleaded for me to promise to return home after my two-year contract was over.

I knew that as soon as my train had pulled out my mother would have to travel back alone on the tube to Victoria station and then on the train back to Brighton. I also knew that she would be feeling very miserable, so I promised her that I would definitely return at the end of the contract... but it was a promise I never kept.

With my mother in New Zealand

The dull pain in the side of my left knee is still there, but I try to ignore it.

I catch up with Rob who has parked in the grounds of a local pub where the Arsenal/Man U game is being shown live. We settle in to watch the game and naturally, to be polite, we both have a beer or two! After the game we book into another lovely caravan camping ground: the Black Horse Farm Club Site near Folkestone.

Today's pedometer reading: 26.70km (16.44 miles).

Notes of Interest: Folkestone

It is said that sometime in the late seventh century this settlement acquired the name of Folcanstan and that it refers to Folca's stone. Others believe that it derives from a Celtic name, and that the suffix of 'ton', might suggest 'place'. It wasn't until the mid-nineteenth century that the modern name of Folkestone was officially accepted.

As with many coastal hamlets Folkestone was constantly under attack from warring, overseas tribes even during the Roman occupation.

The town began to flourish from 1843 with the coming of the railway. It would be the rail system with its relatively cheap mode of travel that would eventually be the catalyst for the tourist boom. The town became popular as a seaside resort but the development of other resorts was to bring about its decline as a holiday destination.

SUNDAY, 17TH MAY 2009

Today is a rest day. Good! It's a lousy day out there anyway.

Rob and I have a bit of a lie-in before getting up to look around the pleasant surroundings of the Black Horse Farm Caravan Club Site. It's a lovely landscaped area with a pleasant rural outlook over surrounding farmland. Set in the heart of farming country in the Kentish village of Densole on the Downs, it has an excellent system of walking paths from which many local attractions in and around the area can be explored with ease.

We discover that many of our neighbouring campers were en route to the continent. What with the great facilities available on site and a good TV and mobile broadband signal, it is an ideal place to spend our time on this rest day. However, tomorrow is going to be an early start and hopefully we'll make it up to Deal.

I say 'hopefully' because yesterday I started having further doubts about my ability to complete this huge trek around England. I know I need to walk an average daily distance in excess of 16 miles or 26 kilometres (similar to yesterday's walk) and that I would need to persevere with that regime six days a week for five long months – that's if I want to finish the walk before the onset of winter!

You need to have a positive frame of mind to take on something like this at my age – or be mad; but my confidence was dented last night while we were in the pub. We were about to leave after the Arsenal/Manchester United game was over when this smartly dressed middle-aged guy offered to buy us a drink. I still had my sign-written hi-vis jacket on as it always increases the chance of receiving donations to our charity, so the man was aware of our project.

Both Rob and I had already consumed two pints of ale each and we were not really interested in staying on, but we thought he probably just needed someone to talk to so we let him order a half pint of shandy for each of us.

He introduced himself as Pete somebody-or-other and told us he was a retired teacher. His first comment was a query about my age. He then wanted to know the distance I had walked since starting and when I told him, he said that I was lucky to have got that far, considering my age.

Now I must mention right here that I was in high spirits before this guy began airing his views about my walk; after all, I had achieved good mileage for the day despite the knee and we had been looking forward to having the following day off. When I happened to mention my sore knee he said, "There you go! And that's just the start! At your age your joints just won't stand up to it". He then went on to say, "I'd be surprised if you make it up to the Thames".

What with my aching knee this was the last damn thing I needed; some negative twit trying to shoot me down before I'd hardly got started. I began thinking again about that room back in Hastings!

He then asked me how much money was I expecting to raise.

The eternal optimist replied, "Around £50,000".

He retorted with, "You *are* an optimist aren't you!" He made the word 'optimist' sound like the word 'idiot'.

Pete then pointed out that if I was a celebrity half my age and was walking half the distance I could easily raise £50,000 or even more, but that I'd be lucky to raise £5,000 let alone £50,000. I was getting more despondent by the minute.

Rob and I exchanged glances; mine was saying, "Let's get the hell out of here".

He then said, "Did you get checked out by your doctor?"

I said, "No...Why?"

He retorted with, "Well, your doctor would have probably advised you against doing the walk".

When I asked him why my doctor would do this he said, "Because at your age, even if you complete the walk your joints would've taken such punishment that you'll be crippled within a year or two".

I told him that what he was saying was bullshit and he answered with something like, "Well, I'm only saying what I know...take it or leave it!"

He continued with more discouraging remarks when I stopped him in his tracks, thanked him for the shandies and quickly left the premises with Rob close behind.

I had gone into the pub feeling great and emerged feeling bloody depressed. I suddenly felt weary and deflated; a feeling that was still with me as we rolled into the Black Horse Farm Caravan Club Site. It was only when I was under the shower that I came to the realisation that my weariness was due to the negative thoughts that lingered on from the discussion in the pub; that the lethargy was not a physical problem but a mental one.

This evening, as I relaxed with Rob, we came to the conclusion that the reason Pessimistic Pete was drinking on his own was probably because no other person wanted to be bombarded with a load of his negative, cynical crap. I then began wondering about his past teaching career and whether there had been a higher than average suicide rate among his students!

Today I've shrugged off Pete's comments altogether and am determined to make it up to Deal tomorrow. My only regret was not getting Pessimistic Pete's email address or phone number so that if I did manage to complete the walk, I could contact him and remind him of our meeting. I would then take delight in requesting that he takes his negative remarks and shoves them up where the sun never shines!

Notes of Interest: Outward Bound Sea School, Aberdovey

(The correct spelling of the anglicised word, Aberdovey, is Aberdyfi and Towyn to the Welsh is spelt Tywyn.)

During the Second World War, emerging data showed that when a ship was torpedoed and sunk, the first to succumb were usually the young, fit sailors. Surprisingly, the older seaman appeared to have a better ability to survive. The explanation for this was that the younger sailors had less life experience; in grim situations they were more likely to yield to their fate sooner than their older compatriots.

These statistics prompted a Gordonstoun School headmaster, Curt Hahn, and a father of one of his pupils, Lawrence Holt, to set up a Training School for young merchant seamen and in 1941 the Outward Bound Sea School in Aberdyfi was born.

The venture was mostly funded by Alfred Holt & Company, owners of The Blue Funnel Line, affectionately known to so many as Blue Flu. It was one of the largest and finest fleet of cargo ships of its time and was heavily involved in the precarious business of shipping goods throughout the war years. The company was well aware of the hazards to young seamen serving on the Atlantic convoys and understood that the need for a crash course in survival training was a matter of some urgency.

Apart from teaching survival skills, the Outward Bound Sea Training School presented young people with challenges and showed that by facing difficult and daunting situations, youngsters can realise their true abilities under pressure.

Nowadays, the school provides a far greater variety of programmes enabling young people to explore their own full potential. Activities such as sailing, canoeing, improvised rafting, rock climbing, gorge walking, mountain expeditions are all part of the school's curriculum. Young people are escorted on supervised expeditions all over North West Wales, including Snowdonia, Cader Idris, the Rheinogs and Arans.

The camping trips can be from overnight to a few days. On the longer courses, the young people will venture out into the unknown with just a rucksack and for the duration of their course, will rely solely on their initiative to complete their objective.

The Outward Bound Training School and their staff fervently believe that everyone, despite their background and academic ability, should be given the chance to realise their full potential.

MONDAY, 18TH MAY 2009
FOLKESTONE – DEAL

We return to Folkestone harbour to resume my walk. It is 7.50am and the weather is fine with a brisk wind blowing from the south-west. This morning I notice that the pain in my left knee is not so bad; hopefully, yesterday's rest might just have done the trick.

On the way towards the coastal heritage walk I meet a guy walking his dog. He walks with me over the clifftop route to Dover. It's an exhilarating walk and although the heavy surf is some distance below, the distinct smell of the briny is in the air. We come down from the White Cliffs, past a stunning view of Shakespeare Beach, and into the West Docks. The distance we have covered is far greater than the road miles due to the winding clifftop tracks. It was great having someone to chat with, but on the outskirts of Dover my walking companion made his farewell and began heading back home with his dog.

I meet up with Rob at a nearby parking lot and after going through the usual leg stretching routine and ploughing through two large bowls of porridge, I prepare myself for the big climb up onto the cliffs of Dover. I arrange to meet with Rob in Deal. It is about 8½ miles away by road, but I know that the big climb and the continuously winding clifftop track will result in a greater distance being covered. Luckily I have a strong south-west wind at my back nudging me along which is a bonus.

The pain in my left knee has all but disappeared and I thoroughly enjoy the walk with the lovely undulating countryside and panoramic views overlooking the English Channel.

While walking this section, my thoughts venture once again to the Outward Bound Sea School at Aberdovey.

I remember feeling a bit nervous as the train pulled into the small railway station. As I alighted from the train, I was conscious of the cold wintery wind and of the lone man in dark blue track pants and polo neck jersey waiting on the platform to meet me. He was one of the instructors and was waiting to take me and two other boys, who had been on the train, to the school. Unfortunately, his name eludes me.

It was late afternoon and after being supplied with our kit we were escorted to our Watch Houses. I was introduced to some other boys who were to be my companions over the next thirty days. I can't remember exactly how many boys were in my hut, possibly 12 to 16; but I do know that our watch was called Beattie Watch. Ours was one of a number of watches, each one named after a famous naval commander, such as Nelson, Drake, Raleigh and so on.

Dinner time was signalled by the strike of bells. I was pretty eager to get to the canteen, for although my mother had packed me a load of sandwiches and fruit, I had consumed the lot before the train had got through the Sussex countryside.

I have almost reached Deal when I see Rob in the distance coming along the seafront to meet me. The previous evening he had been ranting on a bit too much about my left knee; obviously, he had let Pessimistic Pete get to him. I reckon that he was half-hoping it would get worse so that I'd abort the walk allowing him to get back to Australia; with this in mind I thought I'd do something to keep his hopes alive. I start limping quite badly. By the time Rob reaches me I've exaggerated the limp to such an extent that I'm actually dragging one foot along the ground like a zombie in a horror film. I wonder why he is laughing as he approaches me until he explains that he had spotted me earlier from the roof of the van and saw me walking briskly along with no sign of a limp.

"Anyway," he says, "you're dragging the wrong leg."

He's right! Why didn't I think of that? Ah well, thought I'd give it a try.

We look around the lovely town of Deal before driving to the new campsite where we settle in before 7pm.

Today's pedometer reading: 31.06km (19.3 miles).

Notes of Interest: Deal

The village of Deal is apparently mentioned in the Domesday Book, but its history stretches back much further in time according to archaeological evidence.

It's probable that Julius Caesar made landfall on the Deal-Walmer coast in 54 BC. Nelson honoured the town with a visit and Captain James Cook, it is thought, made Deal his first landfall in 1771 after returning from his maiden voyage to Australia.

Because of the constant threat of invasion three castles were built in the area by Henry VIII They were Sandown, Deal and Walmer castles. Both Deal and Walmer castles are, I believe, still open to the public.

By the end of the thirteenth century Deal had grown from a small fishing hamlet to a reasonably active port due to its sheltered coast that made it a timely haven for sailing ships approaching the coast. Many of these ships would be anchored off in great numbers and the victualling of these wind-bound vessels brought business and prosperity to the area.

Deal, like many coastal towns, became known for its rampant smuggling activity. In January 1784, the smuggling prompted Prime Minister William Pitt to send soldiers to Deal. He had chosen a time when stormy sea conditions would keep the entire smugglers' fleet of vessels ashore, allowing Pitt's men the easy task of setting them all alight. It would, however, be no more than a temporary set-back as smuggling had become almost a way of life and a necessity in supplementing a meagre income for these people.

It is said that many of the houses in the seafront conservation area have the remains of old tunnels and secret hiding places used by the smugglers.

The Rattling Cat in Walmer was a good example. Legend has it that the name of this old coaching inn originates from the fact that the proprietors of the past kept cats with pieces of bone attached to their collars. The only time the cats would become active was when strangers were approaching; the rattling of their collars would alert everyone that excise men might be in the area. The Rattling Cat is now a grade II listed residential building.

TUESDAY, 19TH MAY 2009
DEAL – RAMSGATE

We have a few things to do before I can start on today's walk. Then, after a good old English breakfast fry-up, we set off to Deal pier where I am dropped off to begin my trek northward. The time is 8.37am.

The weather is fine, the wind is from the south and the pain in my left knee has disappeared altogether. What more could any man ask for? Well, a few things really, but why push my luck!

I take the coastal route as shown on the Explorer map. With my friendly southerly wind nudging me along I feel confident of making good progress today despite starting late. The views along this part of the coast are quite spectacular and I am enjoying the walk past the golf course and along Sandwich Bay. I am expecting to see a turn-off to my left that will take me to the town of Sandwich so I am on the look-out for it.

As I walk, my attention is divided between the panoramic coastal views to my right while trying to keep an eye out for the turn-off on my left. A little later I see the river mouth up ahead of me and realise I have overshot the turn-off by at least 2 miles. I could kick myself! I begin heading back along the coastal path, but in my frustration I decide to cut across what appeared to be grassy terrain and head for the large chemical plant that I can see in the distance for I know that the plant is sited somewhere in the vicinity of Sandwich. I would normally have checked my map before doing this, but on this particular occasion I had forgotten to take the damn thing with me. It is to become mistake number 1.

The terrain is pretty flat with a sort of marsh grass growing everywhere and although it is firm underfoot, the thick clumpy growth hampers my progress.

After about a mile or so I come upon a narrow but fairly deep ditch. It has wet mud at the bottom so I guess it is a tributary of the nearby river. I jump over the span easily enough and carry on. It isn't long before I come across another. This one is a bit wider, but by walking along the edge to where the gap narrowed somewhat, I am able once more to leap over.

The shin-high marsh grass conceals these tributaries to such an extent that I don't see them until I am almost on top of them. I'm guessing that there might be other ditches to cross but that they might be as easily traversed as the previous ones, and so with a positive outlook I continue on. This was mistake number 2.

I make slow progress through the marsh grass and about 20 minutes later I come upon another ditch. This one is far too wide to leap across. I have no option but to slither down the bank and wade through the soft glistening wet mud. My feet sink about six inches or so into the mire as I feared they would, but I was soon clambering up the bank on the other side.

I walk on with mud caked up to my lower shins feeling tired, depressed and a little worried. I soon come across another wide tributary. I stare at the depressing sight below me and for a moment I consider turning back, but in the hope that this might be the last barrier to get through I once again lower myself into the mud. As I do so, I think to myself: this might be mistake number 3!

Two or three squelchy steps take me to the other side where I grab clumps of the coarse marsh grass to help me scramble up to the top of the bank. I walk on (trudge would be a better word) for another ten minutes or so when suddenly, I am confronted with yet another ditch that is even wider than the previous two. Once again I repeat the process of getting to the other side; then, muddy and bedraggled, angry and tired, I continue on my weary way.

The chemical plant seems much closer now and I can see in the distance what appears to be higher ground ahead. I trudge on for another ten minutes or so and then, to my relief, I begin climbing up on firm ground and can see what looks like the town of Sandwich almost concealed behind trees some distance ahead.

I now check my watch and instantly realise I am about an hour behind schedule and know that Rob will be getting worried. I decide to give him a call and reach for my phone, but it's not there. It's no longer in the front pouch of my waist pack. I just can't believe it! I stop in my tracks and desperately search all pockets but to no avail; gathering my thoughts I quickly realise that it must have dropped out as I was clambering out of one of the ditches. The phone is absolutely essential. Without it there was no way I could make contact with my son. I hadn't memorised his new number, nor had I written it down anywhere, so I was now faced with a problem. I knew that he would be parked up somewhere between Sandwich and Reigate for that is what had been pre-arranged. I now wanted him to return to Sandwich as I was desperately in need of a clean-up and a breather, but without the phone there was no way of making contact. There was only one course of action to take; it was to retrace my steps and hopefully find the phone somewhere along the way.

I began to wearily walk back to the last tributary I had crossed. It was relatively easy to find the exact point of crossing as all I had to do was walk along the bank until I came across footprints in the mud at the bottom edges of the ditch. After all, there would surely only be one set of footprints as no other mad sod on the planet would have been stupid enough to have ventured into this area. I was sure that the phone hadn't dropped into the mud, for I had been upright while walking through it; hopefully it had dropped out while clambering up a bank because then I was often in a crouched position.

I soon found the place where I had actually crossed and I look around carefully, but there was no sign of the phone on or near the bank. I go down into the soft, wet mire, looking all around before climbing wearily up onto the other side. After another ground search

I trudge on for about 15 minutes toward the next ditch. I slither carefully down the steep side looking everywhere as I do so. As my feet sink into the mud, I turn for one last look at the bank I had just slid down and instantly spot the mobile phone quite close to my head, lodged high and dry on a clump of grass near the top of the bank. I immediately grab it and place it in a different pocket in my waist pouch, one that can be zipped closed and after casting my eyes up to the skies in silent thanks to providence, I quickly climb back up the bank.

Once on the bank I immediately phone Rob for I had several 'missed call' messages on the screen. As I expected, he was pretty worried about my absence over such a long period, especially being unable to raise me over the phone. I give him a brief run-down of my situation and my proximity to Sandwich, and then begin walking once again in the direction of the town while Rob drives back there to meet me.

A short while later I'm crossing over a little bridge and then strolling alongside the river into Sandwich.

I should have been quite despondent being muddy and dishevelled, and running well behind schedule as I should have been approaching Ramsgate by now; but at this moment, resting on a bench by the river while eating an ice cream seems like two stops from paradise.

I make another phone call to Rob telling him precisely where I am resulting in his arrival five minutes or so later. He is obviously as glad to see me as I am to see him. I stretch aching legs, have a pasta meal, then continue walking toward Ramsgate. I manage to get to Pegwell on the outskirts of Ramsgate, but here I have to stop as I am now thoroughly exhausted. I had aimed to get to Margate later today as we had already booked into a campsite there, but I am too tired to continue walking and it's getting late.

Today's pedometer reading: 20.81km (12.92 miles).

Note: the above distance is incorrect as I had turned off the pedometer in Sandwich and forgot to turn it back on again. At a guess I reckon I walked about 17 miles, though it felt like 50!

Notes of Interest: Ramsgate

It is thought that the earliest reference to Ramsgate was the name 'Hraefn's gate', meaning cliff gap. In the 1200s it became known as

'*Ramsgate*' *or* '*Remmesgate*'. *Over a century later around the mid-1300s the area became Ramesgate. The settlement then was little more than a fishing hamlet with small farm holdings dotted around the area. Then in 1483 Ramsgate became part of the Cinque Ports Confederation due to its association with Sandwich.*

I believe that Ramsgate Harbour had the unique distinction of being the only Royal Harbour in the United Kingdom.

Around the turn of the seventeenth century Ramsgate became a busy garrison town. Its proximity to mainland Europe made it an important embarkation site for troops bound for foreign shores. The harbour has seen tens of thousands of troops embarking and disembarking throughout the years during periods of conflict.

It is thought that many of the six to seven hundred vessels involved in the operation used Ramsgate harbour in order to rescue our forces stranded on the beaches of Dunkirk.

One of the Dunkirk 'little ships' that I believe is now moored up at the Maritime Museum in Ramsgate is the motor yacht, Sundowner. Built in 1912, it was once the private yacht of the second officer of the Titanic, C. H. Lightoller. He was a survivor of that fateful disaster and yet, many years later, he was busy at the helm of his boat during the evacuation of Dunkirk, where in one trip he succeeded in bringing home 127 soldiers from the Dunkirk beaches.

WEDNESDAY, 20TH MAY 2009
RAMSGATE – HERNE BAY

It was a battle of two minds once the alarm had woken me. One was saying quite sternly, "Come on get up, its 5am; you said you wanted an early start today so get moving". The other mind was sympathetic but just as insistent, "Stay in bed, Dave, you had a really hard day yesterday and you need a break. Pull the covers over your head and go back to sleep". I put my mobile alarm on a ten-minute 'snooze', and waited in anticipation while these conflicting thoughts kept running through my mind. Then, just a mere second after the next alarm began I pressed the stop button, pulled my duvet back and slid out of bed. The stern mind had won.

This early morning conflict of two minds would become a regular event throughout my walk, yet I rarely succumbed to the softer option simply because of the schedule I knew I had to maintain. It is not quite 6.30am when I alight from the van on the Pegwell Road to start my day's walk from where we left off yesterday. The weather, although fine, has brought along a cool breeze that I am happy with.

I had planned to go around the headland to Margate as it would have been a much more scenic route, but I knew it meant walking over a far greater distance than the more direct route. I am behind schedule due to yesterday's fiasco so I am opting for the latter. The weariness from yesterday's efforts was still with me for it took me almost two hours to cover the mere 4.9 miles to Margate. Once in the town, I catch up with Rob who has parked on the promenade below Fort Hill and here we enjoy a meal of tasty pasta while looking out over the sea. The lethargy of the morning had all but disappeared and after another leg stretch I take off along the coast, bound for Herne Bay.

The coastal walk on this section of the Kent coast is exhilarating and Rob is there to meet me at Reculver, our rendezvous point. The old medieval Reculver church ruin is hard to miss for it stands out for miles around. After taking photos of this ancient monument I have another meal before resuming my walk along the coast to Herne Bay. The journey presents me with a mixture of wonderful coastal and rural scenic views, yet surprisingly I have not met another soul during my walk along this part of the Kent coast.

As I walk this section, I'm thinking about that old Reculver church and wondering about the people who would have worshipped there so many centuries ago. It jogs memories of another religious life; one that I had experienced during those long years of evacuation in a Dr Barnado's home in Norfolk, during the war.

We had to attend church twice on Sunday and sometimes on a Saturday, if someone was running a bible class. I remember how Sunday was always the worst day of the week for me. I'd always wake up with a headache looming as I dreaded the hours spent at the church.

There was another reason for my Sunday morning gloom; it was apple pie! The midday meal at Barnado's was our main meal of the day; it was usually a Sunday roast followed nearly always by apple pie as desert. The trouble with the apple pie was that the pastry was hardly ever cooked properly. Once your spoon broke through the upper thin crust it exposed a layer of this blue-grey, gooey stuff. The home had a fairly strict policy with food, for as far as they were concerned it was a precious commodity not to be wasted; a viewpoint shared by many during the war years. We were all expected to eat everything on our plates, apart from bones that is; those that didn't would be given a considerably reduced portion of food at the next meal session. As we were always hungry, especially toward evening, a reduction in food was seen as an effective punishment for any wayward behaviour.

Group photo on front lawn at Dr Barnado's

Trying to swallow this soft pastry was a real trial as I found the taste of it really disgusting. I would try hiding the taste by mixing the sliced apple with it but I would often run out of the fruit before finishing off the pastry. Even now, the taste of partially cooked pastry turns my stomach. On reflection, I sometimes wonder if it was something else other than pastry; after all, there were substitutes for a variety of other foods during the war years.

In the church we'd all sit together in two or three pews. We couldn't even whisper to one another because you had this weird feeling that the beady eyes of the priest were watching every move you made. Having to attend church in the morning and evening on a Sunday was one thing, but for me, the worst part was the dreadful prospect of having to listen to the agonising and fearsome words of the preacher. His sermons would, with monotonous regularity, ring out dire warnings of what would happen to us if we were not good. I must have been pretty young at the time yet I still remember how frightening it was to listen to all the terrible things that would happen to you if you didn't follow the 'path of the Lord'.

I remember him once looking in our direction, for we evacuees were conspicuous in our 'Barnado greys', and with an admonishing stare began ranting about what our fate would be if we displeased the Lord by (among other things) playing with ourselves. I didn't understand what he meant, so afterwards I remember asking my big brother.

I sometimes used to throw a bit of screwed up paper in the toilet pan and bombard it with my pee. I'd make out it was a German battleship and I had to sink it before I finished peeing. If I was successful I would leave the toilet feeling really happy; if I didn't sink it I would feel dead miserable. I hadn't fully understood what my brother told me about playing with myself, but I wasn't going to risk playing games with my willy anymore; entering into a world of hell-fire and damnation for eternity seemed very real and frightening to me at the time.

As I approach Herne Bay I see Rob coming to meet me as I am running late. It's such a relief to have reached my day's destination for I'm feeling very tired after 7½ hours of walking. I have a refreshing shower and another familiar but tasty pasta meal before firing up my laptop. I try to update my diary and progress map as per usual, only to find that the computer has crashed on me; I can't retrieve or record anything. I am devastated as it is essential for me to access my files on a daily basis.

Today's pedometer reading: 32km (19.9 miles).

Notes of Interest: Herne Bay

The name Herne Bay originates from the neighbouring village of Herne, two to three kilometres away. It is believed that the word Herne might have evolved from the Old English 'hyrne', meaning corner, as apparently there's a sharp turn in this vicinity along the Roman Road.

During the early 1800s smuggling was still a source of income for many a ne'er-do-well. To be successful they would operate as gangs, often coming into conflict with excise officials. The government eventually imposed their authority on those active in this illicit trade and by the 1820s smuggling activity had all but ceased.

By the mid-1800s, steamboats began running between Herne Bay pier and London, but it would be the arrival of the railway system that would lead to the town's rapid growth
The first 'Brides in the Bath' murder by George Joseph Smith was committed in Herne Bay in 1912.

THURSDAY, 21ST MAY 2009
HERNE BAY – WHITSTABLE – FAVERSHAM

Rob prepares a smashing breakfast this morning of sausages, bacon, eggs, baked beans and toast. After washing this down with a black coffee I am ready to tackle the day.

I leave Herne Bay harbour area a little before 7am with a cool north-westerly breeze in my face. I take the walking route along a sealed coastal path that reveals lovely seascapes of the Kent coast. The colourful scene ahead, with seagulls wheeling above and the refreshing odour of the briny stirred up by the thumping surf, makes me feel very much alive with the growing awareness that this scenario would have been a perpetual routine on the coastlines of our planet for millions of years.

As I approach Whitstable, a path takes me alongside playing fields and a large area of static homes and then a series of bathing huts. I call Invicta radio as a phone interview had been arranged earlier from Herne Bay, but the Whitstable representative wants me to delay the call till later in the day, but we can't wait. My next concern is to get the laptop fixed so we call into a computer shop on the Whitstable high street. The guy takes a quick look but says he can't do anything as he is very busy. "Call back tomorrow and I'll see what I can do," he says. I tell him that we'll think about it and leave.

I decide to give Rob a break from the wheel, but driving through the town centre, I have to move over to allow a bus to pass on the narrow street, and in doing so hit a shop awning that had protruded out over the kerb. Today is not my lucky day!

We have lunch on the seafront and I finally begin my walk out of Whitstable in the early afternoon. It is such a lovely experience to walk along the seafront again and through the bird sanctuary. How much better it would have been to have had more knowledge of these winged creatures; to recognise certain species and their habitat, to know what exotic land they had flown from or were going to.

The area is again devoid of any sign of human activity – surprising if you consider the sheer beauty of the place – but as I gaze over the remote areas of marshes and mud flats, the solitude brings a strange serenity to the walk. As I continue my journey on the delightful scenic route towards Faversham my thoughts once more return to Wales and Aberdovey.

They say that if you cast your mind back often enough on a certain event, previously forgotten details will often emerge. It's like returning to an archaeological dig and unearthing a crucial element that had been missed on earlier visits. I delve once more into that short but important period of my life at the Outward Bound Sea School.

The first morning at the school was a harbinger of what was in store for us all in the coming weeks. We were woken by the strike of four bells. It was 6am. Our first task was to don shorts, vest and plimsolls (there were no flash running shoes in those days), then a six-mile run halfway to Towyn (Tywyn) and back. Immediately on our return, it was a visit to the shower block where a torrent of ice cold water was sprayed on naked bodies for what seemed an eternity; a whistle then gave us permission to thankfully withdraw and allow the next group to suffer the same fate.

After cleaning up around the hut, we eagerly awaited another strike of bells that would signal 8am, the time for breakfast. We were out on parade after breakfast when the commander of the school appeared and introduced himself. Suddenly a name came back to me... It was Captain Fuller!

Then it was back into our respective huts for inspection by our watch master, before heading back outside to be put through a series of exercises. A little later, although I cannot be certain if it was the same day, we were divided into groups of three and given a compass, a map, and a container consisting of cheese, bread, cubes of butter, an apple and a knife.

We were to climb the hills to the north of Aberdovey and reach the 2,927ft summit of Cader Idris known as Penygadair (Top of the Chair), then return back to the school. I was still only fifteen and I remember feeling somewhat daunted by this new challenge. The night before, one of the boys in our Beattie Watch had said that Cader Idris was haunted and that anyone who gets trapped on its summit for the night will wake up as a madman in the morning. That thought didn't comfort me either!

I walk into Faversham fairly late in the afternoon and soon after, we drive around searching for a decent caravan touring site. On this occasion we are not successful and finally end up at a farm without electricity or water facilities. I feel miserable not being able to shower and Rob is frustrated as we have no TV; worse still was having no satellite signal for internet access. But we survive!

Today's pedometer reading: 23.1km (14.4 miles).

Notes of Interest: Faversham

A settlement in the vicinity had already been established long before the Roman conquest. Durolevum was the name the Romans gave to Faversham, although the Domesday Book records it as 'Favreshant'. Durolevum apparently means 'the stronghold by the clear stream', but its origin is derived from the Celtic language which was in use well before the Roman occupation.

There is a pagan shrine which forms part of the ruined church of Stone-next-Faversham about a mile-and-a-half from the town centre, where it stands as a memorial to the Romans' early pagan culture in Britain.

Faversham, which has an interesting history as an ancient sea port and market town, can now claim to be the centre of the county's brewing industry where it's home to Britain's oldest brewery, Shepherd Neame. It also remains one of the most profitable breweries in Britain.

Oare Marshes is an important reserve for all species of birds, attracting bird-watchers from all parts of Britain to view the many migrant species visiting this solitary and peaceful haven.

FRIDAY, 22ND MAY 2009
FAVERSHAM – GILLINGHAM

Awoke to another fine day! I have about five rounds of toast with marmalade and honey for breakfast before preparing myself for the day's walk. We've run out of bananas.

At this juncture it might be a good idea to acquaint you with my daily diet. My son does most of the cooking, God bless 'im; although

I often do the dishes after the main evening meal. I usually have banana and toast in the morning with a cup of coffee then, if I am walking on the road, Rob will drive ahead about 7 miles then wait for me to catch up around two hours or so later. This first break usually involves a leg stretching routine before consuming two large bowls of porridge. Rob will then drive on again covering the same sort of distance, and by the time I meet up with him it's lunch time when I'd usually have a large bowl of tuna pasta or something similar. I would then start on a third session and would ask Rob to drive ahead no more than 4 or 5 miles depending upon the terrain and on how I was feeling. On reaching the van, I would usually have another bowl of pasta, having finished walking for the day; by then it would be around 2pm. A few hours later, back at the caravan site I would be ready to consume a large evening meal. That's five meals a day!

If I am on coastal or country tracks where Robert can't reach me, I will take a backpack with packed sandwiches, plastic cartons of cold pasta and a banana or two. The beauty of walking a long distance each day is that, no matter what you eat, the calories are easily burned off in the process.

My watch shows 8.15am as I clear the outskirts of Faversham. I continue on the road that will take me to Sittingbourne. I have to follow the road on this occasion as the walking tracks are too far away. I stop at Teynham about 4 miles on; it is where Rob is waiting and where I stretch the legs before continuing on toward Sittingbourne.

Throughout my walk, since starting out on the 10th May, thoughts have been my constant companion. In fact I can't remember ever having done so much thinking. Thoughts would often converge into memories – today those memories were of the street we used to live in many years ago.

Our street was a hotchpotch of poorly constructed houses and an even greater hotchpotch of humanity dwelt within their walls. A street that possessed two public houses, a spiritualist church, an undertaker's premises, an ice-cream factory and one or two dubious business activities that us kids were not privy to at the time.

As I walked, I could picture the house we lived in as if it were yesterday. The living room was on the ground floor at the front of the house. A tiny, inefficient, blackened grilled fireplace that was expected to give warmth to the whole room graced one damp wall, while the feeble attempt to illuminate the room was given to a single gas mantle that protruded from the stained, mottled ceiling. The only other gas mantle in the house gave cheerless light to an even more cheerless kitchen and scullery.

As older children, we were given the task of taking lighted candles upstairs to the bedrooms so that the younger ones could be prepared for bed. We would arrive to bed later, all at different times, each depending on our mother's patience. I would attempt to read under the dismal candlelight until my mother came into the room and started protesting; eventually and with much grumbling, I would have to relent and blow out the candle. Sometimes our mother had to work nights, especially coming up to Christmas. Our older sister Jean would then take charge of the household. She must have been no more than 14 years of age, but as I remember, she took on the role with single-minded dedication; so much so that she would often have conflict with her two brothers both nearer to her age – Mick who was older, and me, 18 months younger.

I often see Jean these days, and occasionally when we reminisce, she will often remark about the times Mick and I would throw her out in the cold while our mother was at work. I remembered only the one time we did this. I think there was snow on the ground at the time, so we threw her a blanket to stop her from freezing to death and left her out there for about 20 minutes. (Jean reckons it was much longer, but she's a bit of a drama queen!) Anyway, she seemed okay when we let her back in, but boy did the waterworks start when our mother arrived home some time later. Consequently, both my brother and I got a real tongue-lashing from a very harassed and tired woman.

I also remembered the time when a scream from an upstairs bedroom had my older brother rushing up the stairs to find that my younger sister Carol had set light to the curtains. As we followed him into the bedroom, the flames had already been extinguished and he was in the process of chastising our tearful sister for her carelessness.

Some nights, especially during holiday weekends, we would hear a rumpus and shouting coming from outside. We would quietly lift up the sash window of the bedroom so that our mother wouldn't hear and watch the drunken brawls that spilled out onto the pavements from the Black Lion pub that lay a few doors up and on the opposite side of the street. I remembered how sometimes we'd look out on a bitterly cold winter's night and see the usual ragtag kids sitting on the doorstep of that same pub waiting for the occasional hand-out of a bag of crisps or bottle of lemonade from their parents who were enjoying themselves in the cheerful warmth of the saloon.

Even though we were quite poor and despite our Dickensian surroundings, we kids thought of ourselves as being fortunate to be where we were at the time and we also felt grateful for having the sort of mother we had. And guess what...you won't believe this but Jean never ever thanked us for throwing her that blanket. That's gratitude for you!

As a gangly teenager with my sister Jean

I catch up with the campervan again on the other side of Sittingbourne at a Wickes store car park. Rob and I have bacon burgers and coffee at the on-site mobile burger bar, (a change for Rob who normally has to prepare meals in the van). While we tuck into the food, the lady behind the counter called Jane, allows me to charge my phone and refuses to take payment for the meal, saying it was her way of giving support to our event. Thank you Jane, you are a diamond!

We are soon on our way again towards Gillingham, with Rob driving ahead and me walking. For some reason I find the going a bit tough over these last couple of miles and am looking forward to resting up for the day. Approaching Gillingham, I'm having some difficulty locating Rob as he appears to be on a different route from the one I am on, but eventually we meet up at the Tesco car park. I gratefully call it a day and together we drive to the caravan camping site. Thankfully the site is equipped with power connection, shower facilities etc allowing us to enjoy the end of the day in reasonable comfort. Due to my defunct laptop, however, I can no longer update my website. Something will have to be done.

Today's pedometer reading: 28km (17.38 miles).

Notes of Interest: Gillingham

The Domesday Book of 1086 records the name of a small hamlet named Gillingham. It is believed that the word might derive from a war lord, named Gyllingas or possibly from Gylla's village observing the Old English 'ham' meaning village or homestead. In 1667, Gillingham was invaded by a Dutch fleet that had sailed up the River Medway. The Dutch eventually retreated, but the incident, named as 'The raid on the Medway' caused much embarrassment and humiliation to the English Navy.

There have been two memorable disasters in Gillingham: on 11th July, 1929 a public demonstration by Gillingham Fire Brigade went out of control, resulting in 15 fatalities, and then in 1951, a bus ploughed into a column of Royal Marine Cadets, killing 24 young cadets aged between 10 and 13.

I was home during this tragic event and I seem to remember that it had happened in December around six in the evening. The column of cadets wearing Royal Marine issue dark blue uniform had been walking on the left-hand side of the road without any rear lights. It was quite dark and the street lighting was poor when they marched past the gates of the Chatham Royal Naval Dockyard. It was about that time when the bus ploughed into them. I've never forgotten the incident for at the time it was big news.

There was national mourning throughout the country and I remember my mother being terribly upset over it, as we all were. The bus driver had an exemplary driving record prior to the accident and had been driving for the company for about 25 years. He was convicted for it, as I remember, but I often wondered about the agony he must have suffered knowing what he had done and whether he carried that awful burden for the rest of his days.

SATURDAY, 23RD MAY TO MONDAY, 25TH MAY 2009 GILLINGHAM

Today is going to have to be a rest day from walking, as I desperately need to get the laptop fixed. After breakfast, Rob and I drive back to the town and park up. Although it was Saturday, I was confident that I would find a computer service shop somewhere in Gillingham.

We decide to split up and take different routes around the city's shopping area to see what we could find. We end up locating two shops that serviced computers, but after cursory checks of my laptop we get the same response from both shops: neither was able to do anything till after the weekend. It was a bank holiday weekend so that means it would be Tuesday before the laptop would be looked at. Four days without the computer was a problem because Wi-Fi access was often not available in places where we stopped overnight, so something else has to be done.

We drive back to the caravan site and over lunch I come to a decision; we'll drive back to Brighton and let Anthony take a look at it. Anthony had created my website; he was also a bit of a whizz-kid when it came to IT stuff. I had already spoken to him over the phone about the problem, so after lunch we take off and head south. We arrive back in Brighton late afternoon. I was hoping Anthony could look at the laptop this evening; however his social life had to come first. He promises to check out the equipment on Sunday morning.

There were a few raised eyebrows when the campervan was seen parked up at the marina this evening. With all the Cancer Research signage on the van, it stood out like a beacon at sea. Now let me explain about life at the Brighton Marina. There is a sort of village/holiday atmosphere about the place. Those that live and socialise there are well acquainted with each other and a major support for my walk generated from the friends and acquaintances I have here. However, there are some who are quick to see the funny side of a situation and over the weekend I was to become the brunt of some wicked humour. Comments like, "Cripes Dave that was quick, you must have sprinted it!" or "I've heard of the Road Runner but this is ridiculous," or "What's next... Australia?" or "That hairpin bend at Land's End must have been a bit scary!" or "Have you contacted the Guinness Book of Records yet?"... And so on. On numerous occasions I'd see someone I knew approaching and I would quickly try to explain my reasons for being back down on the marina before they had a chance to make wisecracks.

But it's all in good fun and Rob and I enjoy the evening having a few beers with friends while listening to the local band, 'The Fog' playing at The Master Mariner. On the Sunday it was bad news from Anthony. In his opinion the laptop really wasn't worth fixing and that it would be better to buy a new one. I wasn't anticipating having to pay out additional money for a new laptop, but as they say, 'needs must', whatever that means! It's Monday morning before we get to a store to buy the new computer. Rob and I depart from the marina and head back up north to Gillingham with a few last-minute, smart-arse comments still ringing in our ears.

TUES, 26TH MAY 2009
GILLINGHAM –TILBURY

After breakfast and some last-minute shopping at Tesco, I begin my day's walk. It is 11.15am before I finally clear the outskirts of Gillingham. The sky is overcast and rain has fallen intermittently throughout the morning, but now it begins to brighten up into a lovely day.

I walk through the outer suburbs of Chatham and Rochester, then walk across the Medway and onto the A226 to Gravesend. Surprisingly, it's a nice walk and once clear of suburbia, the road takes me through open fields with trees and bushes on either side. It was around this time that my thoughts returned briefly to the Cooden Beach Golf Club.

Mr Kincaid's words! I recall now, his later advice that I should attend the Outward Bound School as an apprentice cadet, and that he could arrange it. I politely turned the offer down due, as I remember, to a lack of confidence in my academic ability. The secondary school I had gone to was pretty ordinary; most of the kids like me were from poor backgrounds and their only ambition was to finish their schooling and find employment that would put some spending money in their pocket and hopefully help with the family budget. Higher education was not perceived as an option and even the teachers, as I seem to recall, never brought it to our attention. I was away from school half way into my fourteenth year and glad of it. Although my formal education was quite abysmal, I would regret turning down Mr Kincaid's proposition, for I was to learn later that obtaining a cadetship into Alfred Holt's Blue Funnel Line was no easy matter. Instead I had aspired to become a junior rating in the catering division of that esteemed shipping line; in other words – a cabin boy!

Now that I've reached Gravesend I have to decide whether or not to walk through Greenhithe and up to the Queen Elizabeth II Bridge or get a lift with Rob via the Dartford Tunnel to Tilbury Docks. The distance between Tilbury Docks and Gravesend was a mere 800 metres across the Thames so I choose the ride to Tilbury. We manage to find a suitable camping site near Tilbury and settle in for the evening. Tomorrow I will resume my walk through the county of Essex.

Distance walked: approximately 18.5km (11.5 miles).

Notes of Interest: Tilbury

It is believed that the eighth century name for Tilbury was 'Tilaburg'; the word 'Tila' might have referred to a low-lying marsh area of that time and the Saxon word 'burgh' possibly meaning a fortified place. In the Domesday Book, however, it's thought to be noted as 'Tilberia'.

During the Roman occupation it appears that the sea levels were much lower than today, making the marshes habitable. In fact, there is archaeological evidence of a Roman settlement on the site where Tilbury Docks is situated.

Tilbury has had a long-standing association with Gravesend, the town that lies on the opposite (south) side of the Thames. The meandering River Thames narrows to around 800 metres at this point, making Gravesend its closest neighbouring town and once an important river link. A Tilbury–Gravesend ferry operated there from very early times. In those days, however, it seems that the marsh area was not the healthiest place in which to live; Daniel Defoe wrote a comment on what was then known as the 'Essex Ague'

The building of the Tilbury Docks was to drastically transform the area. Temporary accommodation had to be found for thousands of workers, while others commuted from surrounding villages and towns. Eventually permanent structures were built, but the houses were poorly constructed, becoming tenement blocks that resulted in squalor and living deprivation for many of the occupants. The town remained in this poor state until around 1918, when government assistance gradually brought considerable improvement to the run-down area.

CHAPTER 3
ESSEX

WED, 27TH MAY 2009
TILBURY TO BRENTWOOD

I leave Tilbury Docks at 7.30am in cool, overcast conditions. It soon starts to spit with rain as I trudge up the hill toward Chadwell St Mary, but I soon manage to get on the A128 to Brentwood. It was great to be back in the countryside once more, striding along among tall hedgerows, trees and fields. It isn't the most walker-friendly route to take because the traffic is quite heavy. I walk on a grassy verge running alongside the road but it is overgrown to such an extent that my progress is slow and laborious. I look for public footpaths going in my direction but there doesn't appear to be any that are conveniently situated in this part of Greater London. However, I manage to divert onto the old Brentwood road near the village of Bulphan, but it finally leads me back to the main A128 highway again.

As I walk toward Brentwood a remarkable coincidence of events is about to unfold...

I am about 25 minutes walking distance from the town when my mobile phone rings. It is my daughter calling from Melbourne to tell me that Andrew, my grandson, had suddenly been taken ill and had been rushed to hospital. Andrew had only recently returned from a holiday in India to take up a position as a vet in London.

My daughter, Carolyn, who knew I was walking but wasn't sure of my actual location, asks me if I could stop my walk to visit him. I agree to do this and enquire about the name and location of the hospital. My daughter says she hasn't yet been told but that she would phone Andrew's girlfriend, Jo, (for she was the one who had sent the message about Andrew's illness) and would call me back as soon as she had the information. Meanwhile, I keep walking toward Brentwood. Ten minutes later my daughter calls again. "Dad, he's been taken to Hartwood hospital in Brentwood, do you know where that is?"

I'm flabbergasted and I tell Carolyn that I'm about ten minutes walking time away from the town. She's as astonished as I am, as she realises that he could have been sent anywhere in greater London other than Brentwood.

I have a pre-arranged interview and photo shoot with the local paper so I phone them to postpone the meeting. I tell them about Andrew and they were as intrigued about the coincidence as I was and they request a meeting at the hospital. I agree to this, but Andrew is not in a receptive state to see anyone apart from family. I explain this to the young lady photographer and the journalist and they decide to wait until I return from visiting my grandson before speaking to me.

Andrew's sickness was painful but not too serious thank goodness, for it turned out to be an abscess on the liver.

After the press appointment, Rob and I go to Mason's Restaurant where we are royally treated by Danielle, Ronnie and Emma. Thanks girls! We had previously booked in at a lovely campsite for the night and later, Dave, my cousin's son and his girlfriend Sally, arrive to see us there. This evening we all go out to a pub to watch the Man U/ Barcelona game on TV. It's been an interesting day!

Today's pedometer reading: 22.8km (14.15 miles).

Notes of Interest: Brentwood

It is thought that Brentwood began life as a settlement in a forest clearing that had been created by fire; it was known then as 'Burntwood'.

Its proximity to the old Roman Road influenced its growth, for this was the main London to Colchester route for travellers, including the pilgrims, who would often stay overnight on their way to Canterbury via the Thames bridge. So Brentwood became a prominent coaching stage, a welcome overnight rest for man and horse.

Warley Barracks created a military presence in the town for over 250 years. The barracks was to close in the early 1960s when National Service was abolished. Being less than a day's walk from Tilbury Docks made Brentwood's military establishment in Warley Common an ideal location for armies waiting to serve overseas. Since 1742, thousands of troops, horses and equipment involved in various conflicts from the

Spanish Armada to the Indian Uprising, and from the Boer War to the last World War, have been stationed here.

Today Brentwood has an above average number of pubs and four of the High Street inns listed in 1788 are still trading, so I've been told. The White Hart, Brentwood's leading inn at the time, once retained a sixteenth-century carriage entrance leading to a coaching yard. Today, however, the property shows little of the legacy from its ancient stagecoach past.

THURS, 28TH MAY 2009
BRENTWOOD –MARGARETTING

There is no sense in rising too early today as we have another press meeting, this time with an Essex Echo photographer, at the Hartford hospital at 9.30am. Rob and I duck in to the Brentwood hospital to see Andrew once more and then head back to the campsite as I have an 'on-the-air' phone interview with Essex BBC at 11.30am.

The weather is fine and warm as I start walking out of Brentwood's suburbs and into the countryside. My mind, as usual, gives rein to many thoughts before homing in on the footie match that we had watched last night in Brentwood. I love watching a good game of football, but rugby is my first passion – possibly due to living in New Zealand for much of my life.

I begin wondering why footballers (and sometimes their managers) are allowed to harass an official when disputing his decision on an infringement they disagree with. I have even seen players barge and eye-ball the referee as they try intimidating him. I find it disgusting that these highly paid people are allowed to get away with this sort of prima-donna behaviour. As I walk, I jokingly reflect that if I were a referee, I would red-card every player who confronted me in this way. Trouble is, as a result, there would probably be only three or four players left on the pitch by the end of the game and my career as a referee would undoubtedly be the shortest on record! Seriously though, it tends to sour my view of the game because that sort of behaviour must send mixed messages to the millions of youngsters watching the action either from the terraces or on TV that it's okay to oppose or denigrate the actions of authority, whether it's from referees, teachers, the police or parents.

As I continue my walk, I think about the many international rugby matches I have watched over the years. The managers and coaches usually watch their teams with computers and note books while seated up in the covered stands; unlike football managers, who will often prowl the sidelines displaying their wrath to some official like an ill-mannered parent at a kids' match. In rugby, referees officiate with authority and have the respect of all the players on the pitch. If there were doubts about an infringement, it was usually the captain who would approach the referee. The official was always addressed as 'Mr So and So' or 'Sir' and the discourse was always polite and friendly.

While pondering this issue a certain idiom springs to mind: 'Football is a gentlemen's game played by hooligans, and Rugby, a hooligan's game played by gentlemen.' An unfair generalisation I suppose, as many footballers may not fall into that category; however, the phrase has, I think, a certain degree of veracity. I then begin thinking about how technology has become a crucial factor in decision-making procedures in other sports such as rugby, tennis and cricket; 'it's all for the betterment of the game' their followers will say. I can't help but wonder why FIFA have always ignored the obvious practical benefits of this technology. I thought that maybe the powerful global popularity of the sport allows the hierarchy to smugly believe that improvements to the game are unwarranted? I believe this governing body ought to have introduced the technology into the game years ago, especially to monitor infringements in the penalty area where a wrong refereeing decision could cost a team anything from a place in the European Champions League to being relegated; in monetary terms, millions of pounds of lost revenue.

Those against this technology claim it is a time-wasting exercise that would interrupt the flow of the game. As I see it, every time an infringement occurs resulting in a penalty or a yellow or red card, the members of the infringing team crowd around the referee venting their anger and frustration for minutes at a time; a reaction from spoiled rich brats that also interrupts the flow of the game! At least with CCTV technology the correct decision can be quickly determined; whether it's a fake dive in the penalty area, impeding the goal keeper or if the ball has or hasn't passed over the goal line and so on. Collaboration with this all-seeing, hi-tech fourth official can, in my view, only improve the game.

It's funny, the things you think about as you're walking!

I catch up with Rob at a town called Margaretting and decide to end the day's walk here. I was hoping to reach Chelmsford this afternoon but cannot make it. For some reason I feel very weary today. The Spread Eagle in Margaretting gives us refreshments and lunch on the house. To Graham, Ash and Ged, thanks again guys!

We roll into our caravan campsite at 6.30pm. This evening we buy fish and chips and settle down to relax and watch TV.

Today's pedometer reading was only: 12.8km (7.94 miles).

FRI, 29TH MAY 2009
MARGARETTING

We are having an idle day today... for walking that is.

I rise early, fully intending to start the day's walk but after breakfast I decide instead to fire-up my new laptop. We have good mobile broadband reception here at the site and there is so much online stuff to catch up with that I think it's best to stay and get it sorted.

Usually our day off from walking is Sunday, but we have decided to change this procedure as the traffic is not usually as heavy on a Sunday, so it's easier for the support vehicle to get around. In some of the village areas it can be a nightmare negotiating the wide campervan through narrow streets, especially with busy traffic around, so it makes sense to walk on Sunday and have a day off during the week. Today therefore is our rest day. Hopefully, I will get in a good day's walk tomorrow and by Sunday I should reach Colchester.

Notes of Interest: Margaretting

The village of Margaretting sits astride the Roman Road that ran from London through Chelmsford to Colchester. There is mention of this historic settlement in the Domesday Book. Originally, the community was thought to have settled around the crossroad close to the junction of what is now known as Penny's Lane. According to the Domesday entry, Margaretting was part of the King's land during the reign of Edward the Confessor.

In 1086 King William, (the Conqueror), held the manor in demesne (kept for his own use). Then in 1315 the manor was passed to Edmund,

Earl of Arundel, by King Edward II, but it seems that the Earl was beheaded twelve years later. The title returned to the widow twenty years after the execution and then ultimately to her son.

SAT, 30TH MAY 2009
MARGARETTING – WITHAM

I start walking from Margaretting at 7.15am. The weather is fine and a light southerly wind accompanies me as I make my way onto the A12. It isn't long before I'm skirting around the outer suburbs of Chelmsford and walking again through the countryside.

I veer onto a track that appears to be a byroad running alongside the highway. It's such a relief to get off the busy road and into a quiet country lane that I forget to recheck my map. The path is okay for a while but then it suddenly dips down quite sharply before veering away in almost the opposite direction. I couldn't believe it! I stay on the route for a while in case it turns back again, but I eventually have to retrace my steps to where I had earlier diverted onto the track. This error resulted in a 2-mile walk for nothing! It is bad enough when you find yourself on the wrong route when driving, but at least then it is just a matter of a little wasted time and fuel. But having to walk extra, useless miles due to taking the wrong route can make you feel very resentful and angry for being so stupid. Thoughts help to take my mind off the predicament and soon I find myself back in the Welsh hills during my stay at the Outward Bound Sea Training School.

Walking up the foothills toward Cader Idris was a great experience, with lovely views of Tallylyn Lake far below. I think there were three routes to Cader Idris and I am not sure which we took, but I do remember that the higher we climbed, the steeper it got. After a time I felt exhausted; it had been a physically hard day right from the start, what with the early morning run and everything and I was beginning to wilt. Worse was to come when a cold mantle of mist began to settle all around us. After reaching the summit, we stopped to eat before making our way down by a different route. The mist, as I recall, was quite dense as I followed in the wake of my two older companions.

I vaguely remember walking along a ridge and then, in a short space of time, I had lost sight of them. In my hurry to catch up, I tripped over something and tumbled down a steep bank. Somehow I had managed to get back to the top of the bank and then hurriedly took off after my companions. In the thickening fog I came across a fork in the track and without the map I had no idea which way I should go. I remember just standing there and shouting out at the top of my voice.

I can't recall how long it was before they found me, but I do remember imagining being stranded there overnight and waking up as a howling madman in the morning!

Three and a half hours later I reach Hatfield Peverel where Rob is waiting for me. After the usual stretching exercises I tuck into two bowls of a tasty tuna pasta dish accompanied by pea and ham soup before getting back on the road.

I finish the day's walk at Witham where I meet up with Rob and we drive back to a campsite on the grounds of a village pub. The staff and the patrons treat us incredibly well. We must go back there! Thank you, Debbie & Dave. Also a thank you to Dave senior whom I walked past at the bus stop; also to Steve who offered help with sponsorship forms and to all the others here who donated generously to our cause.

Today's pedometer reading: 27.1km (16.83 miles).

Notes of Interest: Witham

The name Witham is Saxon in origin and appears in the Domesday Book of 1086 as the parish of Witham.

Over the years evidence of Neolithic occupation has been uncovered in and around the town and during the 1970s the remains of a Roman temple and a pottery kiln were unearthed. These finds seem to lend weight to the belief that Witham was used as an overnight stopover on the long journey between London and Colchester.

Another important find was the uncovering of an Offering pool. Several artefacts have been found in the grounds of the temple that would indicate that the Romans, during their early pagan years of occupation, were still making offerings to the gods.

Witham also enjoyed a brief spell of afluence as a spa town after a mineral-bearing spa was discovered during the eighteenth century.

Witham has experienced disasters over the years: on Saturday 1st September 1905, a 14-carriage express train was derailed whilst hurtling through the station. The carriages tumbled and crashed onto the platforms killing ten passengers and a luggage porter; 71 passengers were injured, some seriously. Since then no other railway accident in the county has caused such fatalities.

It is thought that the disaster could have been much worse but for a signalman, whose quick action averted the next train hitting the wreckage.

SUN, 31ST MAY 2009
WITHAM – COLCHESTER

I was up early today and after a breakfast of toast and banana accompanied by black coffee I was ready to start walking. The weather was again fine with a light southerly breeze.

From Witham I make my way down minor roads through Wickham Bishops and then on to a delightful B-road; routes that take me through Great Totham and on to Tiptree where the famous jam comes from. It is here that I meet up with Rob and the support vehicle for my first break of the day.

After a meal consisting of two large bowls of porridge, with cream and sugar I might add, followed by a large mug of black coffee, I was ready to continue on the road towards Colchester.

Staying on the B1022 I walk past Colchester Zoo where a photo shoot by the Colchester Zoo media people has been arranged for the following day. They say a local newspaper will also be on hand to cover the event. I have another break to stretch my legs and load up with carbohydrate before the final push into Colchester itself.

It's around this time that my thoughts stray to an incident in my teenage years. My thoughts are sometimes triggered by something I've recently read or seen on TV. It was at my lunch break today that I read an article from an old magazine we had lying around. It was about a youth who had battered his dad to death, then tried to hide the evidence. The article went on to describe how the boy and his mother had been subject to constant abuse from the father.

The school I attended after returning home to Brighton from evacuation was St John's Primary, but soon after I went to Queens Park Secondary School. It was a rough school with some tough teachers and most of the pupils were from poor backgrounds. I remember this skinny kid whose name I think was Ken, but I can't be certain; anyway I would sometimes try and chat to him as he was often standing around on his own in the playground. He was in a higher class than mine as he was older. It was common knowledge that he got rough treatment at home because he would often come to school sporting a black eye or a bruise here and there. He once came to the school with his arm in a sling.

After he left school I didn't see him again, until I bumped into him while waiting in a cinema queue maybe three or more years later. I don't think I would have recognised this guy who was standing behind me in the queue, had he not called my name; but as soon as he told me who he was, the memory of seeing him at school returned in a flash. He'd changed a lot; not only was he taller, but he had filled out and I thought that he appeared to be quite muscular.

I remember him telling me that he had been working for this engineering firm for a couple of years and was staying in some digs close by. He went on to say that he had joined a boxing gym and was working out almost every evening.

What made this particular conversation stick with me over the years must have been the way he talked about his father. I must have asked him about the boxing because I remember him saying that he'd not lost a fight over the last year or so, and then said something about being almost ready to take on his father. He told me of his plans; that he was going to catch the 'bastard' on his way home from work one evening and give him a taste of his own medicine. I distinctly remember him saying that he was looking forward to beating up his 'old man' and that he'd do it every time his father beat up on his mother. The expression on his face and the quiet tone of his voice left me in no doubt at the time that his intentions were deadly serious.

After finishing the walk we set out to find a suitable caravan touring site. It's just after 3pm when we drive into a delightful campsite north of the city. I find this is the best time of the day, for after a shower we sit back in sun loungers and relax while sipping on a glass of good red wine!

Today's pedometer reading: 22.3km (13.84 miles).

Notes of Interest: Colchester

Colchester, it could be said, is probably the most historically important city in Britain. It is believed that the area has been inhabited since the seventh century BC, although it was first chronicled in the year 77 AD, making Colchester the earliest recorded town in England.

The town became an early target for the Roman invaders (AD. 43), and historians believe that in later years it would accommodate the first community of retired legionaries. Originally known as Camulodunum, it derived its name from the Celtic god of war, Camulos, and the Roman word 'dunum' meaning fort.

Some say that Camulodunum might have been the source of the legend Camelot of Arthurian legend, but this is pure conjecture.

It is believed that the Emperor Claudius, after receiving the surrender from the city's Celtic rulers, decided that Colchester would be regarded as the capital city of England.

In AD 60 Queen Boudicca led a rebellion against the Roman occupiers and she immediately attacked Camulodunum. The defenders took refuge in the temple of Claudius, but the rebels broke in, killed the people and burned the temple. The rest of the town was then set alight.

The rebellion was finally crushed and the Romans then set about rebuilding Colchester.

There's no further mention of the town until 917, when it is thought that the ownership of Colchester was being contested between Danes and Anglo-Saxons.

Years after, the Domesday Book merely records it as being 'a borough of some significance'. However, the Normans recognised Colchester's strategic value and would later use the foundations of the principal Roman temple to build their own castle.

Through every era, from the Saxon, the Norman, the Medieval, to the Modern Age, all have left their mark on this town, resulting in Colchester's rich historical heritage.

MON, 1ST JUNE 2009
COLCHESTER

There's no chance of walking today as I have an appointment with staff at Colchester Zoo for a photo session at 11am. We have a decent lie-in and then Rob cooks up a great English breakfast. It's the classic 'fry-up' with bubble and squeak from leftover vegetables and spuds. Smashing!

We get to the zoo in good time. I ask Rob if he wants to be part of the session, but he prefers to stay in the van and wait. The female photographer says that she wants to take a few shots with me feeding one of the animals. She asks if there is an animal I would prefer to hand feed. "What about one of the lions?" I say jokingly. She doesn't appear to appreciate my attempt at humour; instead she advises me in a serious manner that feeding lions by hand would not be allowed as it was too dangerous. Strange that! I end up having a half-hour photo session feeding the lemurs while she snaps away with the camera. Ah, but what delightful creatures! When you get close to animals like this, you immediately sense what the natural world is all about.

The *Colchester Evening News* photographer arrives at 12.15pm. He wants to take some pictures of an elephant being fed by this guy who is 'walking around England'. It was a bit of a contrast to the little lemurs!

Afterwards, Rob and I go shopping for groceries and other essentials before returning to the town centre at 5pm, where another photo shoot outside the Town Hall has been arranged. I return to the campsite feeling more tired than usual. I have come to the conclusion that having photo sessions with local newspapers is not really my bag. It is also too time-consuming.

I have done some mileage calculations this afternoon and realise I am currently behind schedule. My present walking rate means that I would arrive back in Brighton in November. I realise that I will seriously have to up the ante from now on. But never mind that for now; it's just lovely relaxing here in the late afternoon sun and spending the rest of the day chatting with my son while enjoying a glass of red wine. Tomorrow I will try and reach Ipswich...but then, tomorrow is another day!

TUES, 2ND JUNE 2009
COLCHESTER – WHERSTEAD

Rob drops me off at Colchester Town Hall at 6.27am. It is the ideal time to start walking for the weather is cool and the morning traffic is light. It looks as if another fine day is about to unfold.

Once clear of the suburbs, I set out for the A137, a route that will take me into Suffolk via Manningtree. My first stop is at Ardleigh, about 6½ miles from Colchester where Rob has a huge breakfast waiting.

From Ardleigh the road becomes pretty tedious, with large acres of ploughed fields, others green with unrecognised crop, while some lie fallow. Apart from what appeared to be conifer trees standing like sentinels to my right, there was nothing around to hold my interest, and I begin to let my mind wander once again to Wales and Aberdovey.

Some periods at the sea school emerge clearly in my mind, almost as if it were yesterday, such as the first day we climbed Cader Idris.

It was about 2pm before we arrived back at the School after coming down from the summit. We were sent to the canteen to eat a cold lunch. I was so hungry I remember thinking how I could easily have eaten the whole oven dish of sausages that were embedded in congealed fat and lay out of reach on the stainless steel bench under the window.

Outward Bound Sea School, Aberdovey, Wales - I'm in the centre row, fourth from the left

I remembered that while we were eating, another party of three boys turned up, which made us feel a little better; at least we weren't the last group to come down from Cader Idris.

I vaguely recollect that after we had finished eating our meagre lunch we had to run down to the jetty, where the main group of boys was waiting for us to join them on a large sailing vessel that I think was called Warspite.

We sailed out into Cardigan Bay and each watch took turns in furling and reefing the heavy canvas sails or standing by to winch aboard a lifeboat manned by another watch or carrying out a number of other tasks around the vessel. The sea was quite choppy, as I remember, and many of the boys were seasick. Surprisingly I was okay until I slipped over when walking for'ard. Finding my feet again, I looked at my hands and found they were covered in slimy, yellowish, regurgitated matter that immediately caused me to lean over the railings and retch up all my lunch. Any boys that were sick within the confines of the boat were frowned upon, for at the start of the trip we had all been instructed to vomit over board.

I stop at the village of Brantham where Rob is waiting. I stretch aching legs, feed up on a carb meal of tuna pasta, and change shoes and socks to prepare for the final push into Ipswich.

This section of the A137 is again not walker-friendly and I try seeking a bridle path to take me off the road. The trouble with byroads is that they often divert away from the intended route, adding more miles on the pedometer and consequently, more miles on tired legs. I have been on the road for about seven hours when I finally arrive at Wherstead, a suburb on the outskirts of Ipswich.

I have felt hot and tired through heat exhaustion over the last few miles and so I'm grateful to finish my day's walk here. Rob is waiting in the car park of a local pub. He had phoned me to check on my ETA and is already sitting in the shade of the beer garden when I arrive, and he has a cool ale for me sitting invitingly on the table.

We arrive at the Orwell Meadows camping site an hour or so later, and after a shower and a meal I begin to feel better, although my legs are aching more than usual.

Today's pedometer reading: 34.3km (21.30 miles).

Notes of Interest: Ipswich

During the Roman occupation Ipswich was an important inland route location and a staging post between York and London.

After the invasion of AD 869, it is believed Ipswich fell under Viking rule. The town was eventually overrun and recaptured by the Saxon English.

It was during the reign of Queen Mary that the Ipswich Martyrs were burnt at the stake for not relinquishing their Protestant faith. This terrible event was carried out on the Cornhill and a monument commemorating this moment in time now stands in Christchurch Park.

It is believed that the artist, Thomas Gainsborough, resided in Ipswich and Charles Dickens also had temporary residence there. The author apparently stayed at The Tavern Hotel in 1835 (later known as The Great White Horse Hotel) and some scenes from his novel, The Pickwick Papers, *depict the hotel's meandering corridors and narrow stairways.*

Two of England's most successful football managers had strong connections with Ipswich Town. Sir Alf Ramsey (who is, I believe, buried in the town) and Sir Bobby Robson. The team, under Alf Ramsey's leadership, won the League Championship in 1962 and the FA Cup in 1978. Then in 1981, during Bobby Robson's reign, they won the UEFA Cup.

CHAPTER 4
SUFFOLK

WED, 3RD JUNE 2009
WHERSTEAD – BRIGHTWELL

This morning I awake feeling tired and listless. I need to get to the local NHS to see if I can get another hearing aid to replace the one I happened to have lost near Chelmsford. It's a good excuse to keep from walking!

We manage to locate the Ipswich hospital and we're then directed to the Audiology Dept. I explain how I'd lost my hearing aid and how crucial it is to have a replacement. I inform them of my charity walk and explain about the dangers involved in being unable to hear approaching traffic while walking on busy, narrow roads. Aware of the situation they immediately take a mould of my ear and tell me that they will try to get a new hearing aid to me within the month. I give them an address in Whitby, a town I should be passing through around that time; I then thank the lady for her help and take my leave.

It's 11.30am and I've no other excuse to prevent me from walking so I get Rob to drop me off where I had stopped yesterday. It's not long before I'm walking over the Orwell Bridge and away from Ipswich; it's then onto the A14 before I turn north onto the road to Lowestoft. As I leave the suburbs of Ipswich, I begin musing over the vast amount of traffic everywhere. On my journey northward I often have to walk on roads where a constant, never-ending stream of traffic speeds by, especially when approaching the cities and towns. I begin thinking about a problem that has always concerned me.

I think about this unimaginable volume of traffic in every city and town around the globe and the colossal amount of fuel that is being swallowed up worldwide in just one hour... no, not one hour but each minute. I consider the vast amount of traffic in some of the worlds largest cities... I imagine standing on a bridge spanning a motorway, a freeway or an autobahn and seeing this perpetual flow of moving steel passing under me. I think of the ships plying the oceans and the countless aircraft flying the skies, and I try to imagine the quantity of fuel that must be guzzled up every minute of every day.

"Have a guess, Dave!" I say to myself. So I tried to work out how many litres might be used worldwide every minute of every day, but even a rough estimate was beyond my capability. I wonder if it would be equivalent to all the water in Lake Superior; or by converting those litres into linear metres, maybe they would reach the moon and back... every minute! What happens when they drain these vast subterranean fields of oil, I ask myself; are they left as empty cavities or do they refill them with water afterwards? Then I think: what if we could take our planet from the time when living creatures first evolved onto dry land, right through to the present day, and encapsulate that vast epoch into just a few years.

There's 473 million seconds in 15 years so for the sake of simplicity let's assume this period roughly corresponds to the period in years when fossil fuels were in the process of being formed. According to fossil records the Cambrian period (often referred to as the Cambrian Explosion) was a time when a rapid development of sea life emerged in its many diverse forms. The Cambrian period came to an end 495 million years ago; therefore it can be said that fossil fuel development would have been well underway 22 million years later.

So if we convert 473 million years back into seconds then, by my calculation, it would have taken 14 years, 51 weeks, 6 days, 23 hours and 55 minutes to create the Earth's fossil fuels and just a mere five minutes of man's tenure to fritter them away! Obviously a very loose calculation... but one that should give us an insight into how incredibly ignorant and indifferent we are to our planet's well-being.

I finish my day's trek at Brightwell as it's close to a campsite we have booked into. Not a big walking day today as I'm still feeling knackered. I must get more daily miles under my belt though, if I'm going to complete this walk on schedule. We do some shopping at a nearby Tesco store before driving out to the caravan touring site. It's now 3.30pm. Once we're hooked up to the power we sit outside in an attempt to benefit from the occasional periods of sunshine.

After checking the map to plan the next day's walk, I begin updating my diary and progress map. I'm feeling very tired for some reason and it's not long before I'm curled up in bed.

Today's pedometer reading: 12.7km (7.88 miles).

THURS, 4TH JUNE 2009
BRIGHTWELL – FARNHAM

I'm on the road this morning by 7am. The weather is again cool and overcast, ideal conditions for walking. I'm feeling refreshed after a good night's sleep and I begin my walk where I had finished off yesterday. I soon manage to get onto the old Ipswich road known as the B1438. This route takes me through Martlesham, Woodbridge and the lovely rural surroundings of the Suffolk countryside, and gives me miles of enjoyable walking.

A variety of random thoughts begin to flitter through my head and for a while my mind once again homes in on that time with the sea training school at Aberdovey.

It seems that I have inherited only vague recollections of my four-week sojourn at the school, apart from that first traumatic day; but now as I look back, a couple of incidents begin to materialise more clearly than before.

Memory of the storm that came up suddenly in Cardigan Bay; the five-hour struggle to get back to Aberdovey harbour; the now nameless bearded skipper ordering tacking procedures that required hands on deck to be exposed to the waves crashing over alternate forequarters and finally the sheer relief in entering calmer waters.

I remember now those breathtaking sunsets over the Dyfi estuary and how some days a shroud of grey mist covering Cader Idris would suddenly disperse, bathing the summit and the green hills in sunlight. Then there was that final day and the rousing speech by Captain Fuller before we broke up to enjoy a relaxing day with the Captain, the instructors and the mates we had come to know and rely upon. The memory of that final day became clearer. I remember how we congregated at the railway station waiting for the train that would take us back to our respective homes around England. It was a far cry to that distant day of four weeks ago when I had alighted from the train feeling apprehensive about what might lie ahead.

My thoughts skip to my mother who said how surprised she was to see me looking so fit and tanned. I recall knowing that my days at home were numbered; it wouldn't be long before I would be notified to join my first ship which would be sailing out of the port of Liverpool.

I have my first meal break just before reaching the bustling, thriving town of Wickham Market that lies close to the River Deben. It's the old porridge number again, but I was hungry and enjoyed it immensely.

I eventually have to return to the main A12, but soon after I find the cycle track I was looking for. It's an ideal walking track between tall hedgerow and farmland. Obviously it is little used for the blackbird and thrush, pigeon and crow display their annoyance at my intrusion into their world as I walk by. The delightful route takes me close to Farnham, my final destination for the day. We soon find a decent campsite nearby and I'm sipping on a cup of tea by 2.30pm.

Today's pedometer reading: 28.9km (17.94 miles).

FRI, 5TH JUNE 2009
FARNHAM –YOXFORD – SOUTHWOLD

I start out from Farnham at 6.30am. The climate again is ideal for walking as its overcast and cool. At 10.30am I meet up with the support vehicle waiting just beyond Yoxford. A young lady pulls up on the other side of the road, comes over to the van and gives us a donation. The lady, named Caroline, explains that she has MS but is happy to donate to our charity. Thank you for your support Caroline!

I begin my next session after the usual meal break and walk toward Blythburgh using a bridle path. It's a delightful walk, but it starts to deviate across country taking me away from the main route. I get onto a narrow country road that takes me to a B-road. I'm finding the traffic a bit hazardous now so I hop over a fence and take to the fields. I see another footpath, I'm not sure if it's a public footpath but I follow it as it seems to be going in the right direction. Suddenly I'm walking through this large herd of cows and some young calves.

I must mention at this juncture that I have had considerable experience with cows for I'd worked on a dairy farm in New Zealand for 18 months. I also spent a further 12 months as a herd tester and this meant testing 25 different herds on different farms each month to record the quantity and butter-fat content produced by each cow. So walking through this herd isn't worrying me at all and I think the cows are sensing this for they just eye me casually and continue to chew the cud.

But as I'm ambling though their midst, there's a bit of a disturbance and this young bull appears out of nowhere. I recognise the signs of an agitated bull instantly so I keep an eye on him while staying close to the herd. But he keeps following me through the herd snorting and tossing his head in an aggressive fashion and the cows are beginning to disperse. A few are moving hurriedly toward a boundary fence and I notice this wooden gate nearby. I quickly follow as this bull seems to mean business. The word 'quickly' is really a bit of an understatement, I actually run like mad through the herd with the bull close on my heels and I go over that gate faster than a scared cat up a telegraph pole. I reckon if any scout searching for an Olympic contender for the high jump had seen me at that precise moment he would have signed me up on the spot!

I eventually meet up with Rob at Blythburgh where's he's been waiting for me by the lake. I go through my leg stretching routine then sit down to a meal of tuna pasta and salad, while explaining to Rob about my reasons for arriving late.

It is then back on the road for the final push to Southwold on the Norfolk coast. The last part of this walk is becoming a nightmare! I've been walking on this narrow, winding road and there's no room to get off to avoid the busy traffic. Although I am wearing my hi-vis jacket I'm still thinking that it's too dangerous to stay on this road, what with these farming trucks zooming around corners as if they own these narrow highways I can get bowled at any moment! I can see the headlines: 'Dave Wilson, the 73-year-old 'Around England Walker', had to abort his venture due to being knocked down and killed by a bloody big cattle truck'. . . or something like that! It's funny the things you think of as you walk.

I'm now walking on fields alongside the road again. It means having to climb over barbed wire fences much of the time. The ground is quite lumpy in places and I have to tread carefully to avoid twisting an ankle or knee and it's slowing me up considerably.

As you can imagine I am pretty tired by the time I reach Southwold and grateful to be at last back on the coast; even more thankful that I have made it in one piece!

Today's pedometer reading: 28.7km (17.82 miles).

Notes of Interest: Southwold

The Domesday Book mentions Southwold as an important fishing port and it is believed to have received its town charter from Henry VII in 1489. The town's potential to become a major port declined due to the gradual silting up of shingle across the harbour mouth.

It is believed that a fire ruined much of the town in 1659, badly damaging the fifteenth-century Church of St Edmunds. Overlooking the beach is the aptly named Gun Hill, where 6 18-pounder cannons are installed to commemorate the 1672 Battle of Sole Bay It involved the English and French fleets fighting together against the Dutch.

The battle was fierce and bloody and it was reported that many bodies were washed ashore; despite the loss of life the battle ended inconclusively.

During World War II, Southwold gained the status of a "fortified town". It became the target of many bombing raids by Germany, despite the fact that the cannons on Gun Hill were defunct and unable to fire.

Today, because of the surrounding marshes, considerable restriction of expansion has been adopted resulting in a more pleasant landscape.

SAT, 6TH JUNE 2009
SOUTHWOLD – KESSINGLAND

I usually shower after I have finished walking for the day, but yesterday all the showers were occupied, despite visiting the ablutions on two occasions. So I decide to shower this morning instead. We leave the caravan camping site at Southwold at 7am after a breakfast of toast and banana and black coffee. The weather looks fine, but I have this northerly wind in my face as I begin my walk from where I had finished off yesterday.

I am soon walking on the road that leads to Lowestoft; it's a narrow and winding road with high hedgerows on both sides and once again I have to resort to clambering into nearby fields and walking alongside the road. Once on the coastal path it's a relief to have the noise of the surf ringing in my ear instead of the continual traffic noise. I decide to make it an easy day today for tomorrow I plan for a big push through Lowestoft and on to Great Yarmouth... hopefully!

We find a caravan camping site right on the beach near Kessingland. It's a great site with panoramic views out over the North Sea...wonderful! We have power on site so we hook up and then I'm off for a refreshing shower.

The evening meal is over and I'm now going online to answer emails, update my diary and progress map etc. Just hope I don't get as tired as I did the other night when I fell asleep on top of the keyboard.

Today's pedometer reading: 10.3km (6.4 miles). **Note:** I forgot to turn on pedometer at start, so refer to actual road distance: 8.6 miles.

SUN, 7TH JUNE 2009
KESSINGLAND – GREAT YARMOUTH

Today I've decided to walk to Great Yarmouth.

I leave the Heathland Beach Caravan site at 8.10am and begin my walk toward Lowestoft. I manage to stay on a track along the dunes for a while and then walk past a large area of static homes before reaching a lovely promenade that takes me almost to the marina. At this juncture I have to join the A12 to cross the harbour and then continue my journey through Lowestoft.

Some distance after leaving Lowestoft, cliff erosion presents a problem and soon I am clambering over unstable collapsed substance from the cliff face above. It's tricky and laborious walking.

I eventually get onto a smooth path closer to the rocky shore, but the tide has been coming in and I am soon confronted with heavy seas crashing against the rocks occasionally sending a deluge of spray across the pathway. Rather than return to the unstable cliftop walk I trust to lady luck and continue along the path. But the lady finally gives up on me and I am suddenly drenched from the aftermath of a large wave.

I stand there soaked to the skin and begin surveying the situation. I notice the spray crashing over areas of the path some distance ahead of me and I realise that this is not going to be the most sensible route to take. I remember seeing some wooden steps winding up the cliff face about 500 metres back and so I start to retrace my sodden steps and eventually begin to make my way up the cliff face. It's a fair climb, but I finally reach the top and soon I come into a small village called Corton.

About 2 miles further on, feeling hungry and damp I finally meet up with the campervan at Hopton-on-Sea where the first meal in the county of Norfolk is waiting for me. After the break I make my way through to Gorleston-on-Sea by walking along the river before finally crossing the bridge into Great Yarmouth. I reach the harbour as rain starts to fall and when I eventually meet up with Rob on the far side of Yarmouth I am once again wet through. In the notebook that I always carry with me I had written the words: 'the power of prayer.' It was a reminder of another random thought I'd had during today's walk.

I remember asking myself: is there really such a thing as the power of prayer? I realise it's something that most of us do at one time or another. In fact, I recall raising my eyes and sending up a silent 'thank you' when I recovered my mobile phone from that ditch on the Kent coast only 2½ weeks ago. I remember also having a few scary moments when coming into the entrance to the Brighton marina with about 30-odd passengers on board my tour boat during a relatively rough sea and being broadside on to a rogue wave. It took me close to the Akman blocks on my starboard side, but luckily we reached the safety of the outer harbour with all the passengers blissfully unaware of any danger. I remember casting my eyes up to the heavens, thankful to be in safe water.

However, thanking providence was always an involuntary action after the situation had been resolved, never before. It occurs to me that those of us who are religious will undoubtedly believe in the power of prayer; that somehow the act of praying might possibly bring some divine intervention to a problem. This is something I've never been able to get my head around. I began to think of all the prayers that must have gone unanswered over the years. The millions of people wiped out through the ages by plagues, famine, wars or those that had experienced terrible treatment and afliction, all would have prayed for some heavenly deliverance to end their suffering. I remember thinking about more recent times; about those caught up in the Nazi Holocaust. Jews were taken from their beds or snatched off the streets and packed like sardines into rail wagons to be taken to the concentration camps around Europe.

These nightmare journeys would sometime take days with little respite from the cramped conditions and many would be forced to relieve themselves where they stood. I guess they would have prayed! On arriving at these terrible death camps parents would experience the appalling heartbreak of having their children torn away from them. Would not the mothers have prayed for their young ones? Wouldn't the fathers have done the same? Would not sister have prayed for brother, and brother for sister? Wouldn't prayers have gone out to save elderly parents, the sick, the infirm or those too weak to work, knowing only too well that they were to die in the gas chambers? Did they all not pray for an end to the suffering; to the long and bitter European winters when the harsh, freezing winds would numb their thin, ill-clad bodies to the bone? Wouldn't there have been daily, even hourly pleas to the heavens for some sort of deliverance from their living nightmare?

From as early as 1933 innocent people, mainly political and ideological opponents at first, but soon Jews along with gypsies and other 'undesirables' were being incarcerated in these terrible places. Here in these 'factories of death' they suffered and died and it wasn't until 1945 when the Allies finally overran these despicable institutions that the few pitiful survivors were able to be rescued from their hellish existence.

So was there really some all-encompassing deity up there looking down on the terrible affliction and agonies that these people were forced to endure over twelve long, terrible years? And if so, why did it decide to do nothing? I reasoned that if desperate prayers like these go unanswered why then should this 'God' be expected to answer an individual's prayer to help a sick mother or child, or respond to a prayer for an easy childbirth, or for a painless time in the dentist's chair or to help someone pass an exam or find a job? Why would the footballer who kisses the cross on his neck chain and briefly looks up to the heavens before running onto the field expect to be given divine assistance in winning the game or having it protect him from injury?

And yet, despite my rambling cogitations, I firmly believe that all people should be allowed to follow their own religious beliefs including their right to pray; for the power of prayer can, at the very least, bring solace and comfort to the many unfortunate people in this world who are still experiencing troubled times.

After shopping for groceries at a nearby Asda store we settle into a lovely campsite near a racecourse.

Today's pedometer reading: 24km (14.9 miles).

Notes of Interest: Great Yarmouth

The town of Yarmouth (originally Yernemuth), was without doubt a Saxon settlement of some size, but it is believed to have been razed to the ground by Vikings around 1010. The town sits at the mouth of the River Yare near the site of what once was a Roman fort camp known as 'Gariannonum'.

A thirteenth-century charter was granted to Great Yarmouth by Henry III with the following conditions: "The town is bound to send to the sheriffs of Norwich every year one hundred herrings, baked in twenty four pasties, which the sheriffs are to deliver to the lord of the manor of East Carlton who is then to convey them to the King".

In the early eighteenth century, Yarmouth was vividly described several times in Daniel Defoe's travel journals, with such comments as: "...for half a mile together, they go cross the stream with their bolsprits over the land, their bowes, or heads, touching the very wharf; so that one may walk from ship to ship as on a floating bridge, all along by the shore-side..."

On 2nd May, 1845, the town was the site of a drowning tragedy when a suspension bridge crowded with children collapsed. They had gathered on the bridge to watch a clown who was being pulled by geese down the river while in a barrel. The children all moved to the other side as he passed under the bridge, but this caused the chains on one side to snap. The bridge deck tipped over, spilling the children into the water. It resulted in 79 children being drowned that day.

On the 19th January, 1915, Great Yarmouth experienced an aerial bombardment in the shape of the dreaded Zeppelin L3. Then in April 1916, the town was attacked by the German Navy .

The town withstood considerable Luftwaffe bombing during World War II, destroying much of the old town. It is thought that many bombs were released by the Luftwaffe on leaving our shores just to rid themselves of the load before crossing the channel. However, despite the war damage, much of the original 2,000m protective medieval wall and several of the mazes of alleys and lanes known as 'The Rows' have survived.

The North Sea flood of 1953 badly affected the town, but in September 2006, it suffered even worse flooding.

It is said that the author, Charles Dickens, stayed at the Royal Hotel on the Marine parade in Yarmouth while writing his classic novel, David Copperfield; *and that the author of* Black Beauty, *Anna Sewell (1820-1878), was born in the town.*

Great Yarmouth is sometimes regarded as the gateway from the Norfolk Broads to the sea.

CHAPTER 5
NORFOLK

MON, 8TH JUNE, 2009
GREAT YARMOUTH

Today is a rest day for Rob and me. The day is cloudy but pleasantly warm. We decide to go into Great Yarmouth by bus to shop and look around. At this point I feel I should make mention of my pedometer watch. It's a really useful peace of kit. It just needs a couple of clicks to convert its function from digital watch to pedometer. It records your activity period from start to finish, and then with another couple of clicks, it will display your performance, distance walked, calories burned etc and store the information. The unit can then be converted back as a normal wrist watch. However, I believe there are GPS units that are as good or even better, so while we were in Great Yarmouth we went to a store where they have these gadgets and I have to admit that they were pretty impressive. I'm also told that some mobile phones now have this facility. Anyway, these products were fairly expensive and as I was funding this whole walking venture myself, I thought it prudent to resist the temptation to buy.

Later in the afternoon we return to the caravan site where I get down to updating stuff on my laptop while Rob conjures up a meal. In the evening we walk to a local pub where we indulge in a pint while watching a darts match. Then it was back to the campervan for a good night's sleep.

TUES, 9TH JUNE 2009
GREAT YARMOUTH – WINTERTON-ON-SEA

Today is significant for at its close, we will have been on the road for exactly one month! The skies are overcast and rain is threatening as I start out from Great Yarmouth and head out onto a decent coastal walkway. I make good progress to Caister-on-Sea, but then the going begins to get tough and spits of rain on my face were a forecast of what was to come. I'm soon forced to go down onto the beach as the track I've been walking on is turning to soft sand.

I plod on while listening to the pounding surf coming in from the North Sea on my right. The dark skies ahead of me look ominous; dark enough to create no distinct line at the horizon as leaden skies meet leaden sea. As I walk continuously northward, the driving rain becomes more severe, making it difficult to push into the headwind. I need to reach a place called Winterton-on-Sea where I have arranged to meet Rob as it's the nearest place for him to reach me on this part of the coast. I eventually arrive there at 12.40pm and although I have been walking for no more than 4½ hours, I still felt pretty weary, wet and cold.

The wind and the rain combined with the soft sand underfoot make this 9-mile walk pretty tough; however, after a cup of hot coffee at a nearby cafe I soon feel okay.

Today's pedometer reading: 14.3km (8.9 miles).

Notes Of interest: Winterton-on-Sea

Winterton-on-Sea is an ancient fishing village some 8 miles north of Great Yarmouth. It still contains the charm of a village unspoiled by the tainted hand of tourism. There are no amusement arcades and few fast-food establishments, but the area is blessed with beautiful sandy beaches, and a tern colony has recently made their home in the peaceful dunes.

The dunes nature reserve is an 'Area of Outstanding Natural Beauty' ideal for bird watchers and walker alike and there is a seal colony, 30/40 strong, that can be often seen just north of Winterton.

WED, 10TH JUNE 2009
WINTERTON-ON-SEA – WALCOTT

We are up really early today. After showering and a breakfast of toast and banana, Rob drops me off at Winterton seafront to start my day's walk. By 6.10am I'm back on the coastal path heading northward. Once again I have to resort to walking on the beach as the sealed path soon disappears under mini avalanches of soil from the unstable cliffs above. Walking along this vast stretch of beach in the early hours of the morning is an experience to remember, for as far as the eye could see, no human figure infringed upon this tranquil landscape. The only sounds come from the occasional lamenting cry of a seagull and waves breaking lazily on the deserted shore, while the early morning sun squints through the elongated, orange-tinged clouds in the eastern sky.

About 3 miles before Sea Palling, I come across a colony of seals. I try to get as close as possible, with my camera at the ready, but as I get nearer they quickly become unsettled and prepare to dive off into the sea if I dare to move closer. I retreat a little and when they begin to relax I start clicking off some pictures... but oh for a better camera!

I meet up with Rob who was waiting on a beach front parking area at Sea Palling where I stop and have a meal break. I continue walking on the beach front again for my second session of the day. Walking on sand is a problem; it's okay if it's compacted as it usually is near the sea edge, especially on an outgoing tide, but too often the sand becomes soft resulting in extra effort with each step and this in turn gives rise to rapidly tiring legs. I eventually manage to get onto a decent track among the sand dunes and am making good progress when thoughts, as always, parade across my mind. What I find strange is that it's only since I've been walking that I've pondered over subjects such as religion, fossil fuels, world problems etc. Normal day-to-day existence never allowed me the time to dwell on such matters, despite being retired. Today I particularly remember thinking about how we humans have progressed over the years.

I thought that all the technological advances man has made since the Industrial Revolution have been nothing short of miraculous; but I wondered whether we had made the same progress in the spiritual sense, as greed for wealth and power continue to override all other facets of the human character. Wars and civil unrest continue to erupt around the globe; people still resort to personal and mob violence; drug taking and child abuse still exists and a great proportion of people are still suffering from malnutrition while others on the same planet are over-consuming and over-eating to the point of gluttony.

Yet as I walk, I remember thinking about the progress we have made in moral and ethical terms. After all, we no longer allow the death penalty and yet, less than 200 years ago people would congregate to watch public hangings; and it wasn't just men being taken to the gallows but women and children also. There must have been little pity in those days, because these so-called 'criminals' could be hanged for some small offence that in today's world would be regarded as little more than a misdemeanour.

Watching chained-up bears or bulls being harassed and gradually torn apart by trained pit dogs while people stood around betting on the outcome must have been everyday entertainment in medieval times, for it is said that there would have been a bear-pit in almost every town in England. Yet today most of us would be horrified to witness such a wanton display of cruelty.

I begin thinking about today's world and of the concerns people have for the conservation of our rainforests and about fossil fuels, the husbandry of marine life and the protection of endangered species. To my mind, there seems to be a greater regard for the welfare of our planet these days than there was, say, two generations ago. But is it too late, I wonder…

I walk on feeling a little comforted; maybe my grandchildren's children and their children might bear witness to a much better world after all.

Carol, Jean & me with our families - our mother is in the centre

For another 2½ hours I stay on the coastal path to Eccles-on-Sea. It's an exhilarating walk absorbing the ever changing vista of sand, surf and sea, but now I'm on an inland path that eventually brings me into the village of Walcott where Rob is waiting. I have been walking for over six hours and I am ready to pack it in for the day.

Today's pedometer reading: 26km (16.14 miles).

Notes of Interest: Walcott

The name Walcott is said derive from the Celtic word Walecote, which apparently means 'village by the wood'.

Walcott is about the only place along this part of the coast where the road actually runs along the edge of the sea, making it an ideal sight-seeing stretch.

The coastal erosion along this part of the coast has been a worry and could account for the disappearance of approximately a 2km-wide strip of land since the Roman occupation era. Over the ages this erosion has seen the demise of several medieval villages that have been reclaimed by the encroaching seas.

THURS, 11TH JUNE 2009
WALCOTT – CROMER

I leave Walcott seafront at 7.30am. The skies are a heavy grey and rain is threatening as I start out on the sea wall's concrete path. I am soon walking on what is supposed to be a walking path that lays directly underneath the earthy, unstable cliffs on my left. About 20 metres away on my right the surf tumbles rhythmically onto the dark sand; its whiteness and that of the breaking crests atop turbulent waves are in stark contrast to the dark steel-grey expanse of the North Sea. It isn't long before the path disappears completely, buried under past falls of earth from the adjacent cliffs and I find myself having to tramp through soft sand once again. It's raining steadily as I draw level with Bacton.

I realise that the coast road further along runs closer to the seafront, so I look for an opportunity to get up onto the cliftop to reach it. I knew it would be far less tiring walking on a hard surface than on soft sand. A mile further on I see steps that have been formed on the cliff face and I am thankful for the chance to leave the beach.

As I pass through Mundesley, I decide to try the footpath that runs alongside the cliftop, but after a couple of miles I realise it's too dangerous as the cliffs are again very unstable along this stretch, so I return to the coast road. I catch up with Rob at a village called Trimingham, then stretch aching legs and replace damp clothing before sitting down to a decent meal and a bit of a rest. Too soon I have to reluctantly leave the van and continue my walk. I know I have another 4½ miles or so before reaching Cromer and it looks as if the rain might start falling again so I carry on at a faster pace toward my destination.

During the day, as always, various thoughts come and go, some in rapid formation while others linger for a while like scenes in a stage play. My thoughts finally settle on that brief respite at home after returning from the Outward Bound Sea Training course in Aberdovey.

I can't recall how long it was before I was notified to join my first ship sailing out of Liverpool – possibly two to three weeks or more – but I do remember that I appreciated being back home and away from the strict regime of the sea school. Despite the fact that we were quite hard-up, our family life, as I've always remembered it, was a happy one due mainly to a hard-working but very easy-going and loving matriarch, our mother. In later years all seven of us came to realise what sacrifices she must have made to put decent meals on the table, to have us sleeping in warm beds, to have presents for each and every one of us on our birthdays.

Christmas was a time we looked forward to for there were always presents and goodies in pillow cases at the bottom of the beds of the younger ones, and gifts from under the Christmas tree to be handed out to all of us during the day. Days before the girls would cut up silver paper to use as tinsel and coloured paper would be cut into 1½" wide strips then glued together to make paper chains to adorn the room and be drooped around the tree together with the tinsel.

During my period at home after arriving back from Wales, I would often meet up with my mates and we would usually go off to a cinema to watch a movie. Because we were always short of the readies we'd elect for one of us to pay at the ticket counter while the others would wait at the rear emergency exits. At the interval people would often use these exits to leave the cinema having previously seen the main film, for the programme was on-going throughout the day. Our 'insider' would be waiting for us to slip in and then in the semi-darkness would guide us back to some empty seats.

I recalled there were times when they'd have a man outside waiting to catch kids who were trying to 'bunk-in'. However, if you picked the right time when there were lots of people milling around, you could, nearly always slide in undetected.

Occasionally while you were sitting there, smugly thinking you had got away with it, a torch beam would single one of us out and ask to see our ticket. The boy who had let us in would quickly give his ticket to the one under the spotlight so that he could show it to the attendant. If the attendant (or usherette as they were called in those days) was thorough and asked each of us in turn, we were done for and despite our protests that we had lost our tickets, would have us removed.

But this rarely happened because other cinema goers would often object to the disturbance made by the torch and the interrogations, so the attendant would often be obliged to make a reluctant retreat, especially if the main film was about to start.

When thinking about those times, my thoughts would often stray to the unique and dilapidated street that we lived in and about some of the weird people who lived there.

I have reached Cromer and have caught up with Rob on the Esplanade near the pier. We drive to the caravan site that we had booked earlier, and are soon settled in. After a shower and a cup of hot coffee, I feel as right as the rain that was now falling steadily on to the campervan.

Today my pedometer reading was 23.3km (14.46 miles), although with the dull ache in my legs, it felt as if I had covered a much greater distance.

Notes of Interest: Cromer

The lost church of St Peter is a reminder of Cromer's ancient history; a time when Cromer, a settlement known then as Shipden or 'Shipden-juxta-Felbrigg', was lost to the sea. The name 'Cromer', (possibly alluding to 'Crows' mere or lake), was first noted in 1297.

Over the centuries the town grew as a fishing centre. In the early days you would have seen a variety of catches being landed depending on the season; lobster and crab in the summer, drifting for herring in the autumn and long-lining for fish like cod in the winter. The town has now become famous for the Cromer crab, and most restaurants will more than likely have it on their menus.

In the early nineteenth century, Cromer became popular and the wealthier Norwich residents would invariably have a summer home there.

The Cromer lifeboat station is renowned for the notable rescues the crews carried out between 1917 and 1941. Their bravery brought national attention to the town and to its lifeboat and crew. Most notable of these was Henry Blogg, who received the RNLI gold medal for heroism on three occasions and was awarded the silver medal four times.

The lifeboat station is responsible for a large area of coastline as no harbour exists around this long and exposed stretch of the coast.

FRI, 12TH JUNE 2009
CROMER – BLAKENEY

I begin my walk from the Cromer esplanade at 6.45am. The weather's fine with a cool, light southerly breeze. The resort's long esplanade is a treat to walk on as it stretches northward for some distance. I continue on the coast road, the A149, walking past Sheringham where I have my first meal break. I'm soon off again, but this time I take the coastal path via the Sheringham Golf Course. I stay on the coastal path until the turn-off to Weybourne where I then merge onto a track that takes me through the Cley Eye Bird Sanctuary; a marsh and heather wonderland for a great variety of birds. It is at times like this where the knowledge of the different species of birds, especially those migrating to our shores, would have added another interest to the walk, but sauntering through the sanctuary carrying powerful binoculars, taking photos and making notes was not part of my agenda; my foremost priority was to make consistent headway north.

I divert once again onto the coastal road and walk through the pretty village of Cley before turning off once more onto the coastal path walk. The sign post in Cley reads: Blakeney 1 mile, but I think I have doubled that distance reaching Blakeney by the marshland route. Still, I am well compensated, for the scenic beauty of the place leaves quite an impression on me.

As I walk along the raised track I begin meeting other walkers out for a day's stroll. Some of them know all about my walk as they have been speaking to Rob who's waiting at the riverside parking area, so I'm often being met with handshakes and words of friendly encouragement.

Today's pedometer reading: 28km (17.38 miles).

SAT, 13TH JUNE 2009
BLAKENEY – WELLS-NEXT-THE-SEA – BRANCASTER STAITHE

Today I start walking at 6.15am. My destination: Wells-next-the-Sea via the Moreston Salt Marshlands. To walk through these marshlands in the early hours of the morning is an unforgettable experience. The air is still and there's no sign of human activity to mar the utter tranquillity of the area and as I walk I listen to the delightful sound of the wake-up birdsong of a dozen or more different species.

It's taking ages to get to Wells-next-the-Sea, due mainly to this looping track through the marshland that's going to add at least another hour to the journey, but I'm really enjoying the walk. Rob is waiting at Wells when I arrive and after a meal and a leg stretch I decide to journey on for a few more miles.

This time I think I will take to the road as the track through the marshes is too great a distance by comparison, and my legs are beginning to feel the strain. It's not long before I have to divert off onto the country byways once again for the narrow, winding road has become busy with fast moving traffic and I'm finding it too hazardous to walk on.

At times during today's walk my thoughts wander back to my teenage years and to the school I went to.

Queens Park Secondary School was, I suppose, typical of most learning establishments in the lower socio-economic areas of England in the 40s and 50s. I seem to remember dark varnished doors and windows and the dark green paint that adorned the walls of the large classrooms and gloomy hallways. When I look back I have this impression that the whole atmosphere of the place was impersonal and uninspiring. There was a large hall with a raised stage at one end and a wooden climbing rack was attached to a side wall. Our play time and outdoor PE sessions were spent on a tarmac playground that surrounded (as I remember) two sides of the school. The school was about a quarter of a mile from where we lived and mostly uphill. We all walked to school of course; kids walked everywhere in those days!

As I stroll along I try to recall the names and images of the teachers who were at the school during my time there. Some teachers you never forget; like Mr Phillips our maths teacher, built like a gorilla but twice as mean. If he thought you weren't paying attention a blackboard rubber (an oblong piece of wood with felt attached) would go flying through the air and usually find its target. Sometimes he'd get you up in front of the class and then tell you to write on the board the answer to some equation or other; if you got it wrong you could generally expect a twist of the ear before he sent you back to your seat.

In a way he started me off on my lifelong interest in swimming. The school had a fairly active swimming team and their training sessions happened to coincide with our maths classes, so Moe and I decided that we had to get into the team. We were both reasonably good swimmers, but we began going to the North Road pool to try and improve our sprinting times. Within a few weeks we had met the swimming team requirements, which simply meant swimming a certain length in a certain time limit. From then on we were excused from most of our maths classes with Mr Phillips. Being members of the swimming team saved us from much pain and worry, but it didn't do much for our maths education!

Other teachers spring to mind. There was Mr Shepherd, our science teacher; Mr Martin was, I think, our art teacher then there was a Mr Metcalf and a Mr Shaw, but I cannot recall the subjects they taught. There was also a female art teacher but her name eludes me. The only other female teacher in the school during my time there was our PE teacher, Miss Carter.

Ahh Miss Carter! If there was a graph showing the teacher most disliked at the school to the one most popular, you'd certainly see Mr Phillips at the bottom and Miss Carter at the top. We had PE classes for two hours about three times a week. Our class had Miss Carter on two of those sessions and on those days there would be hardly any truanting and boys who had been off sick would mysteriously turn up for school temporarily cured of their ailment. In the fifties there wasn't much around in the way of glamour to occupy the minds of testosterone-loaded teenage boys. There was no such thing as 'Page 3' or glamour magazines. There was no TV at the time, no internet, and certainly nothing alluring in comics like The Beano and The Wizard. At the movies we might have been enchanted with visions of gorgeous women like Betty Grable, Myrna Loy, Esther Williams, Jane Russell, Marilyn Monroe etc, but they were on celluloid, a world away and almost on a different planet as far as us boys were concerned. But here was Miss Carter, a real flesh and blood attractive woman and one who (perhaps unknowingly) would often reveal much of that flesh to the satisfaction of enraptured young male PE students.

Miss Carter would have probably been thirtyish. She was short as I remember, with dark curly hair. She was also quite buxom with nice legs and she'd wear wide, thigh-length, black shorts. We'd all follow her through a series of rigorous exercises including tumbles and vaulting, during which she'd often show a great deal of thigh and white knickers, much to the delight of most of the boys.

During a respite Miss Carter would give a lecture on the importance of being fit and supple. It was on one of these occasions when a boy (I can't remember who) talked of his difficulty in performing a certain exercise and asked her if she could show him the correct way to do it. As soon as she began to perform the exercise we understood the reasoning behind the request. It was probably the most revealing posture for her to do, but she seemed unaware of the implications involved in performing the exercise in front of a group of students that included about 20 randy young boys. From then on it became almost standard procedure during these lecture periods for someone to ask Miss Carter to repeat some exercise or another. She never seemed to catch on to the skulduggery behind the requests; either that or she was a compulsive exhibitionist. It caused me to wonder in later years that if some of us boys had given as much attention and concentration to the lessons as we did to Miss Carter's anatomy we might have achieved better academic results!

I finally walk into Brancaster Staithe at 1.30 pm and catch up with Rob who has been finding it difficult to locate a caravan site due to the Elton John concert being held over the weekend. Eventually we secure a site at the Pinewood Holiday Park way back in Wells-next-the-Sea, the place we had walked past earlier today.

Today's pedometer reading: 28.8km (17. 88 miles)

Notes of Interest: Wells-next-the-Sea

In the late sixteenth century, Wells (as it's often named) was the major port for the area, due to its prime position on the coast. Wells status as a port continued to thrive well into the twentieth century, but over the years, life in the little town has radically changed.

The name Wells comes from the many springs that were around the town. In the 1800s, the town authorities decided that there was a need to give greater distinction to the town by changing its name, so Wells became known as Wells-next-the-Sea.

In 1880, the Wells Lifeboat was launched in heavy seas to help the Ocean Queen, a ship in distress. The conditions were treacherous, but the lifeboat answered the call and went out to help the stricken craft, making way with only oar and sail power. Of the crew of thirteen aboard the lifeboat, eleven lost their lives after being hit by a rogue wave.

SUN, 14TH JUNE 2009
WELLS-NEXT-THE-SEA – BRANCASTER STAITHE

We have decided to have the day off today, as friends were coming up for the Elton John concert and have arranged to meet us here in Wells later in the afternoon. It was a good opportunity for us to catch up with a backlog of laundry, filling our water tank and emptying our grey water. We finish all the chores then enjoy the rest of the morning relaxing in the warmth of the sun.

Later, after a pizza and salad lunch, we walk into the village to meet Geraldine and Johan and John and Lesley. It's really great to see friends from Brighton Marina, but all too soon they have to leave as they are concerned about getting to the concert in time.

Rob and I spend the rest of the day shopping and browsing in the village. Towards the evening we buy fish and chips and eat them while sitting on a low roadside wall. Afterwards we stroll back about half mile or so along a sort of causeway that leads to our caravan site. We sit outside the van and chat for a while as we watch the sun settle behind the hills. Soon, it's back inside the van to update the diary and progress map on the website. It has been a very enjoyable day, but tomorrow it's back to the serious business of making northerly progress in my attempt to walk around England.

MON, 15TH JUNE 2009
BRANCASTER STAITHE – PEDDARS WAY

The clear, crisp early morning air hints at the likelihood of another fine day as Rob drops me off at Brancaster Staithe at 6.35 am. I continue to walk from where I left off on Saturday and make my way toward Holme-next-the-Sea, where I intend to make my first meal stop. We are only 3 miles from Hunstanton and the name triggers memories from long ago.

It was around June 1940 that I was evacuated with Mick, my older brother, to a Dr Barnado's boys home in this county of Norfolk. The expected blitzkrieg from the Luftwaffe had not materialised since the start of the war, but almost nine months on, there was an expectation that it was definitely about to happen. The War Ofice issued its bulletins in the newspapers and over the radio urging the evacuation of women and children out of the cities and into the country. The mass evacuation began again, but this time in earnest and Mick and I were among the many thousands of children that were being evacuated around this period.

One day the staff at the Dr Barnado's Home decided to take us on a trip to the seaside and it was Hunstanton that we went to. I can't recall much detail except that I remember feeling amazed at seeing the sea. I remember also the smell of the salt air and the noise of seagulls intermingling with the light rumble of the surf. The tide must have been out for I recall walking through shallow pools of water in the sand to reach two fishing boats that were perched near the water's edge, and watching some men in black jerseys selling lots of silvery fish to the people standing around. The beach seemed to go on for miles in both directions and I remember thinking that it was the most beautiful place on earth.

From Holme-next-the-Sea I pick up the well-known walk, the Peddars Way. This public walkway goes straight down for 20-odd miles in a south-easterly direction through some of the loveliest countryside in the heart of Norfolk. But being such a long distance public right-of-way it means that the walker, on occasion, has to cross over country roads that intersect with it.

The walk is incredibly enjoyable and apart from one small group of walkers who are resting under the shade of a tree as I pass, I don't meet another soul. Enjoying the warmth of the morning sun, I walk along a country lane bordered by tall hedgerows, and listen to the delightful chorus of a variety of songbirds; add a bouquet of countryside aromas and you might get some idea of the euphoria I was feeling. Sadly, many people never experience such things. My reverie was soon to be marred, however, by the incident I was to have with a badger.

I had already walked through Ringstead and Sedgeford, then, after about another hour of walking, I come across another tar-sealed country road. As I begin to cross the road I hear a sort of staccato barking noise. I look up and down the road a couple of times expecting to see a dog because it was that sort of sound, but then I catch sight of a muddy grey form that was lying near the roadside, about 30 yards further up. I hear the sound again and see the movement of the head so I knew where the noise has come from. I approach the animal slowly, unsure of the problem.

From the white stripe on the head I immediately realise that it's a full grown badger. It's obvious that the poor animal had been run over and is in terrible pain as the hind legs are askew, bloodied and deformed. I immediately think of trying to phone the RSPCA, but there are no signal bars on my phone and I suddenly realise that I will have to attend to this problem myself. There is no option but to put it out of its agony. I need to kill it quickly but what with? My wooden walking stick is not suficiently heavy enough and will do nothing more than give the poor animal a headache which I am sure it can do without. I wander up and down the road desperately looking for something heavy enough to do the job when I see what looks like a large piece of concrete lodged up against a wooden post. It was actually a large smooth stone embedded in remnants of concrete. It took two hands to carry the stone back to the wounded animal.

I immediately kneel down close to the badger, raise the stone into the air then bring it down with all my force onto its head. There's a slight shudder of the body, the eyes glaze over and the badger lies still. I get hold of the head as I can't find the forelegs and then I pull the animal completely off the road and into the thick vegetation. As I do so I can't help but be surprised at the heaviness of the body.

After this incident I can't focus on enjoying the walk. It has shaken me up quite badly and all I want to do now is get the day's walk over with as quickly as possible. I journey on for another 2½ hours before meeting up again with the camper van. Rob drives to a delightful campsite, but my thoughts still linger on the killing of the badger. While Rob goes to the camp shop I connect the power and put the kettle on. He returns a little later with some groceries and about two minutes later the rain came down in torrents. Boy, talk about great timing! I must now forget about the badger, fire up the laptop, do my diary and plan tomorrow's walk.

Today's pedometer reading: 33.90km (21.07 miles).

TUES, 16TH JUNE 2009
PEDDARS WAY – KINGS LYNN

Today is another fine day. Rob drops me off at the intersection where I had finished walking yesterday. I put yesterday's incident with the badger behind me and start my journey through another section of the Peddars Way.

I had been well aware for some time that I was getting closer to Lexham where Mick and I, along with all the other younger Barnado's boys, had attended school.

This school was run by a head teacher called Miss Pogson. Now if there was ever a name that could sum up the personality and appearance of a person, then Pogson has to be it! I reckon Charles Dickens could have made great use of such a name. Even to this day I can recall my impression of the woman and about how frightened I used to be of her. She was always punishing one of the Barnado's kids for the slightest of reasons. Whenever Mick and I reminisced about those times we would come to the conclusion that we were probably picked on more than the village kids at the school simply because we had no parents around to protect us.

Mick would say that hardly a week would pass without her punishing one or two of us Barnado's boys. Miss Pogson would make it worse by telling those she picked on that she'd see them after school so the unlucky ones would be made to suffer throughout the rest of the day knowing what was to come.

Some of the bigger boys used to put a Beano comic under their trousers to soften the blow of the cane on their backsides and other times, she would hit your knuckles with a ruler during class, which was also very painful, especially in the winter.

Miss Pogson had a big pink wart on the side of her face that sprouted three or four black hairs. When she spoke to you it was impossible to look her in the eye because the wart drew your eyes to it like a magnet. I remember thinking as a kid how horrid she was and we were all pretty scared of her. But what confused me was that I would sometimes see her at church, so part of my juvenile thinking was that she must be a good person really and that it was us kids who were bad. It took some years before I would come to realise that churchgoers are not necessarily always 'good people'.

Bus arriving at Dr Barnado's, Lexham Hall

I know that I longed to be back with my mother during those years, yet I cannot recall being treated too unkindly at the home, apart from a vague recollection of being made to stand by my bed one night because I had wet it. Mick and I can't remember ever being abused in any serious way and that was always something to be thankful for. I do remember that we were in some sort of mansion, but it was my older brother who later told me that the Dr Barnado's Home was in a country mansion called Lexham Hall. The home would have probably been disbanded sometime after the end of the war; its purpose made redundant. Yet surely the mansion as I imagined it was still there, standing aloof and grand, its wide passages faintly echoing the footsteps of homeless boys now long gone. As I walked I wondered if the fields would be as green as I remembered, and whether the hedgerows down the country lane where our mother used to walk with us would be as high; and whether the conifer tree we used to climb would still be there, standing tall and proud in an adjacent field.

As I'm walking down Peddars Lane I know I must be getting close to the junction where the A148 intersects the walkway and sure enough, a few minutes later I see Rob in the distance coming up the lane to meet me.

Once back at the van I give thought to driving to Lexham or Litcham village and making enquiries about the whereabouts of the mansion that had been our home for over six years. I have to make up my mind as this is the nearest and most practical juncture to start on that journey. If I turn to my right, the road will take me toward King's Lynn, my chosen route to take me northward. To my left however, lay Fakenham and the A1065 which will take us inland toward Litcham. After more painstaking thought I decide to continue my walk toward King's Lynn so I ask Rob to drive off in that direction while I follow on foot as usual.

I'm not sure whether it is the incident with the badger or my impatience to get around the Wash and start walking northward again that influences my decision not to deviate from my route, but as the day wears on I begin to regret not spending a little time trying to locate the mansion. After all, it was a place where my brother and I had spent a good part of our childhood.

A few miles further on I catch up with the campervan and have my second meal break of the day. After my customary leg stretch I continue on to King's Lynn where I eventually meet up with Rob in a Tesco car park. We shop here for some much needed groceries before heading off to find a caravan campsite north-east of the city. It's not long before we are parked up and relaxing in the warmth of another summer's day.

Later in the evening I allow Rob to talk me into joining him for a beer at a local pub. We end up having a great time with many of the locals offering to buy us beer in return for stories about the walk. As always, my concern is about being fit for the next day's walk so I have no more than a pint of local ale and half a shandy before heading back to the van.

Today's pedometer reading: 31.60km (19.64 miles).

Notes of Interest: King's Lynn

The Domesday Book recorded the town as Lun and Lenn, but during the Middle Ages it was possibly known as Bishop's Lynn due to it being under the ownership of the Bishop of Norwich. The word 'Lynn' meaning pool might have possible reference to the Wash area or it could have originated from the tidal pools on the Ouse.

During the Middle Ages, Bishop's Lynn was granted the right to hold a weekly fair. At that time fairs would last for a few days. They would be lively events and along with the entertainment there would be trading stalls where people would travel from near and far to buy or sell their wares in the town.

The Black Death hit the town of Bishop's Lynn badly in 1348-49, probably killing at least half the town's population. Many towns and villages throughout Europe would suffer the same fate, their people succumbing to the deadly plague in their hundreds. Another severe outbreak of plague followed in the 1500s, and then again in the 1600s.

It was recorded that in 1531 a woman servant was boiled to death in King's Lynn for poisoning her mistress. It is thought that this was the traditional punishment for murder by poisoning (not very nice!). Legend also has it that the town witnessed the hanging of seven-year-old Michael Hammond for stealing a loaf of bread and, believe it or not, he was executed along with his eleven-year-old sister.

The English Civil War, which began in 1642 between the King and Parliament, caused grief for the town when in August 1643, the populace changed their allegiance and sided with the King. Parliament responded quickly and sent an army who besieged the town for three weeks until it surrendered.

It is thought that Daniel Defoe made some mention of King's Lynn as being 'Beautiful, well built and well situated', yet at that time it appears that King's Lynn was quite polluted and therefore an unhealthy place to live. It is no surprise then that cholera would often break out during the mid-1800s and it was only when the town's network of sewers was

*created, along with a decent public water supply, that the place became
less offensive.*

*During WWII King's Lynn became home to many evacuees from
London as they thought the area would be safe from the bombing.
However, due to its unique location at the Wash the town experienced
a number of enemy air raids.*

WED, 17TH JUNE 2009
LONG SUTTON

Awoke early again and after a breakfast of banana on toast and
black coffee I am back on the road by 6.40am. Leaving the suburbs
of King's Lynn I eventually get onto the main coastal route north. I
liaise with Rob to meet up with him about 7 miles on. During this
session I manage to get onto a country byway, but it begins to veer
away from my intended route and I soon return to the A-road, where
I finally catch up with the van. After the usual stretch and meal break
I continue on toward Long Sutton. During the day my thoughts
wander back to those early childhood years.

My two older siblings would often say that, before the war we
were a happy brood of kids being cared for by a loving mother.
We lived in Leeds and our father was away down south in Yeovil,
Somerset with his army unit preparing for service in France. Our
mother became the main carer of two boys and two girls; the eldest
being Mick who would have just turned seven, then came Jean, then
me, then Vivienne who was the youngest. At that time Carol had not
yet been born.

I give some thought to those old photos that we siblings have all
gazed on at times. One of them was a large sepia-toned photo of my
father standing tall and proud alongside a young and attractive dark-
haired lady who was to become our mother. It was their engagement
photo. Another photo showed our mother on a motorbike with two
relatives in the sidecar; they were among many snaps that showed
our mother and father happy and carefree during the pre-war years,
blissfully unaware of what fate had in store for them.

Our father had been in the Grenadier Guards and on demob had
signed up on special reserves. It was why he was called up at the early
part of the war. Our mother would often say that if he hadn't been

in the reserves he might never have been called up, being 34 years of age and the father of four kids.

Our parents to be in their courting days

It was the War Ofice report on the death of her husband that was to radically change the life of our mother and her young family. In later years she would sometimes speak about that particular time saying that she'd had a sudden wave of depression some days before the arrival of the letter, and that in her heart she knew what the contents in the official-looking envelope were before opening it. The full poignancy of that event must have really hit home when a letter dated the 31st March, 1940 and written by our father reached our mother, two days after she had received the report of his death.

Our Aunt Glad, my mother's older sister, would often tell us how close my mother and father were to each other so his death must have shattered her world. Unfortunately other hardships were on their way.

Mother on a motorbike with two relatives

About 3 miles before Long Sutton and just before reaching Sutton Bridge, I walk into the county of Lincolnshire. I decide to finish my walk early as I am feeling a little under the weather due to getting back late last night!

Today's pedometer reading: 23.61km (14.46 miles).

Notes of Interest: Long Sutton

Set in the fertile silt lands of the Lincolnshire Fens, Long Sutton, like many Fenland towns, has enjoyed an illustrious history. By the early thirteenth century, the town was a prosperous trading centre and less than a hundred years later, Long Sutton was said to be one of the richest communities in Lincolnshire.

The nineteenth century brought a feeling of confidence to the area due to the opportunities opening up through the Industrial Revolution. By the mid-1860s rail travel had arrived.

Long Sutton's St Mary's Church is famous for its thirteenth-century lead-covered timber spire and it is reputed to be the highest, oldest and best-preserved lead spire in England and possibly Europe.

The old Market House became, among other things, a venue for adult education. In the very early years people would be reluctant to be seen at one of these classes in case it gave the impression that they were not well educated; and yet attendance remained high as it was thought to be even more shameful if one was unable to read or write.

No. *104/82/7*
(If replying, please quote above No.)

THE OFFICER Army Form B. 104—82B.

CORPS OF MILITARY POLICE,

MYTCHETT HUTMENTS, Record Office,

ASH VALE,

ALDERSHOT.

15 April 1940

Madam,

It is my painful duty to inform you that a report has been received from the War Office notifying the death of :—

(No.) *292669*   (Rank) *L/Cpl.*

(Name) *Fred Wilson*

(Regiment) _____

which occurred *in France*

on the *13 - April* *1940.*

The report is to the effect that he *died from multiple injuries, the result of a motoring accident.*

I am to express the regret of the Army Council at the soldier's death in his Country's service.

I am,

Madam.

Your obedient Servant,

Mr. Wilson
143 Throstle Rd.
Middleton
Leeds.

P. Stewart Capt.
Officer in Charge Records
Corps of Military Police &
Officer in Charge of Records
Military Police Staff Corps.

(7 11 35) W10443—PP2882 20,000 3/19 HWV(T721) 4 E.F./3528
2792—P2654 15,000 8/19

[P.T.O.

Official notification of my father's death

My father's final letter to my mother

CHAPTER 6

LINCOLNSHIRE

THURS, 18TH JUNE 2009
LONG SUTTON – BOSTON

At 6.54am Rob drops me off at the same roundabout he picked me up from yesterday. The weather is ideal for walking as it is a cool and overcast with a light south-westerly wind. I soon drop Long Sutton behind as I look for a side road to get away from the traffic and its noise. I manage to get onto what appears to be a public path although nothing shows in my navigator book. The path is okay for a while but then merges into a ploughed field, so that is the end of that. I return to the A17 again where I eventually meet up with the camper van about 8 miles further on.

After a leg stretch I tuck into a meal of porridge that Rob has cooked and then prepare myself for another long session. It's strange how a certain melody or something as vague as an aroma or taste can rekindle past memories; memories that otherwise might have remained buried for a lifetime. Sometimes an incident can have the same effect, for as I walk out of the county of Norfolk I feel pangs of regret at not attempting to locate the mansion that had been our home during a good part of our childhood. The feeling triggers memories long forgotten. I begin to recall occasions when, as a young teenager I would listen as my mother spoke about those darker periods in her life; a time when her world had been turned upside down.

While our father was down in Yeovil our mother realised that she was pregnant again with her fifth child. Our father could never make the journey back up to Leeds in the short leave periods he was given but assured our mother that his regimental superiors had promised him a longer leave period in the near future. That period came just before he was shipped over to France. He was home for two days when he was sent a telegram ordering him to rejoin his regiment urgently for deployment overseas. It wasn't long after this that our mother received the news of her husband's death. It seems we were living at that time in Middleton, a suburb of Leeds, our father's home town. She felt she needed emotional support from her parents and also to be nearer to her sister Glad, so she left Yorkshire and took us all down to her parents' place in Woodford, an outer suburb of London. I remember our mother saying that just weeks after arriving in Woodford, Vivienne, who was then just 20 months old, was diagnosed with tuberculosis of the knee joint and was hospitalised.

Since the start of the war in September 1939, regular radio bulletins and newspaper articles had issued forth from the government's War Office giving bleak forecasts about the coming blitz. They warned of dangers like gas warfare, incendiary and mass bombing and hurriedly devised an evacuation strategy to get children out of the industrialised areas of England and into the country.

It was during this period that the two eldest children, Mick and Jean were evacuated to the country. Both were unhappy there. Jean later told me of one incident that happened while they were both in the bath together. Jean wanted more hot water over her side so her brother filled a jug from the hot water tap and poured it around her. He did this several times but on one occasion accidently scolded Jean in the process. Jean screamed out and when the woman came in the bathroom and saw what had happened she slapped Mick really hard on his bare back and bottom. Jean said that even at her tender age she remembered feeling sorry for her brother and angry at the woman as it had been nothing more than an accident. The couple they were with had no children of their own and seemed to have no idea how to care for two very vulnerable young kids.

Jean remembers Mick having to constantly work around the place and both were never allowed out to play. Our mother came to visit them soon after the bath incident and seeing how unhappy they both were she immediately packed their things and brought them home. As it happened many of the children who had been sent away in that first wave of evacuation were returned to their homes for the expected raids had not materialised. It would be another nine months before the German bombing threat became a grim reality. This quiet period would become known as 'the phony war'.

Mick, Jean and me - we were evacuated soon after this photo was taken

By May 1940, further warnings arose from the Government about the coming blitz. Our mother had resisted the constant pressure to have her children evacuated, not just from the appeals emanating from the radio every evening, but also from her parents who basically wanted their daughter and her brood of children out from under their feet. Her parents had grown used to a life without kids, having seen the last of their own children leave the nest more than a decade earlier and they couldn't rekindle the patience needed to put up with a brood of young kids running around the house and a baby bawling its lungs out now and then for its feed.

As time went on our mother's concern for our safety overrode all other maternal instincts and one day she sent my brother and me to Stepney Causeway, a Dr Barnado's home for boys since 1870, but now the head office and reception centre, where evacuees would be registered and sent to various Barnado's homes out in the country. We were sent to the Dr Barnado's boy's home in Norfolk and my two sisters, Vivienne (who had returned from hospital with callipers on both legs) and older sister Jean, were evacuated elsewhere. Soon after my mother and her remaining child, baby Carol, were also evacuated.

Within a matter of weeks our mother had not only lost her husband but also four of her five kids had been taken out of her life.

I'm beginning to feel quite weary so will end the days walk two miles from Boston. Thankfully we manage to get into a decent Caravan Club campsite called Walnut Lakes that's located nearby. I need a good rest up now as my legs and my lower back are aching badly; hopefully after a little shut-eye, a shower and a shave, I will be back to feeling my normal self again.

Today's pedometer reading: 30.3km (18.81 miles).

Notes of Interest: Boston

Boston's bountiful past has seen a mixture of significant events and notable characters come and go over the years.

The town is not mentioned in the Domesday Book so presumably it was nothing more than a small settlement in those days.

During medieval times fairs reflected a town's importance, and after being given that honour by royal charter, the Boston fair became one of the most popular and economically successful events in the region.

The Barditch was the boundary that ran around the east side of Boston, and its likely construction date would have been some time during the twelfth century. Historians believe that it was probably used as an open sewer and rubbish tip maybe until around the sixteenth century; the ditch was then channelled and diverted in order to utilise the sea's tidal flow to regularly flush the ditch and keep it comparatively clean.

The building of the Grand Sluice across the River Witham greatly improved the tidal flow system and prevented the silting-up process. The sluice, with its four pairs of huge sea doors and lock, was probably the largest of its kind in Britain at that time.

By the seventeenth century, Boston became a centre of religious non-conformism led by inspirational Bostonians such as John Foxe and

John Cotton. However, many of these people including Cotton, would eventually leave for a new life in Massachusetts.

In 1953, violent weather conditions and unusually high sea levels resulted in devastating floods along the east coast of England. Boston was insuficiently protected by its existing barriers and suffered great damage. Since then however, sea defences have been significantly strengthened.

FRI, 19TH JUNE 2009
BOSTON – SKEGNESS

We leave Walnut Lakes campsite at 5.45am, and Rob drives to yesterday's pick-up point. I start walking toward Boston arriving there less than an hour later. I skirt the town by staying on the A16 then connected to the road to Skegness. The route takes me through flat countryside where huge, recently ploughed fields intermix with green pastures; while other fields lie fallow amidst large rectangular blocks of young wheat, barley, and other unrecognisable crop. The only good thing about this section of the walk is that, for much of the time, you can see for miles in any direction such is the flat nature of the surrounding countryside. However, the route becomes more scenic as I approach the coast. During the morning's walk my mind once again touches upon the war years. I then begin to think about a more recent conflict: the Iraq war.

My thoughts home in on the terrible event of 9/11 with the destruction of the Twin Towers. I remember being puzzled as to why America had declared its intention to attack Iraq when, as far as I could work out, the country or its people had played no part in the Twin Towers assault. There were no weapons of mass destruction and I wondered whether Iraq's lack of such weaponry was suspected all along, but by using this element as a propaganda tool it enabled the 'powers that be' to continue with the offensive with a great degree of support from the American people.

We went to war against Germany because there was a real threat of invasion of our country and the possible capitulation of all of Europe. Margaret Thatcher responded quickly to the invasion of the Falkland Islands simply because the Argentinian intention was serious and had become an immediate threat to our country's sovereignty over those islands. As far as I could see there were no such threats from

Iraq. The only action that might have been sanctioned would have been the need to effect a regime change and I would imagine that disposing of Sadam Hussein could have been undertaken in a covert method well within the capabilities of the intelligence services of both the United States and the United Kingdom. Why he was not disposed of during the original Gulf War remains a mystery.

I recall those mass demonstrations in London and other cities around Britain where the public showed their disapproval of British involvement in the invasion of Iraq and how the government of the day continued to ignore the ongoing protests. I had always been led to believe that a democratic government acted for and was the voice of its electorate, but the Iraq war proved otherwise. If a referendum had been put to the British public on the issue, the result, I think, would have been very much in favour of dissent.

The conflict has been a huge drain on taxpayer revenue and has resulted in the loss of many of our young men and a countless number of innocent Iraqis; but it has probably been the catalyst to a fresh wave of radicalism within the Arab world. During my walk I began wondering if the 7th July 2005 bombings in London when 52 civilians were killed and around 700 injured would have happened had we not been in Iraq.

I remember thinking that the decision to invade Iraq by the British government against an overwhelming tide of public opinion was a glaring example of the democratic process being ignored in favour of political will; in other words, a government acting with the principles of a dictatorship.

It's amazing the things you think of as you walk; even more amazing when I consider the many times I have single-handedly helped solve many of the world's problems!

I meet up with the campervan where Rob is waiting in a lay-by about 8 miles on from our starting point. After the break I am soon on the road again heading toward Skegness. Another 7 miles on I catch up with the van once again and Rob has another pasta dish waiting for me. I realise I need carbohydrate intake, but I'm beginning to get fed up with this blinking pasta!

I feel pretty much okay after the break and decide to walk on for another hour before finishing for the day. I finally reach Skegness, affectionately known to many as 'Skeggie'! Once again we are very lucky to find an ideal caravan camping site close by and we are settled in by 1.30pm.

Today's pedometer reading: 29.4km (18.25 miles).

SAT, 20TH JUNE 2009
SKEGNESS – INGOLDMELLS

I leave our caravan site at 6.15am and start my walk from the lay-by where I had finished yesterday.

I don't really feel like walking today; I feel tired and listless and for some reason a little despondent, but as I head along under the cool, overcast, south-westerly conditions I begin to feel better. At one stage during today's walk I had been attempting to divert from a bridle path and onto a country road by climbing up a bank through a large area of nettles. My bare legs were now almost immune to their unpleasant caress so I felt little discomfort from the experience. However, thoughts about nettles now begin to germinate in my head; in fact, they were to have the honour of becoming foremost in matters occupying my mind over the next mile or so.

I began by asking myself this question: what real purposeful use do nettles have? They are the most prolific of weeds; they're unattractive; they don't appear to flower; and they can produce a painful irritation just by brushing against them. I suppose a botanist would supply a plausibly good reason for their existence but apart from nettle soup, which I have never sampled, I just can't see what beneficial role they play on our planet. But as I walk I cast my thoughts to mankind and ask the same question.

During his brief existence on this planet man has systematically destroyed or consumed much of our world's natural resources, from the great rainforests to the deep oceans. He has been the catalyst to the extinction or the decline of countless species of 'God's' creatures, all rightful tenants of this planet long before man set his clumsy foot upon its surface. He continues to allow a glut of food and other resources to be used and squandered in one part of the world, yet watches while members of his own species experience extreme poverty, sickness and starvation in another.

His religious fervour incites continual hatred and violence toward others, despite the fact that Gods of all religions are supposed to be peace loving... funny that! Finally, despite man's incredible progress in the world of science and technology, his greed for power and wealth continues to override all other principles. So, considering all these things I asked myself: what real beneficial role has man played during his brief existence on this planet? Maybe if I was the Creator of all living things and had to choose who should remain on Earth, man or nettle, I might just opt for the plain old nettle after all...!

After my meal break in Skegness I decide to walk on further. Skegness is the sort of place that you either like or hate. I walk past what seems like miles of entertainment halls and countless outside attractions that must be mouth-watering stuff to kids of all ages. I wonder about the many parents of young families over the years that would have been coerced into dishing out hard-earned cash for their children's entertainment.

It's not long before all the garish attractions and the many acres of static homes are left in my wake. I am now walking along this lovely coast with the north-easterly wind in my face and the sound of the North Sea surf pounding on the shore. Looking back and seaward I can still make out the faint jumble of offshore wind turbines that manage to tarnish the panoramic vista of the North Sea coastline.

I carry on along the coastal path, enjoying the taste of the briny that's being carried by the north-easterly wind while listening to the continuous cawing of the ever-present gulls swooping over my head. Eventually tiredness begins to set in. I glance at my pedometer, it's showing 20.6 km (12.8 miles); I thought the distance would have been greater. I journey on for another 45 minutes and finally end the day's walk near Ingoldmells where Rob comes to pick me up.

We find difficulty in locating a caravan campsite as most have no vacant sites available, but eventually after phoning around we secure a site at Sutton-on-Sea some distance away.

Today's pedometer reading: 24km (14.9 miles).

Notes of Interest: Skegness

Skegness appears to have had its origin from the Viking settlement period. It is believed by local historians that Skegness derives from the Viking word 'Skeggi', possibly the name of one of the Viking leaders who established the original settlement. However, it is also possible that

Skegness originates from a combination of other Danish words; after all the Viking influence was pretty strong in this part of England.

Like many coastal towns, Skegness would have started out as a fishing village and harbour, but the arrival of the railway in 1875 would bring new life to this sleepy settlement. Excursions were soon publicised attracting visitors from London and other inland towns and cities.

The first of the Butlins holiday resorts was built in Skegness in 1936 and has remained within the area to this day. It is still regarded as one of the more popular seaside resorts in the United Kingdom. The town expanded rapidly, but after World War II the resort had to compete with the growing exotic overseas holiday market that was offering economically attractive package deals to the public.

In the early hours of 5th October 1996 an odd event took place. It became known as The Wash Incident. Many Skegness residents, and even some police officers to the southeast of Skegness, claimed they saw a strange red and green rotating light. The many calls reporting the sighting were not only from Skegness but from Boston residents also.

The incident was reported to the Coastguard at Great Yarmouth. Eventually RAF stations, including the GCHQ and RAF Neatishead became involved in the mystery. It was established that the object was not a conventional aircraft because although it had been seen as a blip on radar, it had no transponder.

The coastguard alerted the RAF's air rescue centre at Kinloss in Scotland, who could find no evidence of aircraft in distress. They asked the radar complex at RAF Neatishead, the most important air defence centre in southern England, for help in identifying the lights.

A local newspaper of the time sought authenticity of the report from the Jodrell Bank Observatory. The observatory concluded that Venus, which had been shining with exceptional brilliance in the early morning sky to the east, was the only logical explanation to the image as seen on the video. This explanation was not entirely satisfactory and to many the strange sighting remains a mystery to this day.

SUN, 21ST JUNE 2009
SUTTON-ON-SEA

It's a day off today and yet I was up and about soon after 6am... I don't know why! Anyway, after a shower and breakfast I work on getting my website entries up-to-date and emailing overdue responses to messages and donations that had come in days before. I have also picked up some mail from home and among it was a final bill from my electricity supplier. Although the bill was not yet overdue I thought I should give them a call as I wanted to query something on the account. Big mistake, David!

The reader will know exactly where I'm coming from when I mention these automated telephone response (ATR) systems that are utilised by all major companies. I find it one of the most stressful and frustrating chores that I'm obliged to go through. Preparing to make the phone call is like sitting in the dentist's chair waiting to have a couple of teeth filled. You hope it's going to be trouble-free, but deep down you know there's gonna be a lot of stress and discomfort before the job's finished.

I dial the number and wait for the sound of that dreaded robotic voice. It's usually a sensuous female voice, the idea being I suppose, to keep you calm and relaxed during the ensuing process. It went something like this: "Hello...Thank you for calling our Customer Support Services...Your call is important to us." That comment always brings a knowing smile to my lips. "We are experiencing a higher than normal volume of calls at this time..." The smile changes to a cynical grin. I've not yet ever had the pleasure of receiving a response where they are not having a high volume of calls. In fact, on one occasion, just to test out a theory, I phoned them at 2.30am. Guess what? Same answer! I tried to think of some logical and genuine reason why their customer service centre is run off its feet at such an ungodly hour.

Of course, it would be daytime in the southern hemisphere so maybe there are people over in NZ and Australia who desperately want to live in this country...(!), and are phoning the company to enquire about electricity costs before making the move. Or maybe there's a horde of insomniacs throughout the UK all busily making enquiries about their electricity bills.

The seductive voice continued: "You might wish to call at another time when we are not so busy; otherwise please hold and we'll be with you shortly". Music meant to entertain or give you pleasure now encroaches upon your efforts to remain calm; or, worse still, another robotic voice starts prattling on about their latest products or services; stuff you are determined never to buy or use just for the hell of it! As I wait I wonder; do they intentionally hold you up so that they can get a message over about all their other products? See how cynical I am!

Another two or three minutes go by before my smouldering reverie is interrupted by the same female voice: "We thank you for your patience, your call is important to us, so please hold and we will be with you shortly". I sit through another few minutes of music or prattle. Then: "We thank you for your patience. Please listen to the following menu..." Out of the five options given, I push No 2. It's a query about my account. Same female voice: "Please hold while I transfer you to a customer service operator." More music and then more prattle.

A minute or so passes before the same female voice says: "Your query is important to us, so please wait and we'll attend to you shortly. You are number six in the queue. Thank you again for your patience". If being forced to endure something against your will is patience, then I must have oodles of it! I look at my watch, over eight minutes already.

After more stressful minutes, the same mechanical voice emerges from the ether: "To enable us to attend to your query in the shortest time possible, please key in your account number". Oh, I love that! The shortest time possible! Oh God! Where's that damned account? Why couldn't I have had it ready? I had the account right here on the table next to my laptop, so where the hell is it? "We don't appear to have received your information... please key in your account number." Now how do I tell this bloody automaton that I have a small problem and need it to wait while I find that damned bill? I put the phone on loud-speaker, click in a few random numbers just to keep the robot there, while I frantically search through the paperwork in front of me. It's not there! Damn!

That blasted voice bleeps out again: "I'm sorry, the number does not correspond, please try again"; I throw in another series of numbers and frantically rummage among the papers once more. Suddenly I find the damned account under a writing pad. With a quivering hand I prepare myself for keying in the correct account number when the syrupy voice breaks in once more: "I'm sorry; please hold while I transfer you to a customer service operator."

Music again... then suddenly a dialling tone: I wait, my heart pounding in expectation. "Hello, my name is Johnee; please give me your account number." At last, a real human voice! You cannot believe how relieved and thankful I am at that moment. I guess it's a feeling like being lost at sea for days on end without radio contact when suddenly a voice comes through asking for details of your whereabouts. I'm exaggerating of course. I call out the digits slowly and then wait a minute or more for a response.

"Ah, Mr Weelson, yes?"

I concur.

"How can I help you today, Mr Weelson?"

The voice is undoubtedly foreign; from India I reckon.

I briefly explain that I need to make a query regarding my power bill.

"Is it your account you are wanting to settle, Mr Weelson?"

"No, I don't want to settle my f.....g account" is what I dearly wanted to say, but instead I politely explained that I didn't want to settle the account... just query it.

"I see Mr Weelson. Well I am afraid you have come to the wrong section. You see this is 'Power Cut Queries'."

Through clenched teeth I quietly explain that I thought they had said 'Power Account Queries'.

"Don't worry, Mr Weelson, I will put you through. Please hold!"

"No don't go, please!"

The phone clicks dead for a moment or two, and then the dreaded music starts again.

I wait while a slow rage builds up inside me.

I start daydreaming about walking into the company's head office where I happen to find the Managing Director sitting at his desk. I am in the process of strangling him ever so slowly with his own tie when I hear that female voice again.

"Your query is important to us, so please wait and we'll attend to you shortly. You are number seven in the queue. Thank you again for your patience."

You cannot begin to imagine the scream that emits from my throat as I throw my mobile across the table where it bounces off the foam squab back up into the air to land back on the table. I was about to give it another go when self-control finally kicked in. Rob, hearing the scream, rushes in thinking that I had done myself a dreadful injury.

After I have reassured him that I am okay, I make us both a cup of coffee (mainly for me to settle my nerves) and I then begin to wonder whether I'm making too much of this; after all I've never heard anyone else complain about it. Maybe I'm becoming another Victor Meldrew!

But seriously, who really benefits from all this stress that the customer is put through? Why the company and its shareholders of course! Automated telephone response achieves greater efficiency and is a cost-saving measure that converts to greater profit for the company.

So what benefits to the customer? Oh, the customer... Well, they get no benefit whatsoever. In fact it's the exact opposite. The customer now spends longer on the phone than in those halcyon days before ATR. In actual fact this cunning system actually discourages customers from bothering the company with complaints or queries simply because it becomes too stressful to make contact. So big business wins out all ways.

Their most genius stroke however, was moving their call centres abroad; a move that has brought them even greater savings at the cost of further stress and frustration to their customers. Such measures simply mean that these companies and their shareholders are laughing all the way to the bank. So what about that old business adage, 'putting the customer first'? Well, that's the biggest laugh of all!

We deliver some of my 'Around England Walk' leaflets around the site before leaving for another caravan ground as the one we are in only had a vacancy for the one day. We arrive at the new site around noon and then relax for the rest of the day.

MON, 22ND JUNE 2009
ANDERBY CREEK

For some reason I feel tired again this morning despite yesterday's day off from walking —must have been that telephone call! It's past 8.30am before we rise from our beds. By the time we'd eaten breakfast, cleared up and checked out of the campsite it was almost 10.30am.

I continue walking from the point near Ingoldmells where I had ended my walk on Saturday. I was going at a brisk pace on the Roman Bank road and had covered about 3 miles when I decide to take a wide and well-worn track that seems to lead to the coast. I can see no public byway sign, although often these small wooden signs can be concealed among overgrown foliage. The track also wasn't shown on the navigator map I had with me so I should have known better than to venture down it. But I was eager to get back on the coast and the blue sea in that direction was beckoning me.

After walking over a wide cattle grid I find myself on farm land walking amongst a herd of cows. I realise I am on private farmland, but as I have been walking through the area for some time and can see the coast road a couple of fields ahead I decide to carry on. As I was walking over the next field a guy approaches me with a hammer in one hand and a big piece of wood in the other. I thought he was about to attack me, but it turns out he had been mending a fence when he had spotted me. He tells me I am trespassing and that I will have to go back to where I had come from. I explain to him that I just need to reach the coast road; a road that we could both see beyond the next fence, but he's unmoved. I glance again at the hammer and the heavy piece of wood and decide not to push my case.

He escorts me back about a mile toward the cattle grid in silence and then just before we get there he glances at my hi-vis jacket and asks me the reason for my walk. I show him a leaflet and explain that I am doing it for Cancer Research. Realising that I've walked all the way from Brighton he seems quite impressed and suddenly quite attentive. He then informs me that he has a close relative living down there in Brighton.

As we approach the cattle grid he gets quite chatty and then his next comment floors me: "If only you had said, I would have let you through a gate to the coast road." If he hadn't been holding that damned hammer and that 3ft piece of wood I think I would have clouted the little bugger! But as it happened I had already phoned Rob and arranged for him to return along the Roman Bank road so going back with the guy was not really an option. Instead I just grit my teeth, shake hands and retrace my steps along the track back to the road. But the exercise had resulted in almost an hour and a half of additional walking... Ah well, silly me!

Once back on the road I continue walking for a mile or so before catching up with the van. After a meal break I journey on and finally make the coastal path where there's lovely hard sand to walk on. It is such a refreshing feeling to have the sparkling blue sea close by me once again and to feel the sea breeze nudging at my back.

It's during this session of my walk that an incident comes to mind. I jot it down as a reminder under 'Thoughts' in the notebook I always carry with me. I suppose the thought was triggered by reading the report I had dug up on the internet while in Skegness a couple of days ago about 'The Wash Incident'. (I gave an account of this strange event in the Skegness 'Notes of Interest' section.)

One of the regular duties at Dr Barnado's was for two boys on a roster system to take empty Billy cans and walk through the woods and over some fields to a dairy shed in the early hours of the morning. The cans would be filled with fresh milk and then taken back to the home. On this particular morning it was the turn of my brother and me. We'd come out of the woods and were about halfway to the dairy farm swinging our Billy cans as we went, when we both saw this whirling sphere low in the sky and to the left of us. I recall being really fascinated because of the flashing rainbow-like colours radiating from it, although the predominant colours seemed to be red and green. We couldn't tell how far away it was as I remember and although it kept spinning it looked as if was stationary. We watched it for a few minutes and then it suddenly took off at an incredible speed and disappeared into the distance.

Mick and I occasionally talk about the incident and our recollections of that event have always been almost identical.

I reach Anderby Creek at 2.30pm and decide to stop at a lovely caravan camping site nearby called Hawthorne Farm. Not much distance covered but never mind – tomorrow is another day!

Today's pedometer reading: 15km (9.31 miles).

TUES, 23RD JUNE 2009
SALTFLEET

We leave Hawthorn Farm at 7am. It was a great Caravan Club campsite, with pleasant staff and clean amenities.

The weather is fine with a light, cool easterly as I continue my walk along the seafront from Anderby Creek. I'm walking along the sand for a while as the sand is quite firm, making the going that much easier. Eventually I take to the promenade that takes me into Mablethorpe. I liaise with Rob there and after a meal break we go into the town.

After buying some groceries we both have a much needed hair cut before heading back to the town's seafront. I continue to walk along the fine promenade, but it soon peters out at the town boundary leaving me walking on loose sand. I soon find a firmer walking track alongside the grass covered sand dunes and I stay on it all the way through to Saltfleet.

During the day my thoughts transcend time once more, taking me back to my mother and focusing on her plight during the first years of the war.

I recall the story my mother told me of her working life at a Vauxhall car plant for the war effort. There was a lot of government pressure on women to work in factories, car plants, munitions factories etc during the war years. With most of the male population in military service there was an urgent need for females to fill countless vacancies in order to keep industry and war production moving. Our mother said that as a young woman she felt obliged to do her duty in some way.

Appeals such as: 'We want British women to voluntarily throw their full energies into the war effort and thus avoid the necessity of compulsion', were enough to get hordes of women walking through factory gates. This era was to create one of the most significant changes in the role of the British female. Jean must have been home temporarily from evacuation when the authorities arrived to take Carol, the baby, for placement in a war nursery for she remembered the scene clearly, despite it happening such a long time ago. My sister has the impression of a large, stern woman coming into the living room and taking the baby out of our mother's arms. Jean remembers her mother crying and heard the woman admonish her by saying, "It's no good carrying on like that; your baby will be looked after; we're at war and everyone has to do their bit," or words to that effect. It must have been pretty hard for our mother for now, with Carol gone and Jean being re-evacuated, she ended up having none of her children around her.

However, the pay at the Vauxhall plant was relatively good so it gave our mother the necessary funds she desperately required for visiting her children. She would visit Jean who had been re-evacuated further north or travel down to Hampshire to see Vivienne in hospital or spend part of her day-off visiting Carol in the war nursery. She didn't get over to Norfolk to see us as often as we would have liked. I suppose she thought that as Mick and I were together we were less of a priority than my sisters who were away on their own. But at least we received letters from her and we always knew that one day we would get back home.

Our mother & baby Carol

I am pretty hot and tired now and very glad to meet up with Rob in Saltfleet. He was waiting in the car park of a country pub so I let him talk me into visiting the establishment for a well-earned pint. An hour or so later we manage to locate a very nice campsite and soon after we are connected up and ready to relax for the rest of the day.

Today's pedometer reading: 25.8km (16.2 miles).

Notes of Interest: Saltfleet

Saltfleet Haven was previously known as Saltfleetby. Probably from the Iron Age salt has always been a major source of income to the district and it helped the town to flourish. Saltfleet was also mentioned in the Domesday Book.

In 1281 Saltfleet was claimed by the Crown as a Royal Port and it continued to experience flourishing economic times during the following centuries. However, in later years the Haven port fell into decline, partly due to a silting-up process, and its prospects were to decline further when the Louth Navigation Canal began to operate.

One of the Haven's greatest tragedies of those times occurred on Saturday 18th February, 1882.

The 39ft sloop 'Try', owned by Edward Adams, was entering Saltfleet Haven with a cargo of coal from Rotherham. The Captain, John (Jack) Adams, and his wife Harriet were on board together with three of their children: Louise aged one year, Hermia aged three years and Robert aged four years. Two older children were staying with their grandparents in Louth. The 17-year-old brother of the Captain, Robert Adams, was also on board as the First Mate.

After taking the pilot and five other crew members on board to assist in the passage up the Haven, the weather worsened so they decided to anchor overnight and wait for the morning's flood tide to assist their passage upstream. As the incoming tide reached the Try they realised that the boat had been holed and was rapidly taking in water.

At 2.15am on Sunday 19th February 1882, they prepared to abandon the boat, but the pumps were managing to control the leak and buoyancy was maintained so they decided to continue up the Haven, despite the deteriorating weather conditions. They began to weigh anchor at around 4.00am but the chain broke and the strengthening wind resulted in the second anchor being hurriedly dropped.

At 4.45am, a rescue mission was ordered by the coast guard, but the rescue vessel's rudder ceased to function due to the severe weather conditions making headway impossible.

The second anchor chain on the Try suddenly parted around 5.00am causing the Try to drift out of the Haven exposing herself to the full fury of the storm.

The vessel became more unstable as huge waves began breaking over the beam tearing the lifeboats free and washing them away. As *the weather deteriorated further the young children were brought from their bunks to be held by the men in order to prevent them from being washed overboard. The Try, unable to keep stern-to to the oncoming sea, was now at its mercy as monstrous waves began to surge over the stern quarter of the broaching vessel, swamping the hatches and often washing crew and children off their feet.*

Throughout those terrible early hours the ferocious storm continued and first one child followed by another began to die from exposure. The coastguard eventually reached the Try between 7am-8am only to come upon the pitiful scene of John Adams and a crew member each holding one of the lifeless girls in their arms. Robert, his four-year-old son lay dead; killed by the broken boom that had fallen and pinned his body to the deck. John Adam's brother, Robert Adams, was found lying dead on the aft deck of the boat.

Harriet who lay floating, apparently lifeless in the hold, was seen to have moved and was quickly lifted from the water, then wrapped in a large coat before being taken off the Try. Although completely exhausted, Captain John Adams boarded the coastguard vessel with the crew and injured members with little help from the lifeboat crew.

Despite medical assistance, Harriet died, it is said, from the effects of hypothermia, although the opinion of many was that she would have eventually died of a broken heart had she lived. Her husband, John Adams, was the only family member to survive the tragedy.

Harriet Adams, aged 27, was buried in Louth on Thursday 23rd February 1882, alongside her daughters Louise and Hermia, and son Robert. John Adams's teenage brother, Robert Adams, was also buried in the same plot. The funeral ceremony in Louth was a deeply sombre event and was attended by approximately 1,000 people, revealing the extent of the sorrow that people felt for this very popular family. 'The Saltfleet Shipwreck' a poem about the tragedy was put to music and sold for one penny per copy in an effort to raise money for the family.

WED, 24TH JUNE 2009
TETNEY LOCK.

I leave the comfort of the camper van at 7am and walk down the road to the coastal pathway.

Saltfleet is soon left behind as I walk briskly northward along a firm grassy track. After a time I cross a small bridge and continue walking alongside a river that lay on my right. About two hours into the walk I enter a military firing range area where a terse notice advises walkers not to stray from the track. The path takes me along the edge of tussock covered sand dunes. To my right the flat, dark grey sands stretch into the distance before reaching the dark blue strip of sea.

About 6 miles into the walk I come across a fork in the path. Directions on my map appear a little unclear so I opt for the right-hand path as it seems more distinct and well-trodden. Wrong decision David! After about another half an hour of walking, the track almost disappears into an area of common reed and marsh grass. As I walk on, the marsh grass grows thicker and I scan the area ahead hoping to spot a continuance of the track but without success. I soon find myself on boggy ground having to feel my way with every step.

About 20 minutes later I try to get back to raised firm ground that I could see about 500 yards away on my left, but after walking in that direction a little way I suddenly come across a wide and muddy river. There is no chance of crossing it so I slowly retrace my steps through the marshland to get back to the walking track. I then plod back a mile or so until I reach the fork in the pathway; this time taking the alternative route.

The error has cost me almost two useless hours and pointless exertion on my legs and body. I feel exhausted and my feet are soaked through, but my overriding feeling is one of anger at wasting so much time and effort on a useless exercise due to my failure to interpret the correct route shown on the chart. The new route takes me up on a rise and over a bridge before leading onto a firm, raised, grass walkway. The track is endless with vast areas of wild marshland while on my right I see huge tracts of undulating sand. Soon broad fields of young wheat or barley and other unrecognisable crop intersected with fields lying fallow or ploughed come into view. With some relief I can now see Tetney Lock in the distance.

I finally meet up with Rob and it's then I realise that I have been walking continuously for over 6½ hours. I decide to finish the walk here as the marshland escapade had really tired me.

Today's pedometer reading: 22.6km (14.03 miles).

THURS, 25TH JUNE 2009
TETNEY LOCK – GREAT LIMBER

Last night we were invited by the publican of The Crown and Anchor in Tetney Lock to park on his premises overnight. He had electric hook-up available and also toilet and shower facilities, so we readily accepted the invitation. Thank you Brian and Cal, we are both very grateful for your generous hospitality.

I leave Tetney Lock at 6.35am and head for Waltham, which lies about 8 miles west, and it's where I catch up with Rob. After a meal and a brief rest I carry on walking in the general direction of Humber Bridge. Today as I walk I think about my mother's first visit to the Dr Barnado's boy's home... It was a few weeks from when we had first arrived there. I was not yet five, and Mick, my brother, would have been eight.

I remember little of those early years, but I do recall feeling terribly homesick. When my mother arrived on that first visit I naturally assumed that she had come to take us back home with her. I started to cry when I realised that this was not going to happen and that she was leaving us again. My mother remembers Mick slapping me hard across the face and telling me not to be such a baby, but at the same time she could see that her eldest son was holding back the tears. She would often speak about that time and about how she sobbed all the way back home on the train.

Mick always reckoned that as the months went by, we as brothers, felt sort of special due to the occasional visits from our mother. Many mothers never seemed to bother to see their children; in fact there were boys at the home who had never ever had visits from one year to the next.

My mother would later explain that it was because some women during the war years found their new-found freedom too good to resist. They were no longer tied to the home and caring for children; no longer reliant on meagre housekeeping money, for they were now working long hours for the war effort in factories and plants around the country and earning reasonable wages. With husbands away fighting and their kids evacuated they now had money in their purse and free time on their hands.

For many of these women the American GIs and other foreign servicemen stationed throughout England added spice to their new lifestyle. They found it hard to resist the temptation to get dressed up and hit the town. Suddenly there were romantic interludes with new and exciting men; eager dancing partners to teach them the new jive craze from across the Atlantic; interesting dates for a trip to the cinema or the theatre. There would be gifts of nylon stockings, chocolate, chewing gum, cigarettes and the like; all vastly appreciated for such items were usually unobtainable or unaffordable during the war years.

Mum's visit to Dr Barnado's

For some of these liberated mothers, visiting their estranged offspring would sit way down on their priority list. During her visits our mother would take Mick and I for a walk holding each of us by the hand while some boys would follow, holding on to her coat vying for her attention and addressing her as 'Mummy'.

After one such visit Miss Livings requested that our mother shouldn't visit too often as it had an unsettling effect on the other children. Years later our mother would often say how she found such incidents with these lonely boys terribly distressing.

Rob has gone on a little further than planned, but I finally reach the van about a mile from Great Limber. After a meal of ham and salad sandwiches I walk the extra mile to reach the village and end my day's walk here.

It has been quite hot for some time, so some liquid refreshment at The New Inn, Great Limber's local village pub, was very welcome. As there are no campsites within a 10-mile radius of the village, Brian, the publican offers us his parking and power facilities for the night. Two nights in succession we have been accommodated this way by the proprietors, this time it was Cal and Brian Vickers. They and their staff and patrons also donate generously to our Cancer Research charity. We send a big 'Thank You' to all of you at The New Inn of Great Limber. It was a special and unforgettable evening; a celebratory occasion seeing that it could be our last evening in Lincolnshire for I plan to walk over the Humber Bridge tomorrow.

Today's pedometer reading: 31.4km (19.49 miles).

This is the second section of the walk.

It took 5½ weeks to walk 527 pedometer miles (848km) through 6 counties before reaching **Kendal**

A dense fog spoils the view while crossing the **Humber Bridge**. I am invited into the **Stadium of Light** in **Sunderland**. Pete relieves Rob and becomes my support driver for a week on the **Yorkshire** coast. Jamie and his mother, Joan, meet us near **Seahouses**. Embarrassment on the road near **Wooler**. Wet and weary on the remote **Northern Pennines**.

A strange sighting near **Hadrian's Wall**. We take the ferry to cross **Lake Windermere** in the **Lake District**.

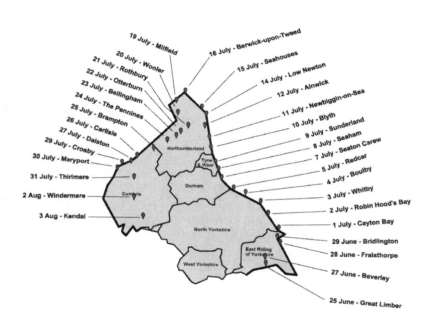

CHAPTER 7
SOUTH HUMBERSIDE

FRI, 26TH JUNE 2009
BARROW-UPON-HUMBER

We leave The New Inn premises in Great Limber at 6.05am, with Rob driving and yours truly by Shanks's pony. I am soon into a good walking rhythm as I start out on the A18; destination, the Humber Bridge. The route takes me past the Humberside International Airport then, further along the road I catch up with Rob at Barney's, a truckies roadside restaurant. We decide to have breakfast there for the aroma of fried bacon and sausage wafting from the establishment is almost irresistible. Rob relishes the meal more than I for it's one of those rare occasions when he hasn't had to cook the breakfast himself.

From the B1206 I take a minor road that leads me to Barton-upon-Humber, finally arriving there at around noon. I am quite tired and happy to stop earlier today, especially as we have been given details of a campsite near Barrow-on-Humber. I decide we'll cross over the bridge early tomorrow morning rather than go today. It's such a lovely evening so Rob and I walk to a vantage point to view the bridge. It is a wonderful sight with the reddish tinge of sunset making a dramatic backdrop for this huge single-span suspension bridge. I had read somewhere that it was the fifth largest bridge of its type in the world and the largest in Europe; it is also said that there is almost enough wire in the suspension cables to circle the Earth! I'm looking forward to a closer look when I travel over on foot tomorrow.

Today's pedometer reading: 24.6km (15.27 miles).

Notes of Interest: Barrow-upon-Humber

The town, known for its Saxon church tower of St Peter's, has also been the site where many Saxon archaeological finds have been discovered

The town of Barrow became the home of John Harrison in 1697. Although being trained by his father to become a joiner, John developed a keen interest in clock making; this interest would one day bring him worldwide acclaim.

In October 1707 an English fleet of ships was sailing off the Scilly Isles in thick fog. According to their navigation calculations they were in safe waters, but a section of the fleet ran aground causing the loss of around 2,000 lives and a good number of ships. The incident highlighted the maritime problem of the inability to calculate longitude.

After this terrible tragedy the British Parliament's Board of Longitude decided to offer a financial inducement to anyone who could develop the means of measuring accurate time at sea and thereby determining a vessel's longitudinal position. They offered a prize of £20,000 (probably around £2½ million in today's currency). It was to become the catalyst to John Harrison's fame.

Harrison's answer was his chronometer; a revolutionary clock that would give seafarers accurate longitudinal position at sea. His struggle to engender interest in his invention and win the huge cash prize was revealed in the novel Longitude. The book was eventually adapted into a television series starring Jeremy Irons and Michael Gambon.

The chronometer was designed to keep accurate time at the home port, so by the use of sun sights, 'local time' at sea could be assessed; then by correlating both time zones, longitude could be accurately established.

Harrison knew that the earth rotated 360 degrees in 24 hours (1440) minutes, so every 4 minutes would give 1 degree of longitude. Therefore, if a vessel's 'assessed local time' was 1 hour behind their home port time it would signify to the officer on watch that the vessel was 15 degrees west of their starting point; or 30 degrees west if it was 2 hours behind.

After almost 300 years, one of John Harrison's creations is still in good working order at nearby Brocklesby and I believe that a 1731 sundial made by John Harrison's brother, James, still stands in the local parish churchyard as a monument to the Harrison Family.

In May 2007, the Saxon church of St Peter's became an ossuary for the bones and skeletons of some 3,750 people and a centre for medical research into the development of diseases.

CHAPTER 8

EAST RIDING OF YORKSHIRE

SAT, 27TH JUNE 2009
BARTON-UPON-HUMBER – BEVERLEY

We leave Barrow and drive through Barton-upon-Humber at 6.25am, where I'm dropped off at yesterday's pick-up point. I start making my way toward the pedestrian and cycle approach to the Humber Bridge. A further couple of miles and I reach the bridge itself, but to my consternation the early morning mist seems to be getting thicker by the minute. I have a feeling of expectancy as I begin my foot journey on this great bridge, but I am completely surrounded by the densest fog imaginable. I can't believe it! I was looking forward to getting some great camera shots as the views up and down the Humber would have been incredible. But apart from a few photos of structural details on the bridge itself, shots of the landscape are out of the question as the fog has swallowed up everything beyond a 20-metre radius.

If I had I known the fog was going to be this bad I could have easily gone over late yesterday afternoon. Ah well, that's life! It takes me about half an hour to walk the Humber Bridge's 2,220-metre (1,380-mile) span and another 15 minutes to clear the northern approaches. I have now entered the county of Yorkshire, my eighth county since starting out from Brighton on the south coast.

I eventually meet up with the camper van and after my usual routine break I continue on toward Beverley. At one stage I deviate onto a public byway, but this leads me away from the A164 and into the village of Skidby. This has meant walking unnecessary extra miles, but at least it's a very scenic route. I now take the Beverley road and eventually arrive at the outskirts of Beverley in East Riding at 11.45am. I could easily continue walking but decide to finish here as I have to acquire a Navigator or Ordnance map for this new county.

It is market day in this very pretty town so Rob and I enjoy a period of shopping and browsing around. We locate a campsite about 4½ miles out in the country and are hooked up and settled in by 2.30pm.

Today's pedometer reading: 24.9km (15.46 miles).

Notes of Interest: Beverley

Originally known as 'Inderawuda', this 1,300-year-old town's origins can be traced back to the seventh century.

Athelstan, the King of England, happened to visit Inderawuda just before the Battle of Brunanburh. That night he was believed to have seen a vision saying he would be successful in vanquishing his enemy. His victory in the following conflict was realised and in gratitude, he became a mentor in the town's prosperity. In the tenth century the name of the town was changed to Bevreli or Beverlac; a possible reference to the colonies of beavers that might have been in the River Hull at that time.

After the Norman conquest of England, many pilgrims congregated at Beverley upon hearing that the town's founder, John of Beverley had performed miracles.

Norman reprisals in northern England for revolting against Norman rule in favour of Viking occupation were harsh and resulted in the destruction of many Yorkshire towns. Beverley, however, due to the reverence it received as being a place of godly happenings was untouched.

During the fourteenth century, Thomas More and Cardinal John Fisher of Beverley were martyred for refusing to recognise King Henry VIII as the Head of the Church of England.

An uprising in Beverley, that would later become part of the larger 'Pilgrimage of Grace', was held in York when around 30,000 people rebelled at King Henry's new religious laws. The King responded by dissolving the Monasteries, the Dominican Friary and stripping them of ownership of their land and in 1540, the Knights Templars of Beverley would experience similar retribution.

During the seventeenth century the plague caused the death of many people in Beverley and the surrounding district.

There are a variety of interesting public houses in the town, such as the Sun Inn, which date back to around the mid-sixteenth century and which is believed to be the oldest pub in the county. Then there's the White Horse Inn, or 'Nellie's' to the local population, one of the last pubs in the world to still use authentic Victorian gas lighting. A few of Beverley's public drinking establishments have been in existence for over a century.

SUN, 28TH JUNE 2009
BEVERLEY – FRAISTHORPE

I look at my watch; it's 6.50am as I start walking from the outskirts of Beverley. The weather is foggy and cool, but the mist is clearing and it's developing into a warm but cloudy day.

To get onto my northward route I need to walk through the town centre of Beverley and through the northern suburbs. Within the hour I am out into the lovely Yorkshire countryside and walking well. I catch up with Rob about 7 miles on where I stop for my first meal break. The walk up till now has been enjoyable as there has been a cycle lane adjacent to the main road. The next session is a little less comfortable as the cycle lane has petered out and I am left walking on a narrow two lane winding road with little room on each side to keep clear of oncoming traffic. A nightmare really!

I eventually stop at a village called Beeford where I meet up with Rob. I stretch the legs and have a tasty pasta meal with salad before continuing my walk. As usual, a variety of thoughts parade through my mind as I walk. It is during this session that my thoughts focus once again on my evacuation days in Norfolk.

In the beginning our mother would bring my brother and me presents, but the Dr Barnado's staff would not allow us to keep them as they thought it would cause dissension among the other boys. They confiscated them and added them to all the other charity items that came in from the public during the year, to be given as presents at Christmas or on birthdays.

As young kids, Mick and I thought that it was terribly unfair to have presents taken from us as soon as our mother had left, but the staff had previously advised our mother that it was their policy to do this to which she had readily concurred.

Nevertheless our mother always brought something with her when she came to visit, but now it was usually in the form of liquorice allsorts or wine gums; things that we could eat while she was with us or share with some of our friends when she'd gone. My brother would often mention, in later years, the curiosity that some of the boys at the home showed toward our mother after her visits. They wanted to know if she lived in a big house, where she worked, when she was coming back again and whether she would be bringing sweets and so on. It was as if some of these motherless kids had in some way adopted our mother as being their own.

Both Mick and I knew in our minds that we would definitely be going back home one day, but today as I walk I begin thinking again about those 'parent-less' boys and wonder what their thoughts would have been during those times and what sort of future fate had bestowed upon them.

Vivienne sitting between her two brothers with her leg in plaster.

From Beeford I carry on toward Fraisthorpe village about 6 miles from Bridlington before finishing for the day. We find a lovely little caravan camping site, but unfortunately all the sites are taken.

However Margaret, the lady who owns the Shasta Camping Club ground finds a special site for us next to her house. Thank you, Margaret, for your hospitality!

Today's pedometer walking: 31.8km (19.74 miles).

MON, 29TH JUNE 2009
FRAISTHORPE – BRIDLINGTON

Rob drives me back to the Fraisthorpe turn-off to start the day's walk. The weather is cool and the skies heavily overcast, ideal for walking if the rain stays away. The grass verge on both sides of the road make my journey to Bridlington most enjoyable. On either side high untrimmed hedgerows, trees and bushes of all description border the grass verges allowing occasional glimpses of the rural landscape beyond. Now and then a freshly ploughed or harrowed field comes into view, while here and there I catch sight of fields of sprouting young barley or some undefined crop of dark green that makes dramatic contrast to the rectangular blocks of what appear to be yellow mustard or oil seed rape crop.

Further along, the roadside foliage grows thinner and I soon find myself on a sealed walking track that leads me into the outskirts of Bridlington. The 6½-mile stretch is over before I know it and I now decide to stop here for the day. It will be an early finish, and by having tomorrow off from walking it will give both Rob and me a really good break.

I catch up with the camper van in a B&Q car park where we purchase some DIY items before driving on to a Tesco site for fuel and groceries. We have some difficulty for a while in locating a caravan camping site with empty spaces, but finally we manage to locate a country site about 2½ miles out of Bridlington.

Today's pedometer reading: 10.9km (6.76 miles).

Notes of Interest: Bridlington

The history of settlement around the Bridlington area is somewhat vague although occupation can be traced back to ancient times. The Domesday Book holds the earliest written evidence of the town, recording it then as 'Bretlinton'. Bridlington might also have once been the site of a Roman staging post or some similar activity for there are traces of a Roman road in the town and Roman coins have been discovered.

The 'old town' of Bridlington contains the historic site of The Priory Church of St Mary. It was built on the site of an Augustinian Priory which was dissolved in 1538 by Henry VIII, and was subsequently destroyed during the Dissolution of the Monasteries. It was around this time when the last prior was executed for taking part in the Pilgrimage of Grace.

In 1643 Queen Henrietta Maria, in support of the Royalist cause, landed her troops at Bridlington during the English Civil War.

Bridlington sits on an area of the coast which is said to have the highest seacoast erosion rates in Europe and it's something I had often witnessed along this part of the coast during my walk. Erosion is protected somewhat by the sea wall and the wooden groynes that help to retain the expansive sandy beach area.

TUES, 30TH JUNE 2009
BRIDLINGTON

It feels good to have the day off today! However, although I thought it would be great to sleep in this morning I find I'm up and about at 7.30am. Must be force of habit. It is quite cool with a dense ground fog, but by around 11am the sun breaks through and it develops into a lovely day.

The farm chickens keep us company as we relax outside the van on lounge chairs. This afternoon we watch the Andy Murray match. It's a desperately fought 5-set contest that exhausts both Rob and I so afterwards we have to laze in the sun for the rest of the afternoon just to recover. I've now walked around 600 miles since leaving Brighton Pier and although I have suffered no injuries I still worry that a joint injury such as a twisted ankle or knee might force me to abort the venture sometime in the future, but such worries are rarely entertained.

WED, 1ST JULY 2009
BRIDLINGTON – FILEY – CAYTON BAY

I am eager to start walking this morning for I'm feeling refreshed after yesterday's day off. I leave the campsite (and the chickens) and begin walking from the B&Q parking area. It isn't long before I'm out of the Bridlington suburbs and into the country once more. I decide to stay on the most direct route that will take me to Scarborough via Filey. This section of the walk is in distinct contrast to that of the previous day as there are very few hedgerows or trees bordering the road, just grassy banks and verges. There is heavy morning dew on the grass so within minutes my shoes are soaking wet. Eventually I come onto a narrow walking track that takes me through fields of grazing cattle before widening out into a sealed path as I near Filey.

A little way out of Filey I divert off onto a road that leads me to a coastal path which goes all the way to Scarborough. It was great to be away from the traffic and even better to have the sea as company once again, but the terrain underfoot is irregular, making this part of the walk quite tiring.

All through the day's walk thoughts would come and go and memories of events during the war years returned. One in particular was about Vivienne; another I recall thinking about was Jean's experience during the bombing of Coventry.

Now that Vivienne was hospitalised, our mother's spare time was mostly taken up with visiting her whenever she could. This was during the early years when our mother had also been evacuated with the baby Carol. She was also trying to visit Jean and very occasionally seeing us in faraway Norfolk; but Vivienne, she would say in later years, had needed her more than ever. The prognosis, at that time, on Vivienne's leg deformity was tuberculosis of the knee joints. The condition meant that Vivienne had to go down south to a sanatorium wing attached to the Lord Mayor Treloar Hospital in Alton, Hampshire, compounding our mother's difficulties in visiting us all.

Jean, my older sister, said she remembered the time when our mother visited her at the children's home she had been sent to. Jean had initially been evacuated to a private home in the country but had contracted scabies. The woman there didn't want the responsibility of looking after my sister while she was in that condition so she sent her on to a children's home without our mother being informed.

Our mother would later explain how it took ages for her to find her daughter and when she did, she quickly realised that Jean was showing signs of neglect and had been pining for her. She immediately packed her daughter's things to take Jean back with her, despite protests from the matron of the home.

They got as far as Banbury by bus when the air raid sirens went off and they were hurriedly escorted to a public bomb shelter. Our mother was still breastfeeding Carol the baby and was desperate to get home but had no option but to leave the bus and go with the warden. Jean remembered lying next to her mother on a camp bed among other people in the shelter. The date must have been 14th November 1940 for it happened to be the same night the German's had bombed Coventry. They had to stay in the shelter until the 'all clear' sounded in the early hours of the morning.

During that evening Jean remembered a warden bringing them each a mug of cocoa, but the drink made her mother quite sick. I recollect our mother's views about that night and about the difficulty she had experienced of getting back to her baby and the home to which she had been evacuated. She spoke of the overnight bombing raids and of the transport disruptions the following morning that made travel arrangements almost impossible. When our mother finally arrived back she was confronted by an angry Mrs Bottoms holding an even angrier baby who had been bawling all night for its feed.

I meet up with Rob at Cayton Bay about 3 miles short of Scarborough and shortly after Pete, a good friend from Brighton turns up. It's good to see Pete again and I'm grateful that he's given his time to allow my son Rob a break away for a week.

We soon find a campsite at West Ayton and quickly get powered up, while Pete strikes his tent close by.

Today's pedometer reading: 22.2km (13.78 miles).

Note: I had forgotten to turn on pedometer at the start of the walk so reckon the walk was closer to 15 miles.

Notes of Interest: Coventry

The first and ultimately the most devastating bombing raid in Britain on a single town (apart from London) during the Second World War was in Coventry. Birmingham and Wolverhampton were hit on that same night but with nowhere near the same intensity.

It was approaching dusk on the 14th November, 1940 when the Luftwaffe's Heinkel 111s began droning in toward the town. During a 12-hour blitz, they dropped around 500 tons of High Explosives (HEs), over 50 tons of incendiaries and a considerable number of parachute mines. It resulted in the destruction of over half of the residential homes and for many civilians it brought death and serious injury.

But the most soul-destroying experience for many of the townsfolk was to see their ancient cathedral lying in ruins; only the spire and tower stood in stark reminder of what once had been. A survivor remembers the night as being one of 'unforgettable horror' and another described the 'incredible relief' when the all-clear sounded at 6.16am the following morning.

Amazingly Coventry survived the onslaught and within weeks the factories were once again turning out aircraft machinery parts, some of which would most probably be used by the RAF to retaliate for the attack on the city.

It is probable that the bombing of Coventry was the catalyst for the 'revenge' bombings of German cities like Hamburg, Dresden, Cologne and finally Berlin by Bomber Command.

Indiscriminate bombardment was to become the norm and the scale of destruction of the German civilian populations would far exceed the 'collateral damage' done during the Coventry raid.

CHAPTER 9
NORTH YORKSHIRE

THURS, 2ND JULY 2009
RAVENSCAR – SCARBOROUGH – ROBIN HOOD'S BAY

We leave the West Ayton Caravan Club campsite at 7.47am. It's a great campsite, well run with friendly staff. Thank you, Terry and Sandra for your hospitality and the staff donation.

With Pete driving the camper van and Rob beside him, we drive back to Cayton Bay with me following behind in the car.

We eventually say farewell to Rob who's taking the Toyota back to Brighton for a week's break. Pete then drives off in the direction of Scarborough while I continue on foot. We meet up at the Sainsbury car park where there is defunct railway line close by. It was once a popular steam train route but was eventually shut down and the lines and sleepers removed; the track was eventually surfaced to make an excellent public walkway through to Whitby.

I meet up with Pete at Claughton, a converted station area. From Claughton I walk on to Ravenscar where we stop for refreshments at a cafe.

From Ravenscar I continue on to Robin Hood's Bay, where the scenery is absolutely breathtaking. The coastal views compete with the lovely Yorkshire countryside in capturing my attention and the experience sharpens my appreciation of all that is beautiful on this island of ours.

The journey is thoroughly enjoyable, so much so that I could have easily walked on further if Pete hadn't already located the Middlewood Farm caravan camping site; it's an ideal site just off the rail track path so I decide to finish my walk here for the day.

Today's pedometer reading: 33.1km (20.55 miles).

Notes of Interest: Scarborough

Iron Age tools discovered on Scarborough's rocky headland would indicate the existence of a settlement being there as early as 500 BC. A Roman signal station might have been established there around 370 AD for there are signs of Roman activity on that site.

There are a variety of theories about the origin of the name Scarborough, but it is likely a derivative of the Viking word 'Borg' meaning 'stronghold'. It is thought that a Viking settlement was established there around 960 AD by two brothers one with the nickname of 'Skarthi' and that the settlement was known then as Skarthi's stronghold (Skarthi Borg) or Skarðaborg.

This settlement was later attacked by a rival band of Vikings led by the brutal Tostig Godwinson, the younger brother of King Harold who was defeated at the Battle of Hastings. A massacre took place and the place was burned to the ground.

Scarborough revived under King Henry II, who then built a stone castle on the headland. In later years, Piers Gaveston, a favourite of Edward II was gifted Scarborough Castle and he remained there until the castle was besieged by barons. He was then captured and taken to Oxford to be executed.

In the Middle Ages Scarborough was given permission to hold a fair in the town. The event became an annual affair attracting merchants from all over Europe. The trading festival began on Assumption Day, finishing on Michaelmas Day, and in a later age this six-week fair would be commemorated in that well-known song by Simon and Garfunkel 'Are you going to Scarborough Fair? — parsley, sage, rosemary and thyme...'

Scarborough began to develop as a holiday resort when, in 1620, spa water was discovered. Some prominent people claimed that the water had beneficial qualities resulting in the birth of Scarborough Spa and the town's reputation as one of Britain's finest seaside resorts.

Scarborough's Grand Hotel was completed in 1867 and it would become one of the largest hotels in the world, with four towers representing the seasons, 12 floors, the months, 52 chimneys, the weeks and presumably the original design contained 365 bedrooms to complete the concept of annual time. However, today it appears that the hotel has 382 bedrooms.

I believe there is a blue plaque near the entrance that marks where the novelist Anne Bronte died in 1849.

Overlooking the North and South bays is Scarborough Castle, which was unfortunately bombarded by German warships during the First World War.

In June 1993 a landslip caused part of the Holbeck Hall Hotel and its gardens to slide into the sea; an incredible event that became worldwide news.

FRI, 3RD JUNE 2009
WHITBY – SANDSEND

I leave the Middlewood Farm campsite at 6.50am. Once through the gate I'm immediately on the walking path and into my journey northward. I somehow lose my way after crossing a road at what I think is the village of Fylingthorpe. I get onto a track that takes me up a steep hill amongst a flock of sheep and lambs before coming to another camping site where a local man directs me to the correct route. I retrace my steps and walk back down the hill before finally getting back onto the rail track path. Ah well, it's all grist to the mill you might say, unless you're the one doing the walking!

Before long I am once again travelling through the delightful terrain of the undulating Yorkshire countryside, before eventually skirting past the small village of Hawsker. I now find myself walking on some sort of viaduct into the attractive town of Whitby. Pete and I look around the town for a time while I'm seeking out the Cancer Research shop that has received my hearing aid from Ipswich Hospital. I pick this up then walk across the bridge for my meeting with the *Whitby Gazette*. After a brief interview and photo shoot we reluctantly take our leave of this lovely town allowing me to make headway north once more.

Pete drives on to the next pre-arranged location, which is Sandsend, while I walk on toward the seafront passing some really lovely quaint shops on the way. I am soon walking along the lovely Whitby shore; the weather is fine and people are strolling everywhere along the wide expanse of sandy beach. I walk close to the shoreline that stretches away into the distance and listen to the calm metallic-blue water of the North Sea as it splutters lazily over the hard buff-coloured sand. Much of today's walk is along gentle terrain allowing my thoughts to hold sway; memories of my early family life surface again and I remember in particular thinking of Janice, my young half-sister.

Jan was very stubborn as a kid. I remember the time when Dick, her father, was trying to get her to eat her vegetables and Jan was having none of it. Her father, who had a short fuse at the best of times, was running out of patience and began raising his voice and threatening her with all sorts of dire consequences if she didn't open her mouth and take a forkful of greens that he had hovering close to her lips.

We were all seated around the table wishing that Jan would relinquish for once, but she kept her lips tightly shut as she glared at her father with a look that said 'do what you like but I'm not having any more of that stuff!' I think it was our mother who defused the situation by saying something for I recollect Dick banging the fork down and leaving the table. We siblings were all relieved for we knew what Jan was like; Dick could have beaten her with a stick for hours or thrown her around the room breaking every bone in her body, but she would never have given in.

But what we all used to find terribly amusing in those days was how she used to swear as a child. Our mother never liked to hear any of us swear so she was mortified when she heard such profanities issuing from the mouth of her two-year-old baby daughter.

It took us a while before we realised where Jan was picking up all these terrible words. During warm, sunny days Jan would be put outside in her pram. The Black Lion pub lay nearby on the other side of the road and during summer months it would often be crowded with visitors, many from the East End of London. With the pub's doors and windows open for fresh air you could hear the discourse and banter from way down the road. Most of us older siblings would often be away doing our own thing. Our mother would usually be inside the house where she could keep an eye on the pram through the window or Jean would be given the responsibility if our mother happened to be at work; so the only one in constant earshot of the pub's noisy clientele was an innocent little kid sitting or lying all alone in her pram!

It was not uncommon for working class men in those days to use bad language, especially when involved in heated discussion. Often fights would start and the ructions would spill out onto the pavement where loud profanities and insults could be heard from protagonists and onlookers alike. We reckoned that Jan must have subconsciously absorbed these words for months on end and then would echo them parrot fashion at the most unexpected and ill-timed moment. But that was not all; sometimes the swear word would be accompanied by a pronoun, another adjective or noun and maybe a verb or two, putting even greater emphasis on our baby sister's crude expletives.

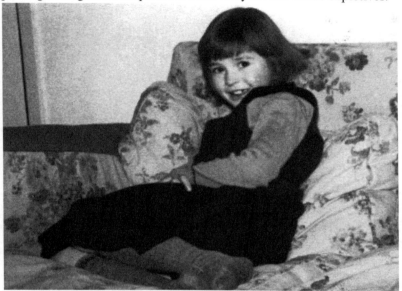

Janice our youngest

What made it worse for our mother was that all her other children, me included, would just roll about in hysterical mirth whenever this little sister of ours uttered some awful word or phrase. Hearing this little kid with the angelic face coming out with such a prolific array of foul language was so delightfully incongruous that it was impossible to remain serious, no matter how hard we tried.

Years later even our mother would laugh about those times and would often recount some of the embarrassing occasions she had experienced while Jan was going through this phase. She told us of the time she was travelling down to see Vivienne who was in hospital at Hayling Island. She happened to visit a cafe with her small daughter and was drinking a cup of tea when suddenly Jan, for no apparent reason, began coming out with all these terrible words. Our mother tried to quieten her but to no avail. In desperation she took Jan to the toilets and gave her a right telling off threatening her with all sorts of retribution if she continued to speak in this way. Our mother might as well not have bothered because our little sister carried on swearing even worse than before. Finally our mother had to hurriedly leave the cafe followed by stares of disapproval from the other patrons seated within.

Then there was the time when a Salvation Army lady, who had been talking to our mother, suddenly leant over the pushchair and began giving sweet talk to the baby girl only to hear "Piss off bloody cow" or words to that effect issuing from Jan's lips. What really worried our mother of course was the opinion of strangers who happened to hear Jan swear, for they would naturally assume that the poor little kid was being raised in dreadful surroundings by terrible parents.

It has been a delightful 2½-mile walk, but I am pleased to meet up with Pete at Sandsend. He had located a caravan camping site not too far away so I decide to end my day's journey right here.

Today's pedometer reading: 23.3km (14.46 miles).

Notes of Interest: Whitby

It is believed that in 656 AD the town was founded under its Old English name of 'Streonshal'.

The Christian king of Northumbria, Oswiu, the founder of Whitby Abbey, had in the previous year been confronted by the pagan king of Mercia's mighty army. Before the conflict he prayed for victory over an army greatly superior in number to his own and in return, he vowed to sacrifice his infant daughter Aelflaed's life to one of piety and give land for the creation of monasteries.

After the victory Oswiu was good to his word; the young Aelflaed entered the monastery under the care of her second cousin Hilda who years later would become an abbess of distinction, and under her guidance Whitby would become a great centre of learning. Hilda would, in later years, be venerated as a saint. Aelflaed succeeded Hilda as abbess in AD 680, and died at Whitby on 8th February AD 714.

The Northumbrian King issued grants for the building of monasteries throughout the area including one at Streanæshealh, which we now know as Whitby Abbey.

In 867, Danish Vikings landed west of Whitby at Raven's Hill, to attack the settlement and to destroy the monastery, but after the Norman Conquest it was allowed to be restored again.

The settlement later became known as Hwytby; eventually changing to Whiteby, referring to the Old Norse word meaning 'white settlement' – possibly due to the colour of the houses.

In 1540 Whitby was only a small fishing village and would have had no more than around 20 to 30 houses and about 200 inhabitants. It was the same year in which Henry VIII dissolved the monasteries including Whitby Abbey.

Whitby, of course, is where the famous explorer Captain James Cook first set out to sea and where his ship the HM Bark Endeavour was built.

The first whaling ship to set sail from Whitby was in 1753 AD. It was the start of a new maritime era and Whitby was to become an important whaling station.

Eighty-five people died on the 30 October 1914, when the hospital ship Rohilla sank within sight of those watching from the Whitby shore. Most of the victims are buried in the churchyard at Whitby.

That same year Whitby was bombarded by German battle cruisers and the Abbey sustained considerable damage during the attack.

Whitby, noted for the discovery of entire skeletons of pterodactyls and numerous other interesting fossils, is also renowned for the well-preserved ammonites that can be found on its shores.

The seaside town has at times featured in television and cinema productions, most famously that of Bram Stoker's novel, Dracula. Tourism is now Whitby's main economy, although its fishing industry is also very much alive.

SAT, 4TH JULY 2009
RUNSWICK BAY – THE CLEVELAND WAY – BOULBY

At 6.18am Pete drops me off at Sandsend where I continue my walk northward. I now have to climb up a steep track to locate with the rail-path walk. I am happily walking on this wide cinder track for about a mile when suddenly the track comes to an abrupt end at a rail tunnel that is completely bricked up. There is an alternative route close by that takes me to the Cleveland Way, a walk that follows the contours of the cliffs; a lovely route providing panoramic views of the Yorkshire coastline. Despite its stunning scenes the route is quite circuitous, penalising me into having to cover a far greater distance compared to the journey by road; an aspect of no great worry to the rambler out for a day's stroll, but it's always a concern for someone with a time and distance agenda to think about.

Approaching Runswick Bay, I climb down what must have been at least 600 steps to reach the sandy beach below (I wish I'd have counted them), then walking another ½ mile along the sand before reaching Runswick Bay itself, where Pete is waiting for me.

After stretching aching legs and having a meal break I am soon on my way again. I have another very steep climb out of the bay before returning once again to the Cleveland Way.

While on the beach I pick up a couple of attractive sea shells as a memento of walking this part of the coast and it casts my mind back to the time when I was walking on the edge of a freshly ploughed field in Lincolnshire... or was it Norfolk??

I had noticed there were sea shells here and there along the length of the field. The significance of it didn't dawn on me till days later. I thought about it again today. This field, I recalled, was miles from the sea, so how the shells got there is a mystery. It was very flat country so possibly its height above sea level would have been minimal. Had there been a huge flood or tsunami in the distant past or were the shells the legacy of a time when sea levels were much higher? If it's the latter, then the seas must have covered a much greater area of our island in those historic times. I wonder what England would have looked like then? The coastline would have shrunk considerably and walking around it would have probably taken no more than a couple of months. They say that there were probably wolves in the country in those days; if that were so, I reckon you'd have got around England even faster! It's amazing the weird things that go through your mind while walking!

I am pretty fagged out on reaching Boulby as the route has been quite demanding at times and the heat from the sun has also taken its toll. A little distance away we find a caravan touring site and it's not long before we are both relaxing in lounge chairs and enjoying the remainder of the day.

Today's pedometer reading: 20.9km (12.97 miles).

Notes of Interest: The Cleveland Way

The Cleveland Way is one of the many designated National Trails walking routes around England; it is also one of most interesting. The 109-mile track follows the 3-sided contours of the North York Moors National Park ending on the coast at Filey; or it starts there if you walk the other way! The trail twists and turns northward as far as Saltburn-by-the-Sea before tracking back south to run along the coast to Filey.

I only walked the coastal section which forms part of the North Sea trail, for to deviate from the coast would have been time-consuming and would have meant walking a much greater distance than was necessary.

They say it takes around nine days to walk the entire length of the Cleveland Way. Most people tend to do the walk in a clockwise direction from Helmsley to Filey, but there's no reason why it cannot be done going anti-clockwise.

The Cleveland Way can easily be walked throughout the year in normal weather conditions, but walk it during autumn and you'll see the moorland's purple-coloured heather at its best; however, journey there in the spring and you might easily spot curlew and red grouse among the bluebells.

The walk offers wonderful views of the North Yorkshire Moors and, at various viewpoints, spectacular visions of Yorkshire's coastline will be revealed. You'll walk through remote fishing villages like Robin Hood's Bay and Hawsker-cum-Stainsacre, on your way through to Whitby.

Along the coastal walk there are Roman ruins; some are believed to be signalling stations that were sited there to observe and send warnings of enemies approaching by sea.

At the early stages of the walk you might visit Helmsley Castle and the historic ruins of the twelfth century Rievaulx Abbey. This Cistercian abbey (now owned by English Heritage) was once the spiritual home to 145 monks who were responsible for the welfare of the many communities in the area.

CHAPTER 10
CLEVELAND

Pete drives me back to Boulby to continue my walk. The weather is cool with a brisk south-easterly, although at times it seems as if it is coming directly from the south. I now decide to take what appears to be a deserted country road instead of the Cleveland Way path, as from the map it seems that the road runs parallel to the coast for some distance and it means faster walking. I climb the steep hill and walk the road for a distance but then decide to rejoin the Cleveland cliff walk again. I soon begin climbing down to Skinningrove, a small but attractive seaside village.

I am making good progress up to this point, but as I walk along the beach from Skinningrove, I miss the partially concealed Cleveland Way sign. About half a mile on I come to an impassable rocky outreach and immediately realise I have over-shot the turn-off track. I retrace my steps along the beach and am redirected by a local resident who points to the partially hidden sign that directs walkers toward the cliff face steps leading up to the Cleveland Way track.

The south-easterly blows in from the North Sea and brings with it a strong smell of the briny. It is so exhilarating just to be walking up on the cliftop track with the wind buffeting my body and the odour of the sea in my nostrils. I feel alive and somehow grateful that I am able to be where I am right now, doing and seeing things that many people, through ill health or physical disabilities, will never ever have the chance to experience.

On nearing Saltburn I come back down onto the road then cross the bridge to meet up with Pete at a parking area south side of the Saltburn Pier. This seaside town of Saltburn I think is quite captivating and I would love to stay a while but, as always, my agenda for covering maximum distance each day takes precedence. After the customary meal and leg stretch I continue my walk along a wide sandy beach that takes me past Marske-by-the-Sea and into Redcar. I have really enjoyed the day's walk but am now looking forward to getting settled into a caravan camping site. After a shower I'll feel as good as new, although I can't say the same for the van's service battery. Its life is effectively coming to an end so we replace it in Redcar while shopping for groceries.

Today's pedometer reading: 24.9km (15.46 miles).

Notes of Interest: Redcar

Redcar, as with many coastal towns and cities, began life as a fishing settlement in the early fourteenth century. The name Redcar appears to have originated from the Old English 'read' and possibly the Old Scandinavian word 'kjarr'. Alternatively the word 'red' might be derived from the ancient word 'hrēod'. Whatever the case, it's likely to have had some reference to the low-lying reed marshland that was predominant in the area.

With the advent of the railway system in the mid-nineteenth century, Redcar became a popular seaside resort for Victorian holiday-makers. Both Redcar Pier and Coatham Pier were to suffer misfortune in their early years. Coatham Pier was wrecked before completion when two sailing ships battered through it in a storm. Then, in October 1898, a barque collided with the pier ruining any chance of its resurrection and from that time on it was left to the ravages of nature.

Redcar Pier experienced a series of accidental shipping collisions and later a major fire caused considerable damage. During the Second World War the pier was deliberately breached, (as were most piers around Britain in order to discourage enemy landings), but additional structural weakening was caused by a nearby mine explosion. Subsequent storms caused further damage and finally led to its demolition in 1981.

MON, 6TH JULY 2009
REDCAR

No walking today as it's my day off! I relax during the morning then Pete and I drive to a retail park to find a DIY store. We return to the caravan camping ground and after a late lunch we do some essential DIY work... or rather Pete does! Later we drive into Redcar for an evening meal. We have a pint of beer at an ancient local inn before heading back to the campervan where we end the evening watching TV.

TUES, 7TH JULY 2009
MIDDLESBROUGH – SEATON CAREW

Up at 5.15am. The weather is cool and cloudy with a northerly breeze. We drive to the seafront at Redcar where I had finished the walk on Sunday and I start on the road to Middlesbrough's Transporter Bridge, a unique cable-driven ferry reputed to be the largest of its type in the world.

I soon manage to divert off the busy main trunk road and onto a public footbath that takes me through a scenic rural park before leading me onto a minor road that goes through part of Redcar's industrial area. I meet up with Pete for a meal break on Middlesbrough's Dockside Road before arriving at the 'Bridge' around 11am. Within 20 minutes we are cabled over to the northern side of the River Tees, campervan and all. Once on the other side I immediately begin walking again, this time on the Seaton Carew Road toward Hartlepool.

I remember casting my mind back into the past again as nostalgic thoughts hold sway during this session of the walk.

I recall my mother's words about the early war days when she would visit Vivienne at the Lord Mayor Treloar Hospital's sanatorium clinic in Hampshire. Visiting hours in those days were very different from today, with the children only allowed visits from parents or guardians for two hours on the first Sunday of each month. In the war years strict fuel rationing made public transport erratic and unreliable and sometimes almost non-existent.

Our mother remembers on one occasion arriving at the hospital late and was only allowed 10 minutes with her daughter. When she arrived at Vivienne's bedside her four-year-old daughter was lying completely hidden under the bedcovers. She was distraught and had been crying profusely for she had thought her mother wasn't coming to see her.

I remembered Vivienne herself reminiscing about that occasion. She recalls seeing all the other children sitting there with presents and sweets scattered on their beds while cuddling and talking to their parents. After a while she couldn't bear to watch any longer so she hid her face under the covers and cried. By the time our mother finally showed up Vivienne had worked herself up into such a tearful state that she cried for most of the visit, angry that her mother had arrived so late. After her mother had left, Vivienne threw all the toys she'd just been given across the ward.

Vivienne also remembered the times when, as a four or five year old, she'd try to prevent her mother from leaving by putting her fingers into the large button holes on each lapel of her mother's coat. Whenever our mother tried to rise from her bedside she'd have to prise her daughter's fingers off her coat so that she could leave.

It wasn't until Vivienne was 13 years of age that the original diagnosis of tuberculosis of the knee joint was changed to one of Still's Disease or Juvenile Rheumatoid Arthritis (JRA).If they'd known that from the outset maybe she wouldn't have been left with her current disabilities. By the time Vivienne was 15 years old, she would have spent ten of those years in one hospital or another.

A few miles on, after another break, I continue on toward Hartlepool, walking into a strong headwind. I decide to finish the day's walk at Seaton Carew as the wind has tired me, but I am disappointed not making it to Hartlepool only 2½ miles away.

Today's pedometer reading: 30.6km (19 miles).

Notes of Interest: Seaton Carew

Seaton Carew is a small and attractive seaside resort. It is situated on the North Sea coast between the town of Hartlepool and the mouth of the River Tees.

The word Seaton might mean settlement by the sea and the word Carew derives from a Norman French family called Carou who owned lands in the area and settled there.

During its heyday in the early nineteenth century the town became popular as a seaside resort. The feature I enjoyed was the long promenade that took me from Seaton Carew to Hartlepool Marina giving stunning and unrestricted views of the North Sea.

In December 2007, the John Darwin case brought Seaton Carew into worldwide prominence. Considered to be dead after an apparent canoeing accident off Seaton Beach in 2002, John Darwin arrived at a London police station reporting in as a missing person.

His sudden appearance started a major police investigation and both John Darwin and his wife were later charged with fraud and each sentenced to over 6 years in prison.

It is said that sometime after these events someone erected a new road sign near the railway station with the words: 'Welcome to Seaton Canoe twinned with Panama'. Of course the sign was taken down, but I imagine it produced a few chuckles from those who saw it.

CHAPTER 11
COUNTY DURHAM

WED, 8TH JULY 2009
HARTLEPOOL – EASINGTON COLLIERY – SEAHAM

At 6.15am Pete drives me back to Seaton Carew to continue the walk. I am soon walking briskly along the lengthy promenade while the sun makes its appearance on the eastern horizon. About 3 miles further on I find myself walking on Hartlepool's coastal path revelling in the uninterrupted panoramic vista around me. Soon I am travelling along a delightful sand-dune track with a sparkling blue sea on my right and below me on my left, Hartlepool's golf links. After passing a large caravan site I am once again in the lovely Cleveland countryside. It's another period of enjoyable walking before connecting up with the van for my first meal break.

I am soon back onto an interesting part of the coastal track where I meet up with a few hikers; not surprising really, as the route goes through some stunningly scenic country and coastal landscape. The path I'm on runs alongside the railway track for some distance, although at one stage I have to walk on the actual train track while crossing a bridge as the path seems to have disappeared.

While walking this section I meet up with John Young and his partner, Sue. We chat for a while and Sue takes some photos. It turns out that John has recently been treated for prostate cancer. He tells me he's feeling great and that the prognosis after treatment was encouraging. I wish him the best and we part company with Sue promising to send the photos on to me. At 11.30 I reach Easington Colliery where Pete is preparing a fry-up in a lay-by. After a great meal and a power nap I am ready for another walking session.

I start off again at 12.30 and take the coastal walkway to Seaham, about 5 miles further north. The track is surprisingly good and on this occasion it will cut a few miles from the road route. I meet more ramblers on this picturesque section and it's where I finally decide to call it a day. I meet up with Pete who's parked on the cliftop at Seaham and find that he has not yet been successful in locating a caravan camping site. We eventually find ourselves at a lovely pub called The Crow's Nest.

Vicky, the manageress, offers the use of their parking lot for the night and also gives us a free beer and a meal. This evening they are holding their weekly quiz night and the place is buzzing. After the quiz is over Sue, the lady running the event nods to me and introduces me the crowd; it's the cue for me to stand up and say a few words about this Around England walking venture. The talk seems to go down well and in response we receive donations from many of the patrons. Thanks, Vicky for your hospitality and please thank your patrons for their generous donations.

Today's pedometer reading: 29.9km (18.56 miles).

Notes of Interest: Seaham

Seaham, formerly Seaham Harbour, is a small coastal town in County Durham

On 2 January 1815 sleepy Seaham became more widely known when the local landowner's daughter married Lord Byron at Seaham Hall.

Apart from his fascination with the sea, Byron appeared to have got bored with the quiet life in Seaham, as indicated by comments he made in a letter to a friend: "Upon this dreary coast we have nothing but county meetings and shipwrecks; and I have this day dined upon fish, which probably dined upon the crews of several colliers lost in the late gales." Although the marriage was short-lived it appeared to have been a drain on the Milbank's (Byron's parents-in-law) resources.

Seaham began to experience hard times when their collieries began to close. The situation had been exacerbated by the UK miners' strike during 1984-1985, and the cheap coal coming in from Eastern Europe. The pit closures were to hit the local economy extremely hard, and Seaham sank into a depressed state during the 1980s and 1990s.

Seaham's long mining history was depicted in the 2000 blockbuster film Billy Elliot *that portrayed life during the UK miners' strike. Seaham and Easington Colliery both feature in the film, particularly* the Miner's Club scene when Billy's dad rushes in to celebrate his son's success in winning an audition at the dance school.

The 'Seaham Lifeboat Disaster' was to have a drastic effect on the local community. It referred to the tragic loss of eight men and one boy on the RNLI lifeboat, the George Elmy, when it sank on 17 November 1962.

Seaham's fine beaches have also been luring a growing number of surfers to the region.

CHAPTER 12
TYNE AND WEAR

THURS, 9TH JULY 2009
SUNDERLAND – TYNE PEDESTRIAN TUNNEL

On the road again! I think that's the title of a song... Anyway it's 6.25am, and I'm taking the coastal route from Seaham to Sunderland. I'm in high spirits as I begin today's walk. My thoughts dwell on a number of things before settling on the subject of climate change and related issues.

I begin thinking about how adverse climate conditions brought about by climate change could sooner or later critically affect all our lives; that major catastrophes such as floods or drought over huge areas of arable land might have a crucial impact on the world's diminishing food resources. With the global population mushrooming to unprecedented levels, future food shortages are already becoming a concern to many governments. I remembered reading somewhere that our world population now stands at around 7 billion and that the daily population increase, after allowing for the global death rate, is thought to be over 200,000. On those depressing figures I calculated that there would be another million human souls arriving on our planet every five days.

After walking another kilometre or so I came to the conclusion that, although some countries are now experiencing negative population growth, the world population will have nearly doubled by 2050. My high spirits were sinking by the minute!

I thought about the world's fishing industry and how fish stocks were becoming depleted to the point of collapse due to over-fishing and indiscriminate netting. I imagined that if this were to continue it would put even greater strain on our land-grown food resources.

Such developments I thought would have huge environmental and social impact worldwide; food scarcity and subsequent high food prices would create political instability, giving rise to social upheaval through mass migration on an unprecedented level.

By now I was dead miserable! My thoughts at this point, I remember, took on a different tack. I reckoned that roughly half the world's population are suffering from malnutrition due to poverty, famine, civil wars and so on, while those of us in the developed countries are over-consuming to such an extent that it could easily be described as gluttony.

In fact, it is my belief that most of us in the developed world could easily halve our consumption of food and still be well nourished. It is also estimated that in the west we waste over 30% of all food produced for consumption. I thought of all the food that ended up in supermarket waste bins after reaching their sell-by-dates, the food thrown away by restaurants, the surpluses discarded after functions and, most important of all, the food disposed of by us – the wasteful public. Suddenly, that wastage figure of 30% didn't seem unreasonable.

I remembered thinking that governments in the developed world should be tackling this problem head-on; that they should, first of all, discourage over-eating with Anti-Excessive-Eating campaigns. After all, they spend huge resources on Anti-Smoking campaigns, and yet the health risks of obesity, although different, must surely be on a par with those of smoking.

Obesity-related illnesses affect a significantly high proportion of westernised populations and I read somewhere that this growing problem is becoming a real concern with health authorities in many countries. I thought about how much all-round benefit could be achieved for our society if the government had the balls to issue some no-nonsense, anti-excessive-eating policies combined, of course, with sound nutritional advice:

(1) The individual would become healthier and, in the long run, happier.
(2) By consuming less the family would be spending less.
(3) Fewer NHS beds would be taken up by individuals with obesity-related illnesses.
(4) Last but not least, the country would spend less on foreign food products, thereby reducing its carbon footprint while simultaneously creating less pressure on world food resources.

However, to me the most important issue of all (and the most frightening), is the rapidly escalating world population. I believe that there are simply too many people on the planet. Almost as frightening is the knowledge that governments around the world are not brave enough to face up to the problem.

I see three waves steadily approaching, waves that when they converge are likely to create the deadliest of periods for mankind; a catalyst to an era of misery on a global scale. They are:

•Overpopulation
•Climate change
•Diminishing food resources.

I remember being in high spirits when I started out, but now I am feeling quite depressed. I must try not to dwell on such negative thoughts and think of more positive issues instead.

I'm now on a coastal path heading out of Seaham, but soon I'll be joining the B1287 until I reach Leechmere. From there another coastal path takes me to the outer suburbs of Sunderland where I catch up with the camper van. After a short break I carry on through Sunderland's city centre where I find a W.H. Smith store. I purchase a Phillips Navigator map and an Ordnance Survey map before walking over the bridge that spans the River Wear.

On the north side of the bridge a photographer has pre-arranged a photo shoot and an interview for the local paper; soon after I rendezvous with Pete in the city's inner suburbs.

As I pass Sunderland's Stadium of Light football arena I decide I would try to get a look inside the famous ground. In the large foyer I meet a couple of security guys who, after making a couple of phone calls, give me permission to enter the arena under escort. They also allow me to take some photos of the stadium before leaving for the road once more.

About 3 miles out I pass Sunderland's football training ground, so I ask at the Entry Control Centre for permission to visit. The official named Gavin tries his best, but the request is denied. He asks me to leave my leaflet and other details saying that there was a good possibility that the footballers would make a donation in support of my charity walk. Thanks Gavin!

I journey on the coast road, but once past the South Shields Golf Club I have to walk inland through the Tyne suburbs to get to Jarrow and the Tyne Pedestrian Tunnel. It's hard to describe the mind-numbing effect of walking alongside suburban roads that are continually busy with traffic on pavements crowded with busy shoppers or trudging along miles of terraced houses and unsightly high-rise buildings.

It takes another three hours of dreary walking before I finally reach the tunnel. Pete is waiting on the other side and once I arrive there we decide to call it a day.

Rob has just arrived back from his week's break in Brighton and is meeting us near the Old Hartley Caravan Camping ground that we are booked into. By 4pm we were all settled in for the evening.

Today's pedometer reading: 30.6km (19 miles).

Notes of Interest: Sunderland

Stand on the northern bank of the river where it overlooks the coast at Wearmouth and try to imagine what it might have looked like in 674 AD when the King of Northumbria granted Benedict Biscop the land to build a monastery. The legacy of that monastery is there today in the Anglo-Saxon church of St Peter's, which remains one of the most historic in England.

The area on the north bank known as Monkwearmouth has the most revealing past; in fact, Sunderland was once part of Monkwearmouth.

The name Sunderland actually derives from 'Sundered Land', in other words, land that was sundered or separated from the monastic estates of Monkwearmouth in ancient times.

Sunderland was granted a charter and elevated to 'town' status and then in 1348/49, the Black Death struck. The plague hit most towns, including Sunderland, where probably half the population would have died.

By the fourteenth century shipbuilding had begun and salt was also to become a major form of income for the town. However, in 1565 a writer described Sunderland's economic woes in the following vein: "ships and boats are loaded and unloaded but there are neither ships nor boats (belonging to the town). This town is in great decay of building and inhabitants".

Sunderland's fortunes changed after the seventeenth century when the town became involved in the mining and shipping of coal and the production of salt; industries that Sunderland would thrive on over the years.

Sunderland, as with all industrial towns during the nineteenth century, experienced terrible living conditions for the working class, a situation that became even grimmer as Sunderland's population grew. The overcrowded slum areas were filthy and unsanitary, conditions that resulted in an outbreak of cholera during the years of 1832 and 1849.

Shipbuilding was to boom in Sunderland and its name became synonymous with this industry. During World War II Sunderland withstood German bombing raids that killed 267 people, destroyed about 1,000 houses and caused damage to around 3,000 properties.

Sunderland's people experienced impoverished times during the depression of the 1930s when almost a third of the men were unemployed. The declining shipbuilding industry finally closed its gates in 1988 and the collapse of the coal-mining industry was soon to follow.

Despite its disruptive past Sunderland has become a thriving city. The Stadium of Light was opened in 1997.

FRI, 10TH JULY 2009
TYNEMOUTH – WHITELY BAY – BLYTH

Rob drives me back to the Tyne Pedestrian Tunnel to start my walk. We have said our goodbyes to Pete who had taken off in the Toyota to return to Brighton about an hour before. I make my way toward Tynemouth through a series of minor roads via North Shields.

During yesterday and today I had been walking for some hours through nothing but the dreary suburbs of Tyne and Wear. It's not just Sunderland; it's the same in all city suburbs. All you see are houses, high-rise buildings, cars, traffic lights, shops, pavements full of busy, intense people, relieved occasionally by city parks and recreation areas, although the constant noise of traffic remains. Sometimes you can't help getting depressed, especially while walking through some of the seemingly poorer urban areas of the cities.

I suppose the only positive aspect is that you acquire a greater appreciation for the open countryside; the delight of being back among nature's adornments or walking along a remote coastal path with a friendly breeze and the sound of the surf in your ear.

Through Tynemouth and on through Cullercoats I soon find myself back on the seafront walkway. The scenic views around this part of the coast are quite incredible and it's making the walk so much more enjoyable.

I continue on toward the outskirts of Whitely Bay where I meet up with Rob who is preparing a meal in the van. After having a meal of porridge with a black coffee, I stretch leg muscles again and then it's back on the road to the town of Blyth. Walking along the seafront promenade out of Whitely Bay is a delight, with the rolling waves coming in from the North Sea on my right and wide leisure greens to my left.

There is a flock of seagulls up in the sky. With wings outstretched and motionless apart from an occasional movement to make aerodynamic adjustments, they hover in the stiff south-easterly breeze. Now and again they tilt their wings and glide off sideways at speed before heading up into the wind once more. My only guess as to why they are performing this act is that it must be out of pure enjoyment. I have witnessed it on many occasions during the walk and have also watched them perform the same ritual on the Brighton promenade and am always fascinated by the spectacle.

I am walking on a coastal track alongside a golf course and hugging the coast I see St Mary's Lighthouse at the end of a causeway. I think about taking a closer look but decide to continue on the delightful scenic route to Blyth.

Arriving in the town I make my way through to the Asda car park on the northern side of Blyth where I have arranged to liaise with the camper van. As I reach the vehicle I see Rob coming toward me with a trolley full of shopping. I help him store the groceries in the van. It's then I notice the three bags of pasta. I groan inwardly thinking about all the pasta meals they're going to produce. I'm beginning to suspect that Rob's got shares in the industry.

We finish the day's walk here and drive back to the Old Hartley Caravan Club site where we stayed last night.

Today's pedometer miles: 28.9km (17.94 miles).

Notes of Interest: Blyth

Early development of the Blyth area is relatively unknown, although there have been some archaeological finds, the oldest being an antler hammer dating back to the late Neolithic or early Bronze Age period. Human skulls, a spearhead, a sword, a bronze axe and a dagger have all been unearthed at one time or another. There are signs of Roman presence in the area, but the evidence is far from conclusive and, to my knowledge, has not been verified.

In the mid-twentieth century Blyth had one of the largest shipbuilding yards on the North East coast, with five dry docks and four building slipways. Many ships were built in the Blyth shipyards during the First and Second World Wars, mostly for the Royal Navy; one of the most important being Britain's first aircraft carrier, HMS Ark Royal, built in 1914.

After the end of the 1950s Blyth would enter a period of steep decline. The railway into Blyth was to close, and by 1966, economic depression resulted in the closure of the shipyards. It wasn't long before the demand for coal fell drastically and closure of many collieries soon followed.

Blyth Power Station became redundant in 2002 and was subsequently demolished, but a renewable energy source in the form of wind turbines now feature on the opposite side of the river and the Blyth Offshore Wind Farm is clearly visible out at sea.

The non-League football club, Blyth Spartans, will also be remembered for their monumental FA Cup victories in 1978.

On my way

Public footpath through a corn field

Walking track near Cromer

Serenity - near Beadnell

Bridge along the Lancashire Canal

With Andrew on our way to Porlock

View near Whinlatter Forest

My son and me on the SouthWest Coast Path

The dramatic Jurassic cliffs

Canal towpath walk

Lovely Robin Hood's Bay

Up on the breathtaking Hergest Ridge

Offa's Dyke Path - through a copse

Beautiful Blackpool Sands

Lovely Slapton Lea

A welcome back celebration with friends at Brighton Marina

CHAPTER 13
NORTHUMBERLAND

SAT, 11TH JULY 2009
NEWBIGGIN-BY-SEA – CRESSWELL – DRURIDGE BAY

We leave the Old Hartley Caravan Club Site and drive to my start point at the Asda car park, on the outskirts of Blyth. Soon I am travelling along the A189, a reasonably walker-friendly dual carriageway as it has about 3ft-wide walking strips on either side. On the Blyth Bridge a barrier-protected pedestrian pathway for walkers and cyclists leads me safely to the other side. Once over the Blyth River, I veer onto the town's curved promenade past a static caravan site before continuing on another coastal track.

Today I'm thinking of some of the people I met while walking through Wearside and Tyneside on Thursday. I found them to be the friendliest of people, but it was their accent that I found really fascinating. They are economical in their use of words and phrases. The word 'canny' for example, is primarily used to describe something 'good' but can also be used to mean 'great' 'impressive' etc.

I remember asking directions to the Tyne Pedestrian Tunnel that lay some miles away. I enquired on a number of occasions for I was walking through a variety of roads and streets in semi-commercial and urban areas to avoid the busy main motorway. There was always a friendly readiness to point me in the right direction, often accompanied by the comment, "Tha's a canny walk, mind!" My nearest interpretation of that phrase would be: "You realise that it's a very long walk, don't you". That's using double the amount of words to say the same thing! Canny, eh?

Once past the Newbiggin golf course I enjoy the coastal journey to Cresswell and from there I travel for about an hour and a half on lovely hard sand.

The North Sea today is a sparkling blue and every sixth step I take seems to correlate to the rhythmic sound of the waves as they tumble lazily onto the shore. All too soon I have to make my way over the sand dunes onto a firmer track that takes me to Druridge Bay. As I approach I realise that I have somehow overshot the place where Rob had been waiting for me, but after a phone call we finally meet up at the Druridge Bay Country Park where I finish my day's walk.

Today's pedometer reading: 27km (16.76 miles).

SUN, 12TH JULY 2009
AMBLE – WARKWORTH – ALNWICK

It is 8am and the weather is warm but cloudy as I begin my day's walk from the Druridge Bay Country Park. I decide to walk on the coastal pathways again as the road seems to be too walker-unfriendly, although by road it's a much shorter route. The wide gravel path goes through the beautiful Northumberland countryside all the way to Amble. Although the route takes me on a wide detour I become absorbed with the remote landscape and don't begrudge walking the extra miles.

I have an MP3 player that I quite often use, especially while walking through uninspiring terrain. I have about 400 pieces on it ranging from favourites like Matt Monro, Nat King Cole, Frank Sinatra etc to some of the classics from musicals of the past including *Les Miserables* and *Phantom of the Opera*. I also have a fair selection of arias from some of the great operas. Rather than have them played in ordered groups I prefer to have them selected at random. That way you never know what's coming up next.

The problem with this method is that as you listen while walking your pace gradually correlates with the beat of the music. Now that's okay when you're listening to something with a fast tempo because then you're inclined to walk faster; the problem arises when you are suddenly confronted with pieces like 'The Nun's Chorus' or 'Nessun Dorma', for then your pace involuntarily slows with the music. It took a while before it dawned on me what effect these slow pieces were having on my walking. I wondered if anybody had ever observed me during these times, for if so, I reckon they would have thought that I was either on the point of collapse or rehearsing for a part in a new zombie movie about the walking dead. While listening to these arias today memories of my childhood returned once more.

I pictured my big brother, Mick, as if it were yesterday; sitting on a chair with his wind-up gramophone on the bedside cabinet and his collection of 78s strewn on the bed. Most of them were illustrated with the familiar logo of 'His Master's Voice' circled over the 'dog and loudspeaker horn' on labels that were a sort of plum/maroon/ red colour. There were a few records with a vivid blue centre, but I can't recall the brand name. Mick must have been no more than 16 or 17 at the time, yet he had a great love of classical music including many of the superb arias of the day. Because we shared the bedroom I would often go to sleep listening to the great opera singers of that era, singers like Enrico Caruso, Beniamino Gigli, Fritz Krauss, Jussi Björling, Joseph Locke, Richard Tauber, Paul Robeson, Maria Callas, Montserrat Caballé and so on. Mick had 'em all! I suppose it is where I get my own appreciation for that kind of music.

There were times I remember, after Mick had finished playing his records that we'd be lying in bed only to hear Kitty, the young kid from next door start bawling again. Her constant wailing would usually prompt Mick out of his bed to open the window that looked out over our back yard. I can still hear his plaintive cry to Kitty: "Please Twiddles, (that's what everyone called her) please stop crying, we can't sleep." I don't know whether she detected the maniacal desperation in my brother's voice, but it usually had the effect of quietening her down to a whimpering grizzle.

We never ever knew why she cried as often as she did; all I know is that she had a pair of lungs on her that those opera singers would have given their eye teeth for. She was neglected, that's for sure, but our mother didn't think she was being physically abused for she seemed happy enough during the day. As for the authorities they wouldn't have wanted to know. In those days, if there wasn't conclusive evidence to prove abuse they just kept well away.

From Amble I return to the A1068 and begin walking through the lovely village of Warkworth. From here I walk on a narrow, winding, two-lane highway for about 800 metres before getting onto a cycle track that goes all the way to Alnmouth. Here the cycle track ends and I reluctantly return to the main road. I continue walking toward Alnwick (pronounced Anick), still on the same narrow, winding road. There is little edge room to avoid the traffic so I'm quite relieved when I eventually reach Rob and the campervan.

It is 1.20 pm; I am hot, tired and happy to stop for the day. We soon find an ideal camping site at the Alnwick Rugby Club. We enjoy a good evening meal before visiting their social club where we have a great night watching an international rugby match on a big TV screen, accompanied by many boisterous rugby enthusiasts. We arrive back at our van fairly late, but it doesn't matter because tomorrow is going to be our day off. Whoopee!

Today's pedometer reading: 24.6km (15.27 miles).

Notes of Interest: Alnwick

The town dates back to approximately AD 600. It is believed that Alnwick, in medieval times, might have been a staging post for travellers on their long journey from Edinburgh and London.

In 1174 William the Lion of Scotland was captured during the Battle of Alnwick, and in the town there's a tablet of stone that marks the spot where the event took place. It is believed that Scottish raiding parties would often attack the town and in the winter of 1424 much of Alnwick was thought to have been burned to the ground.

Alnwick Castle, situated above the River Aln, overlooks the area west of the town. Apart from being a great tourist attraction Alnwick Castle is also the hub of a number of commercial and educational interests. The castle, I've been told, is reputed to be the second largest inhabited castle in England, after Windsor.

This ancient structure has also been used by film-makers to shoot scenes for projects ranging from the Harry Potter films, Robin Hood: Prince of Thieves *and the long-running TV comedy,* Blackadder.

Alnwick was once described by a leading magazine as being "the most picturesque market town in Northumberland, and the best place to live in Britain".

MON, 13TH JULY 2009
ALNWICK

Today is our rest day. I say 'our' because it's also good for Rob to have a break from driving. There's always daily pressure on the support driver, even more so if he's unfamiliar with the area. Many of the country roads in England are pretty narrow, especially through some of the villages; negotiating a fairly wide campervan through some of these places can be a bit of a nightmare.

Both of us take advantage of the break in our daily routine and I catch up with internet stuff, emails, updates etc, while Rob gets some work done on his own websites. In the afternoon we have an on-the-air interview with the local radio station in Alnwick.

TUES, 14TH JULY 2009
CRASTER – BEADNELL – LOW NEWTON

I start walking from Alnwick at 7.12 am, and meet up with Rob about two hours later in the village of Craster. We have run out of gas for the cooker so are unable to cook anything; instead we buy bread rolls, milk and partake of the famous Craster kippers from the local shop. I was soon on my way again on a cliftop track that takes me past the prominent ruins of Dunstanburgh Castle and on toward Beadnell. It's there that I hope to meet up with Jamie, a Geordie friend from Brighton who is planning to come up from Newcastle to meet us.

It's slow going on this session as I divert onto the sandy beach, stopping occasionally to chat to people coming my way. I finally meet up with Jamie and his mother, Joan, at Low Newton where I end my walk for the day.

Shortly after, accompanied by his mother and me, Jamie drives to Seahouses with Rob following in the van. We have a great pub meal there before taking a tour around the fascinating Bamburgh Castle. We finally say goodbye to Jamie and Joan and then it's off in the campervan to replace a gas cylinder, refuel the van and look for a suitable caravan camping site.

We find an ideal site that miraculously has a vacant space for us, but the real bonus is getting the site free of charge and having the owner write a cheque for a hundred pounds to our Cancer Research charity.

Today's pedometer reading: 19.5km (12.10 miles)

Notes of Interest: Low Newton

Low Newton, considered one of the most picturesque villages on the Northumberland coast, was once an isolated eighteenth-century fishing hamlet.

The village I believe is owned by The National Trust and comprises attractive cream-washed cottages surrounding an expansive green with views out across the sheltered bay of Newton Haven; a place where safe anchorage provides security for all craft large or small.

The Ship Inn (originally known as the Smack Inn), is probably regarded as the hub of the village. I was also told that there had been an inn on the site since the 1700s.

Not too long ago The Ship Inn was visited by Oz Clarke and James May when the television programme Oz and James Drink to Britain *was featured there.*

This is also a great area for bird watching, especially at the Newton Pool Bird Reserve.

WED, 15TH JULY 2009
SEAHOUSES – BAMBURGH CASTLE

I leave the lovely village of Low Newton at 7am and immediately set out on the coastal walking track that I find amongst the sand dunes. There is a cool easterly breeze, but the clear skies and the gentle murmur of wavelets lapping the shore seem to promise another fine day. From the village of Beadnell I stay on a coast road to Seahouses as I need to make up for yesterday's lost time.

Rob is parked up just north of Seahouses where I have my first meal break of the day. After the break I continue on toward Bamburgh Castle, the place that we'd visited as tourists yesterday.

I take to the beach from the castle grounds where I notice the darkening skies and I realise that my earlier assessment of the day's weather might have gone slightly awry! I walk hurriedly on.

It isn't long before the rain starts to fall. I phone Rob and arrange to meet him near an access road close to the beach as I need to collect my wet-weather gear. I shouldn't have bothered because by the time we finally rendezvous I am soaked through to the skin. I have a mini-break at Waren Mill to dry off and change clothing and as the rain stops I decide to go on for a third session. I take a minor road that leads inland across the countryside taking me to the small town of Belford. During these last few miles I begin to experience again this strange sense of euphoria.

It's hard to give a full explanation as to why I have these occasional bouts of sheer exhilaration while walking. It can occur in open countryside or on remote coastal tracks. Almost without warning this profound sense of freedom comes upon you. I imagine it's the sort of sensation people get when taking certain drugs. You tend to notice the smallest of details in the world around you with startling clarity. Walking through a copse and seeing the spidery pattern on the leaves of the trees or noticing the glazed surface on a flint stone embedded in a nearby wall; observing in minute detail the thin blackthorn branches within the tangled confusion of a nearby hedgerow or watching cumulonimbus clouds rising up in majestic procession as they emerge over the horizon.

Every sound becomes more acute, from the melodious warbling of the blackbird to the mournful tones of lowing cattle. The rhythmic sounds of the sea plays on the ear in tumultuous fashion as the waves clump on a nearby shore. You hear the cry of a lone gull or the crunching of sand beneath your feet; each sound, every sight, brings with it this strange feeling of being in complete harmony with the world around you. The sensation becomes so profound, so overwhelming at times that you hardly realise you're actually walking!

This last section of my walk takes me from Waren Mills to Belford and onto a little place called Middleton where I decide to end the day. I should be feeling tired for I normally do on the last session of the day, but strangely enough I feel quite refreshed, despite having walked a longer distance than normal.

We drive back to Belford to search for a caravan camping site for the night but with little success. We finally drive into the car park of a delightful country inn to get local knowledge of campsites in the area. It's great just sitting there savouring local ale and listening with eyes half-shut to the fascinating lingo of the locals. Understanding our need to find a camping place for the night, some of the patrons offer helpful directions to the nearest and most popular caravan camping sites in the area although their broad accent meant having to ask them to repeat certain details more slowly. It isn't long before we are driving into a lovely caravan touring site near Belford.

Today's pedometer reading: 34.3km (21.3 miles).

Notes of Interest: Bamburgh Castle

The first documented reference of a castle at Bamburgh is around the sixth century when it was the seat of an Anglo-Saxon King.

Northumberland became a notable centre for education for well over three centuries, but Viking raids resulted in the capitulation of many Northumbrian settlements and in AD 993 the Castle itself was destroyed.

It is believed that Rufus the Red built the first stone castle on the crag but that King Henry II re-enforced it considerably during his reign.

The castle has had an eventful history such as the siege it came under in 1095 during an attack by William II's army. The siege was to put down a rebellion led by the Earl of Northumbria and supported by the owner of the castle, Robert de Mowbray. Robert was eventually captured, but it took a threat by the King to blind him before his wife relinquished her ongoing defence of the castle.

Bamburgh then became the property of the reigning English monarch. As an important English outpost, the castle was the target of occasional raids from Scotland. In 1464 during the Wars of the Roses, it became the first castle in England to be defeated by artillery.

Eventually the crown granted ownership to the Forster family who remained in possession for generations. However, when Sir William Forster was posthumously declared bankrupt, his estates, including the castle, were sold, under an Act of Parliament, to his brother-in-law, Lord Crew, Bishop of Durham.

In later years Bamburgh Castle came under the ownership of the Victorian industrialist, William Armstrong, who undertook a full restoration programme for the castle.

Archaeological excavations were started in the 1960s when the gold plaque known as the Bamburgh Beast and the Bamburgh Sword were discovered.

There used to be a training dig on the site for 10 weeks every summer for students to learn more about archaeological techniques and to research further into the castle's rich history, but I'm not sure if the project is still going.

THURS, 16TH JULY 2009
BERWICK-UPON-TWEED

The weather is fine as I start walking from yesterday's pick-up point near Middleton. An hour of walking brings me to the turn-off to Holy Island. I arrive at the Lindisfarne causeway only to find that, due to the incoming tide, it's going to be a few hours before we can get over to the island. After a meal break I decide not to wait so Rob drives northward in the campervan while I head off on a coastal pathway in the direction of Berwick-upon-Tweed. Holy Island will have to wait for another time!

The route opens up more panoramic views of the beautiful Northumberland countryside. In the foreground are fields of young wheat amid other obscure plantations while other pastures lie fallow or freshly ploughed, all glimpsed now and then through 10ft-tall hedgerows.

I walk on in the warm morning air and eventually the hedgerows disappear and the wide gravel path merges into a narrow grassy track. On my left cows and sheep graze contentedly in green meadows while on my right, tussock-covered sand dunes signal the close proximity of the dramatic Northumberland coast. Eventually I find myself walking alongside a lengthy golf course, before emerging onto an almost deserted, narrow bitumen road. I stay on this road for another mile or so before coming onto a gravel-surfaced track that brings me down into Tweedmouth, a town on the south side of the River Tweed and about a mile from Berwick. Walking alongside the Dock Road I eventually meet up with Rob who is parked close to the Berwick harbour.

I stop to chat for a minute or so then head off in eager anticipation toward our final destination on the east coast. A half an hour later I stroll in to Berwick-upon-Tweed, the most northerly town in England. We have made it!

I have promised Rob that we'll have two days off once we get to Berwick as a celebration for our achievement. Soon we will need to plan our route over to the west coast, but for now we both can relax and savour this moment of accomplishment! We call in at the Seaview Caravan Club ground and successfully secure a site for two nights.

Today's pedometer reading: 27.3km (16.95 miles).

Notes of Interest: Holy Island, Lindisfarne

The Holy Island of Lindisfarne is said to appear in the ninth century under the Old Welsh name Medcaut. It's believed to be a Celtic word of unknown meaning, although it might derive from the Latin 'Medicata' or 'Healing' but this assumption is speculative. King Oswald of Northumbria, who had recently accepted the Christian faith, requested that a mission be sent to him in order that his pagan people might learn about Christianity. Among the mission of twelve monks was the Irish monk, Saint Aidan, who founded the monastery of Lindisfarne in AD 635.

The monks of Lindisfarne went out to spread the Christian word to the people of Northumbria (which was then part of Mercia) and eventually the island became the base for Christian evangelising throughout the known world.

Northumberland's patron saint, Saint Cuthbert, who was believed to be a shepherd in his young life, became a monk and later Bishop of Lindisfarne. He died on the 20th March, 687 and was buried on Lindisfarne. It is said that around eleven years later, his body was moved by the monks and was discovered to be without any sign of decay; it was certain proof that Cuthbert was indeed a saint.

In 793 the Vikings raided Lindisfarne. The news caused consternation throughout much of England's Christianised North as a Viking assault was seen as a grave threat to the progress of their divine cause.

The causeway to Holy Island is usually open from about 3 hours after high tide until 2 hours before the next high tide, but these times need to be checked, and in stormy weather it's advisable to seek local advice.

Despite prominently displayed tide tables and warnings, a number of vehicles become stranded on the causeway each year, incidents that require the Seahouses Rescue Services to give assistance either by boat or helicopter.

FRI, 17TH JULY 2009
BERWICK-UPON-TWEED

We awake to a terribly wet and windy day. It's supposed to be a well-earned rest day, but I am unable to lie-in as I have an appointment at 9am at the local newspaper ofice. The photo shoot is made as brief as possible by both the photographer and myself for the rain is pelting down. Afterwards, Rob and I shop for groceries and I manage to pick up a Navigator and Survey map for Cumbria.

I am a bit concerned about the excessive rainfall, as if it continues it will make walking the Northern Pennines a bit risky. The weather conditions deteriorate further during the afternoon so we spend the rest of the day in the warmth of the camper van.

Notes of Interest: Berwick-upon-Tweed

The market town of Berwick is likely to have been an important settlement during the time of the kingdom of Northumbria. The first part of the name 'Ber' might possibly come from an Old Norse word 'baer', meaning barley, and 'wick' might derive from the word 'vik', meaning bay, although there are alternative theories.

It's unique and strategic position on the English-Scottish border has been the predominant reason for Berwick's rise and fall over the years. Over a period of 300 years or more the ownership of the town was often contested between England and Scotland and the English-Scottish border wars were often traumatic periods for the populace.

King John of England observed in person the barbaric razing of the town in 1216. About eighty years later, after Berwick had sanctioned King John Balliol's new treaty with France, King Edward I, in his anger, decided to attack the town. After a drawn-out siege the King's army stormed through the town slaughtering practically everyone, even those who sought refuge in the churches. It is possible that over 8,000 inhabitants might have been put to the sword.

It is said that: "From that time on the greatest merchant city in Scotland sank into a small seaport". Ownership of Berwick was also one of the primary reasons of the bitter border conflict in the Scottish Wars of Independence.

In the thirteenth century the town again became one of the wealthiest trading ports in Scotland. A reliable source of the day made this comment of Berwick, "so populous and of such commercial importance that it might rightly be called another Alexandria..."

Since the last conflict in 1482, when the town was captured by Richard Duke of Gloucester, the future King Richard III, the town has been administered by England.

In 2008, politician Christine Grahame announced in the Scottish Parliament that Berwick should become the province of Scotland again. A poll was conducted by a TV company to gauge the feeling of Berwick residents; apparently 60% were in favour of rejoining Scotland.

SAT, 18TH JULY 2009
BERWICK-UPON-TWEED

Another day off, that's two days in a row...we're getting soft! I had a real lie-in this morning. Later we both try to connect to the internet with limited success. Every now and then the signal goes and we risk losing what online stuff we had gathered so in the end we put our laptops away. We guess the atmospheric conditions might have something to do with it for the skies are very heavy with dark cloud. Although rain is threatening Rob and I walk into Berwick as we need to visit the Tourist Information Centre to obtain as much local knowledge and info as possible on the Pennine Way and Hadrian's Wall. Afterwards I visit an outdoor activities store to buy another pair of walking boots, (obtained at a very healthy discount – thank you Mountain Warehouse!) before returning to the caravan camping site.

I intend for Rob and I to have a meal in a restaurant this evening to celebrate and hopefully organise someone to take a photo of us both drinking champagne, as it is quite a significant accomplishment for us to have reached the northernmost town in England without any major setback. But as the day wears on the weather worsens to such an extent that it becomes too dangerous to drive the van into Berwick. The day ends up with Rob concocting a meal out of various food items he finds in the cupboards. At least we have a decent bottle of Australian Shiraz to enjoy and celebrate with after the meal! During the evening we pour over the maps to plan our schedule for tomorrow.

SUN, 19TH JULY 2009
CORNHILL-ON-TWEED – MILFIELD

I leave the foot bridge at Berwick at 6.32am, and head out onto the road for Coldstream. Once across the bridge that spans the River Tweed, I am again in the beautiful Northumberland landscape.

Unfortunately most of the road is tricky walking for although there are often wide, grassy side verges much of it has been neglected resulting in overgrown weeds and tall grass making the walk quite slow and tedious. I've now located a bridle path and I begin to enjoy walking through the wide expanse of the Northumbrian countryside. My spirits are high due to having actually reached the northernmost town in England. There have been occasions when I have said to myself: "if I happen to sustain some sort of injury or any other reason that forces me to abort the walk after reaching Berwick, I would quite happily return to Brighton with the knowledge that we'd given the venture a pretty good go". I'm now starting to think that maybe... just maybe... we can go the whole way! I use my MP3 player quite a bit on this section and a certain operatic aria I have been listening to makes me start thinking about an event that happened long, long ago.

I had just returned from a 3½-month trip at sea and was enjoying my leisure time at home with my family in Brighton. My mother wanted to go to the theatre (I think it was the Hippodrome) to watch a great comedian of that time. We had been on a few occasions to watch different comedians for my mother had a great sense of humour, but I'm not too sure of the one that had this particular supporting act on its bill, although I think it might have been either Frankie Howard or Vic Oliver. I thought Frankie Howard was hilarious, but Vic Oliver was one of my mother's favourite funny men.

He was an accomplished violinist but would usually play badly on stage with hilarious effect. Being a Jew and with his scathingly humorous remarks about Hitler during the war years, his name was listed on a Nazi blacklist of people to be arrested or killed immediately after their presumed occupation of Britain. Vic Oliver was married to Winston Churchill's daughter, Sarah, but I believe they divorced in 1945.

It was a supporting act on the bill that was to impress both my mother and me. The comedian (whoever it was) introduced a singing sensation from New Zealand. She was a soprano with very little previous publicity so she was generally unknown to the public. We found out later that although she was born in New Zealand, she was actually living and having all her operatic training in Australia.

As this ordinary-looking lady called Joan Hammond quietly appeared on the stage, there was a lot of hubbub going on in the packed auditorium. There were two naval ships anchored off the Brighton coast at that time, as I remember, and consequently a great number of sailors were in the audience giving derisive calls and whistles to the lone figure waiting for her pianist to prepare the entry for her first song. She began with the Aria from Puccini's Madame Butterfly and from the moment she uttered her first beautiful note an immediate silence came over the audience, including those from Her Majesty's Navy.

She gave a flawless rendition of 'They Call Me Mimi' and assorted Puccini numbers before singing other favourites like 'Oh, My Beloved Father' and 'The Last Rose of Summer', while the audience, including myself, remained spellbound. She responded to two encores before preparing to make her exit from the stage. As she was walking off there was such a tumultuous response from the standing crowd that even the lady herself seemed overwhelmed by it all. She returned to the centre of the stage to sing again when an official beckoned from the wings. Apparently she had overstayed her time and the main act was ready to come back on. Amidst groans of disappointment from her enraptured audience Joan Hammond quietly left the stage to an even greater acclamation.

Dame Joan Hammond spent most of her life in Australia. She was to lose her house and much of her career's memorabilia at her home at Airey's Inlet, Victoria, during the major disaster of 'Ash Wednesday' in February, 1983. This was a time when raging bush fires caused the death of 75 people, the destruction of 2,545 buildings and the burning of over 390,000 hectares of countryside.

After 6 miles I have my first break in a lay-by before continuing on toward Cornhill-on-Tweed. Seven miles further westward I meet up with Rob again near a traffic roundabout, and after another break I carry on walking; but from here I take the road to Wooler, bypassing Cornhill-on-Tweed altogether. After ending the day's walk 4 miles further on near Milfield, we call into the local Red Lion Inn to enquire about caravan touring sites in the area and while doing so, we partake of some well-earned Northumbrian ale.

The proprietor, Iain Brown, is very helpful and offers us the use of his own facilities if we have difficulty in finding a suitable camping site. He also donated to our charity. Thank you, Iain! However, we manage to locate a decent caravan site in Wooler and by 3.30pm we are powered up and Rob's putting the kettle on.

Today's pedometer reading: 27.8km (17.26 miles).

Notes of Interest: The Cheviot Hills

I believe the Cheviot is the highest summit in the Cheviot Hills in England's far north. The Cheviots are quite remote and much of the terrain is boggy especially during the winter months. I think there are a couple of mountain shelter huts situated along the way for those needing respite from the challenging conditions.

Most routes up The Cheviot usually start from the Harthope Burn side to the northeast for it's the place that provides the nearest access by road. The other route is via the Northern Pennines.

The rounded summit of The Cheviot (the highest hill in the range) is an ancient, extinct volcano and it is covered with an extensive 2-metre layer of peat bog. On the main route there are stone slabs which have been laid down by the Northumberland National Park Authority to provide walkers with easier and safer access to the summit, and which also help to prevent erosion damage to the area.

A network of bridleways that were once used for droving cattle and other shepherding work still remain and are sometimes traversed by mountain bikers.

They say that the remains of a crashed B-17 bomber are still evident to the north of the summit. It collided with the mountain in World War II due to a navigational error and crash landed in the peat bog. Identifiable pieces of the wreckage have been removed.

MON, 20TH JULY 2009
WOOLER

I resume the day's walk from yesterday's pick-up point. Everything is going okay until the call of nature beckons. I'm suddenly dying for a pee! Unfortunately there were no bridle paths to take me off the highway that was growing busier with traffic by the minute.

As time went on the call became more insistent, but there was nowhere that I could discreetly answer the call without being seen by all and sundry. Eventually to my relief I come across a secluded lay-by. Small trees and other foliage conceal the lay-by from passing traffic, affording me some modesty in answering what was by now a very urgent command. I have no time to do anything but hurriedly take down my weatherproof trousers that unfortunately lack a fly opening and drop them to my knees so I can reach the fly on my shorts.

So here I am standing there, merrily relieving myself into a profusion of wild nettles when suddenly, a coach full of tourists draws up and stops right beside me. I don't believe it! Talk about embarrassment; I'm wondering what Basil Fawlty would do in this situation – faint on the spot I suppose! Anyway, I turn and wave weakly to all the faces staring out of the window and surprisingly, they all wave back ...well, most of them do. I finish what I was doing, hastily pull up my weatherproof trousers and gather up my walking stick to leave. I think about braving it out by getting onto the coach to hand out the 'Around England Walk' leaflets that I always carry with me, but seeing as they knew I hadn't washed my hands I hurriedly discarded the thought.

As I continue my walk I begin to wonder why the coach had stopped there in the first place; it suddenly occurs to me that maybe some of the passengers also had a need to answer the call of nature.

I catch up with Rob about 6½ miles on, at a place near Milfield and after another meal of dreary old pasta I continue on a southerly direction towards Wooler. About 6 miles further on I catch up with the van for another much needed break; I passed Wooler some time ago and Rob is parked 3 miles beyond the town.

After the break I carry on for another hour before calling it a day. It is a relief just to climb into the passenger seat and relax while Rob drives the 6 miles or so back to Wooler where we have booked in for another night's stay at the campsite. As soon as we get into Wooler we take the van into a local garage to get the 12-volt system sorted out, as it has started playing up again.

The guys at the Mike Hope Garage are really helpful. They find the electrical fault and sort it; then put the van on the hoist, check the gearbox oil, change a tyre, check air pressures, and give us a bill for just £10. On top of that they donate to our charity. Thanks Tony and Jamie for giving us such great service, also thanks to the Garage Management.

Today's pedometer reading: 28.9km (17.95 miles).

Notes of Interest: Wooler

It has been suggested that the name Wooler might derive from the Old English, 'wella' (well or spring) and 'ofer' (a ridge or hill) as the name of Welnfver appears in an 1186 transcript suggesting such a possibility; however, this theory is discounted in various quarters.

The name Wooler does not appear in the Domesday Book and maybe the reason for that was because northern Northumbria might not have been under Norman control when the survey was recorded.

Wooler, an attractive, stone-built market town in Northumberland, is perched above the Wooler Water in the foothills of the Cheviots and to many it is the natural gateway to Northumberland National Park.

Authors Daniel Defoe and Sir Walter Scott both visited the district in their day, as did the Victorian heroine, Grace Darling.

TUES, 21ST JULY 2009
POWBURN – ROTHBURY

We leave Wooler a little late today due to having to update a four-day backlog of diary entries, progress map and email replies. We have found difficulty in getting internet connection since before Berwick so the proprietor of the Black Bull Hotel in Wooler invites us to use their Wi-Fi facilities. Christine also gives a generous donation to our Cancer Research UK charity. Thank you, Christine! The weather is clear with just a light breeze as I continue walking along the A697. I am now in the heart of the Northumberland countryside. The broad expanse of green fields in the rolling landscape and the distant hills of Northumberland's National Park make delightful viewing and I stroll along thinking about nothing in particular until thoughts about my teenage years begin to emerge. I start thinking once more about the street we lived in and of some of the characters domiciled there.

There was a woman called Mrs H, who lived close by. She had this wild mop of jet-black hair that looked as if it hadn't seen a brush or comb for years. She had three sons and two girls, as I remember. There used to be four boys, two of the youngest being twins but one had died before Mick and I had returned home from evacuation. David, the remaining twin, would be stuck outside in his high chair in all weathers. His mother, apart from giving him a cold bottle of milk every once in a while to suckle on, completely neglected him. While playing in the street we kids would give the highchair a wide detour due to the constant smell of excrement wafting from the child. When our mother was home during the day, she would sometimes wait for Mrs H to go out in the afternoon, usually to visit a pub, and then take David back home to clean him up. She would put cream on his sore backside, clean his bottle and feed him before putting him back outside in his chair. Mrs H would acknowledge what had been done for her son and give thanks, but according to our mother the woman never appeared shameful. Maybe that was because she just didn't care. I think she had been reported to the authorities on a number of occasions, but because there were so many similar cases in those days and because of her known violence, she was left well alone.

I remember once standing in Mrs H's passageway waiting for her son, Reggie, to come out. The odour in the place was hard to describe; it was like a mixture of stale cheese and bad eggs. The passage was very dark and littered with all sorts of debris including cigarette butts, matches and crumbs etc.

She had a husband or a partner called Charlie, a smallish man who was hardly ever home and when he was there he nearly always appeared to be drunk. I can't remember what happened to Johnny, the eldest son, or the two girls, but I do know that Reggie, who was about my age, hanged himself while in the army. As for young David, who knows…

I come through Powburn about 2½ hours later. From here the route becomes even more scenic with the road passing through extensive wooded areas. It's quite strange how certain terrain can have a noticeable psychological effect on you as you walk. I feel it especially when walking through heavily wooded or forested areas. There seems to be a sort of stillness, almost as if the trees are like sentinels, watching and listening. You want to be a part of that solitary atmosphere for any sound you make seems to evoke a feeling of intrusion.

Today I am walking on a busy road that meanders through heavily wooded areas; yet despite the traffic and the noise, the feeling is still there. It is not as intense as walking alone on a track through a remote forest area, but I feel it all the same.

I eventually catch up with Rob who is parked up near the Aln Bridge. After the meal break I carry on for another two hours or so, walking through more picturesque Northumberland countryside before eventually turning right onto the road that takes me into Rothbury. The route is very hilly, with numerous dips and sharp turns making the walk strenuous and hazardous. I arrive in Rothbury with rain threatening.

In Rothbury we call in at the Tourist Information Centre. The lady is very helpful providing us with information and literature on the Pennine Way and Hadrian's Wall. We eventually book into a caravan camping site 5 miles out of Rothbury.

Today's pedometer reading: 26km (16.14 miles).

Notes of Interest: Rothbury

As I walked through this small market town of Rothbury, which straddles the River Coquet, it certainly had a village feel about it; the river also adds greatly to the charismatic nature of the place. Even in the depths of winter, Rothbury would attract nature lovers for it is surrounded by Northumberland's dramatic and peaceful countryside. It's an area ideal for those who love walking, fishing and other countryside pursuits. It would also be a haven for the landscape artist or photographer.

The panoramic views are stunning, and in the far distance the Cheviots make a wonderful backdrop. The country air around here has a fragrance of its own and the fast-flowing streams and rivers seem as clear as crystal. I have also been told that in autumn the changing colours of the trees are something to experience.

Rothbury has had a turbulent and bloody history. The Coquet Valley was a pillaging ground for bands of renegades who would frequently attack the town during the fifteenth and sixteenth centuries.

Lord Armstrong's home, Cragside, which lies just a mile or so east of the town (now in the ownership of the National Trust), was said to be the first house in the world to be lit by hydro-electricity.

The Cheviots, Hadrian's Wall, Holy Island and the Scottish border are all within easy driving distance from Rothbury.

WED, 22ND JULY 2009
THROPTON – OTTERBURN

I return to Rothbury from the campsite to start the day's walk. It is 6.30am and the weather is clear with a slight westerly breeze. I walk through Thropton and about 2 miles further on I locate the camper van. I wonder why Rob has stopped this early, but the reason soon becomes clear. A farmer is driving his livestock from some sheds to a field some distance along the road. Three horse riders and a couple of people on foot are helping to herd the cattle toward a gate being opened by another farmhand. As soon as the gate is closed an adjacent gate is opened and the horse riders and their dogs bring another herd back down to the sheds. It is a chore that blocks the road for about an hour, so Rob cooks up some porridge and we have an earlier than usual first meal break.

The next session of the walk is quite strenuous. There are numerous steep hills that really test my resolve. I think I must be pretty fit by this stage so can handle it okay, but I wonder how I would have got on had I been confronted with such terrain in the early stages of the walk. I remember the second day out from Brighton (seems like an age ago now), when I walked up Cuckmere Hill and the hilly stretches past East Dean. Some of these hills in Northumbria seem like 'big mommas' in comparison! After more than two hours slog I come to where the campervan is parked at the top of the Otterburn National Park. After a quick meal of pasta and a leg stretch I am on my way again... destination Otterburn. Again more hills, more breathtaking panorama, more twists and turns on an unfriendly road that I am unable to get off before arriving in Otterburn village.

We go to one caravan camping site, but they want £19.00 for the night, so we call in at a farm caravan site near the town of Bellingham. The farmer, a nice guy called Robert, charges us only £3.00 for the electric hook-up, showers etc.

Today's pedometer reading: 27.9km (17.32 miles).

Notes of Interest: Otterburn

Otterburn lies within the Cheviot Hills.

It is said that the village was made famous by a battle that took place just outside Otterburn between an English force under the command of Sir Henry Percy (Hotspur) and a Scottish army commanded by the Earl of Douglas. The Scots emerged victorious in a fierce battle, but the Earl of Douglas was killed.

Outside the village stands Otterburn Tower, a manor house founded in the eleventh century by a cousin of William the Conqueror. This historic building sits in picturesque parkland surroundings and has now been converted into a luxury hotel. Otterburn is situated alongside the River Rede and is 16 miles (26km) from the Scottish border.

THURS, 23RD JULY 2009
BELLINGHAM

It is early morning when Robert drives me back from Bellingham to the day's starting point at Otterburn. The sky is clear in the east, but there is a build-up of clouds approaching from the west. There seems to be something about walking in the early hours that gives one a real sense of the perennial beauty of our world. The dew on grass reflecting the weak rays of the rising sun, the cacophony of sound from unseen birds in nearby foliage, a rising wind rustling the leaves of a solitary tree, the rumble of thunder signalling an approaching storm or the lazy rhythmic sound of the surf as it spends itself on some remote shore. Observing such natural phenomena makes me think how transient and out-of-touch we are; busy lives that never heed the steady, eternal pulse of our planet.

Walking across a narrow stone bridge just out of Otterburn, I am again confronted with winding roads and steep hills. I suppose the positive side to this is that the constant winding roads exercise my brain by keeping me alert to the hazards of oncoming traffic, while the long steep hills further improve my cardiac fitness. I am about 2 miles into my walk when Rob phones to say he has broken down due to running out of fuel. I am in no position to help him, so apart from making a couple of suggestions, I continue walking. I am surprised when about 15 minutes later a car drives toward me then stops. Suddenly, Rob leans over from the passenger seat and informs me that the lady is taking him to the petrol station in Bellingham.

It is amazing how quickly Rob has the van going again. I am even more astounded to hear that the manager of the petrol station actually drove Rob back to where the van was parked, and waited to make sure the van was mobile again before driving back to his forecourt. That's North Country hospitality for you! A lesson was also learned in watching the fuel gauge more closely in future!

The other day I had passed by some apple trees. The apples were those small, hard green ones that had slight smears of red on them to indicate that the fruit was not yet ripened; nevertheless, I grabbed one and took a bite without breaking step and was pleasantly surprised that, although a bit tangy, they were actually quite sweet to the taste.

I went back and collected a dozen or more that were overhanging the wall and put them in my pouch. I wasn't sure if it was what you'd call scrumping per se, but as there were quite a number that had dropped to the ground in various stages of decay I didn't think anyone would mind. Today, as I am eating the last but one of my ill-gotten harvest my mind traverses back over the years, to the time I was caught scrumping apples as a teenager.

I went off on my bike with my friend, Moe, to a place in Patcham, an outer suburb of Brighton, where we would often go scrumping for apples. Patcham in those days had quite a few orchards in the area; targets for many boys around my age for doing a bit of the elicit harvesting of fruit. Trouble was there had been a few complaints of late and the police were on the lookout. We were on the way home in semi-darkness, for it was winter time, when we got stopped by a copper on the London Road. He told us we shouldn't be cycling because we had no lights; not many of the poorer kids had lights in those days so I think it was just an excuse to stop us. He then wanted to know where we'd been and what we'd been up to.

I had one of those army tunic jackets that when you tightened up the strap at the waist it made an ideal cavity for carrying stuff. This particular day I had it stuffed to my neck with apples making me look like one of those birds that strut around with inflated chests in order to attract the female.

It was no use trying to refute the copper's next question because when he had walked onto the road I'd frantically braked hard to avoid banging into him and a couple of apples had rolled out of the jacket and onto the road in front of him.

He came up to me without waiting for an answer and just said, "Scrumping eh?", and with that he gave me a clip around the ear. I was still holding onto my handle bars so I couldn't avoid the swipe. Funny thing was he never tried to clout Moe; probably because, although we were about the same age, I was much taller, so he obviously thought I was the ringleader. I was also the one carrying all the apples!

The policeman then asked us to follow him up the road where a black police van was parked; in those days we called them 'Black Marias', why, I'm not sure.

With our bikes in the van, all our hard earned fruit stowed into a black canvas bag, and Moe and I crushed up beside him in the front, he drove away. My first thought was that he was going to take us to the police station and throw us in prison, but then he asked us where we lived and drove us home.

My mother came to the door in answer to his knock. He then proceeded to tell her what we had done and that he'd already given me a clout for doing it. It was as if he was saying that I'd already had my punishment. I guess he realised how violent some parents could become in situations like this. He went on to explain that if kids got away with stealing apples it would encourage them to go onto stealing bigger things, and that if I was ever caught scrumping again I would be put into a remand home.

Looking back I think it was just said to scare me. My mother vented her wrath on me as I sidled past her by ordering me to go to my room. As I went upstairs I remember hearing her thank the policeman for bringing me home. As for me, I was happy to be in my bedroom and away from the clutches of the law. I think it must have been about an hour or so later when my mother, being worried as always about the welfare of her children called me down for dinner. It was then I noticed the brown paper bag full of apples on the sideboard. My mother explained that the policeman had asked her for a paper bag and returned with a few of the apples saying something like, "Make sure these are the last stolen apples he eats". I think eating those apples had more effect on me that the clout round the ear! Moe told me afterwards that the policeman did the same with him.

I still wasn't quite out of the woods though because with my dinner came a lecture from my mother about stealing and being dishonest. Our mother needn't have bothered; my greatest fear was being put back into some sort of boy's home again and that threat was enough to deter me from ever scrumping again.

I decide to stop walking early today as I need to prepare for the long Pennine Walk tomorrow. I have a feeling it might be hard day! Today's pedometer reading: 14.7km (9.12 miles).

Notes of Interest: The Pennine Way

Dubbed the backbone of England, the Pennines run through a variety of landscapes from the Peak District in northern Derbyshire, through the southern Pennines then on through the picturesque valleys of the Yorkshire Dales before hitting the wild uplands of the northern Pennines in Northumbria. It crosses Hadrian's Wall to mark the Pennines northernmost section.

The upland areas, particularly those of the lesser-known northern Pennines, can resemble a turgid swamp when the rain falls. It is home to a wealth of wildlife, but very few humans tread there – apart from a 73-year-old walker from Brighton!

A great deal of the more muddier parts of the Pennines such as the footpath over Kinder Scout and Bleaklow in the Peak District and the Great Shunner Fell route in the Northern Dales have been laid with limestone paving slabs to facilitate walkers.

The Pennine Way was the first national trail in Britain and its 268-mile footpath walk takes about three to four weeks to complete. The walk can be quite strenuous in parts, but it provides an opportunity for people of all ages to appreciate the ancient landscapes of northern England.

The town of Bellingham is the gateway to Kielder Water & Forest Park and is an ideal base to explore some of Northumberland's best-known attractions.

FRI, 24TH JULY 2009
BELLINGHAM - WARK – THE PENNINES

I start out from Bellingham under a leaden sky. Although I was close to the Pennine Way, I thought it best to take to the road due to the recent heavy rainfall in the area. The road passes through stunning wooded countryside; a bonus for drivers, but the road's constant twists and turns make it a nightmare for walking. At Wark, I realise I've had enough of playing Russian roulette with the traffic so when I see a wooden sign saying 'Public Footpath to the Pennine Way' I decide to take my chances on higher ground and follow it... despite the wet conditions. A misty fine rain accompanies me as I make my way up toward the Upper Pennines. It is slow going and the signage is poor.

At one point I call in at a remote farmhouse to ask the way as there are two footpaths that fork off from each other close by and the chart map doesn't help me differentiate between the two. The lady at the house points me in the right direction but warns me of the remoteness up on the Northern Pennines. I thank her and continue on my way. Luckily my compass from then on helps keep me on the right course, but it doesn't prevent me from trudging through boggy areas that lay everywhere along the upward track. It isn't long before the inevitable happens and my feet sink well above the ankles in a grass-covered swamp. I can hardly believe it! Here I am, still with a long climb ahead of me and already with mud up to my ankles and soaking wet feet.

On reaching the Pennine Way I face the same problem. For another 3½ hours I am constantly confronted with muddy or waterlogged tracks; but even cold, wet feet and tired limbs don't detract from appreciating the ever-changing scenery and the utter remoteness of the place. I've mentioned before about the peculiar psychological effect that walking through a forest or heavily wooded area has on me. It is happening again on this part of the Pennines. The path leads me into a pine forest that instantly shelters me from the misty rain. The stillness is immediate; a peaceful, profound quiescence that is a little unnerving. I decide to put on my MP3 player, but halfway through the first track I turn it off. I want to merge with the silence of the forest and enjoy the experience – don't ask me why!

The track underfoot is firm and dry and for once I manage to travel at a good pace. About half an hour later I emerge from the trees onto fairly steep, rolling terrain. I stop here to rest while I bite into an apple, my last remaining bit of food. My water supply was consumed a while back. It isn't long before I come through another forest of young pine trees.

I haven't met a soul throughout the walk, yet as I am approaching the end of the forest track I have the feeling that someone is following me. I look back a couple of times but see no one. It is the first time I've ever experienced this feeling over the 2½ months of lone walking around many remote parts of England.

Once out of the forest I emerge out onto more steep, rolling country. It isn't long before I catch sight of Hadrian's Wall away in the distance. The feeling of being followed is still with me and I glance back, half expecting someone to appear out from the forest. It isn't until I am approaching Hadrian's Wall that the feeling comes over me again. I look back for an instant and see what I think is a group of ramblers about 30 metres behind me. Some minutes later I approach the Wall and start to climb over a wooden stepping structure that will take me up and over to the other side. As I do so I glance back expecting to see the group close behind, but I am startled to find that they are no longer there. I look around frantically trying to catch sight of someone, but it's as if they have vanished into thin air. There is nowhere in this wide open landscape for a single person to hide, let alone a group of people.

As I walk along the Wall I try to work out some explanation for the strange sighting as it perturbs me. Possibilities range from the onset of Alzheimer's disease to the likelihood that they had run back into the forest the moment my back was turned. I naturally preferred the latter explanation, but in truth I found it hard to give credence to the idea because at the time of seeing them, the forest would have been a good half a mile away. I dwell on the matter for a while and come to the conclusion that I might have been hallucinating. I've heard that this condition can be brought on by tiredness and dehydration and I had been without drinking water for a few hours and the going had been pretty tough to say the least. I plod along for a time, but I'm beginning to feel very weary. Hours of walking over difficult terrain with wet socks and boots is having its effect, so when a path presents itself I leave Hadrian's Wall and make my way down to the road to have Rob pick me up.

As I walk down I begin to wonder what it must have been like for the soldiers who manned the Wall all those centuries ago, especially the Romans who hailed from Southern Italy. A passage from a recovered letter sent home by a Roman Centurion from a fort on Hadrian's Wall gives some idea of what the average Roman soldier thought of the place: "The climate is cold, the men are cold and bored and long for the good wine and warm women of the southlands".

Rob drives back from where he was parked while I trudge down to the road from the hills to intercept him. I come down near the Housesteads Roman Fort and Museum. I am feeling very weary and looking forward to relaxing somewhere with a cool beer. We call in at a pub aptly named the Twice Brewed Inn near to a village that's also known as 'Twice Brewed' although there seemed to be some confusion about this because some of the locals said the village was really called 'Once Brewed'.

Regardless, it was just wonderful to rest in comfortable surroundings while savouring the taste of a Northumbrian pint of cool malt ale. Rob mentions my 'strange' sighting to a man drinking at the bar. The guy shrugs his shoulders and in a Northumbrian accent says, "We hear a lot about strange goings-on up there on the Wall". He then begins to elucidate on the matter. Apparently, from what the guy said, a number of odd sightings have been reported by ramblers over the years; stories of seeing a Roman soldier on horseback to the sighting of small groups of people in leather tunics wandering around the countryside near the Wall. Maybe I'm not going senile after all! Strange though, eh?

Today's pedometer reading: 28.7km (17.82 miles)... Felt more like fifty!

Notes of Interest: Hadrian's Wall

Hadrian's Wall (Latin: Vallum Aelium) is probably the most popular of all tourist attractions in Northern England. It became a UNESCO World Heritage site in 1987, and was described as being 'The most important monument built by the Romans in Britain'.

The construction of the wall began in AD 122, during a visit by Hadrian, the Roman emperor of that time, and was completed in AD 128. Some historians believe that the wall was created by the emperor Hadrian in order to express the might of Rome, for he was experiencing uprisings against Rome's oppressive rule in many of their conquered territories.

The wall also marked Rome's most northerly frontier and it became an effective barrier against attacks from the troublesome Picts and the Scots, north of the new border. But the inclement weather must have taken its toll on the morale of soldier and officer alike as some of them would have hailed from a warm Mediterranean climate.

The course of Hadrian's Wall can be followed on foot as it tracks over the heights of northern England from the River Tyne near Newcastle in the east, to Carlisle in the west. Countless garrisons of auxiliary troops would have been involved in building the Wall and it is thought that at the height of Roman activity the total number manning the full length of the Wall was probably around 10,000 soldiers.

During the centuries of occupation, it is quite likely that many of the garrison troops would have married and integrated into the local settlements that had sprung up near the wall. Hadrian's Wall remained occupied by mainly auxiliary troops, many from conquered lands, although it's possible that Britons might have been conscripted into manning the Wall during the latter period of the Roman occupation.

The Romans left Britain around AD 410. From that time on, Britain was told to 'look to its own defences'. They were on their own and vulnerable to attacks from the many aggressive tribes from across the North Sea and the English Channel.

CHAPTER 14
CUMBRIA

The day dawns clear and still, but also chilly. Rob drops me off near Housestead's Roman Fort and Museum to begin my walk at around 6.45am. I contemplate the thought of heading back up to Hadrian's Wall, but my walking boots are still wet and my legs still ache. The only sensible option is to continue on the road toward Carlisle.

The road is almost devoid of traffic so the walk is quite enjoyable. Now and then I glance up at Hadrian's Wall snaking over the distant hills and feel a pang of regret not being up there, but I know it would have been crazy to tackle such terrain after yesterday's effort. I only had to twist an ankle or knee and the walk would be over. I owe it to myself and to others not to let that happen.

I catch up with Rob who has pulled off onto a wide grassy verge in a wooded area about 6½ miles further on. After a thorough leg stretch to get the more than usual stiffness out of my legs, (mainly from yesterday's exertions), and a double helping of porridge I set out once more, heading toward the west coast.

As usual a conglomeration of thoughts is going on inside my head. Often it's about the terrain that lies ahead of me or what the weather might have in store, but other thoughts are always waiting in the wings. I begin thinking again about my mother and about the trials and tribulations that accompanied her during the post-war years.

About three years after our Dad died, our mother met another man. He had got to know our mother through working at the same Vauxhall plant for the war effort. His name was Dick. In many respects Dick was quite a talented individual; he could play the piano exceptionally well without the need to read music. He was quite witty, with an infectious laugh (his sense of humour was, I suspect, what had attracted our mother) and had a great rapport with other men. He was also extremely generous, (whenever he had money to be generous with). But it was his negative traits that would become a future burden for our mother. Dick was a get-rich-quick merchant, and typical of that personality, he was a gambler. He suffered a lot from asthma and also had a foul temper. Although our mother never married him he became her partner. However, he contributed little to the family budget; in fact, he was usually a financial burden to her.

My sister Jean with Fred

There were times when our mother would give him money to pay for something she had on the 'never-never', as they used to call it in those days. The item would usually be paid off with monthly instalments and she would regularly give the money to Dick to pay into the company's local ofice in Brighton, Months later she'd have someone knocking on her door to take repossession of the cleaner, or whatever the item was, because no payments had been made. This sort of thing would usually result in our mother and Dick having arguments that we'd often hear late into the night.

At around the time that Mick and I arrived back home from evacuation Dick had been sent to prison for stealing a truckful of tyres with another guy called Johnnie Morgan. In the end Dick became such a burden to our mother that Roy, a grown son from his first marriage, was instrumental in forcing Dick out of the house for good. The only positive thing that sprang from that union was the birth of Fred in 1944 and Janice in 1947. Incidentally, Roy had become my older sister's boyfriend. He and Jean would marry and raise three boys during a long and happy relationship.

I liaise with Rob again 7 miles further on at the turn-off near Greenhead. After a small break and a meal of pasta, I set off for my third session of the day, this time diverting onto the A69 toward Brampton and Carlisle. I have to stop for the day about 2 miles past Brampton as I am shattered. We drive back to Brampton where a young lady called Sharon invites us into the Conservative Club to watch the All Blacks play the Springboks and then helps us find a local camping site. Thank you, Sharon!

Today's pedometer reading: 31.7km (19.68 miles).

Notes of Interest: Twice Brewed

Yesterday, after coming down from Hadrian's Wall, we called into a pub called the Twice Brewed Inn for a much needed refreshment stop. It is located near the village of Once Brewed; well that's what we were told, although we noticed a sign saying: 'Welcome to Twice Brewed'.

We aren't sure, even now, of the true title of the village, or how it acquired its strange name, although we have been assured by the locals that the village is definitely known as Twice Brewed. We reckon it's the confusion that comes from drinking too much at the local pub. But what we gleaned from our very enjoyable evening at the Twice Brewed Inn was that sometime around the end of the fifteenth century, there was an Inn named West Twice Brewed, and around the eighteenth century, an Inn was named East Twice Brewed.

From the nineteenth century the Inn was probably used as a small coaching stop. Since then, the Twice Brewed Inn has grown in size to meet the demand of discerning tourists who, after experiencing the tranquillity of Northumbria, need to sample the brew of Twice Brewed in the village of Once Brewed or is it Twice Brewed . . . ? Oh, who cares! 'Ave another pint!

SUN, 26TH JULY 2009
CARLISLE – THURSBY

With rain threatening I begin my walk from yesterday's pick-up point. I realise I have only 7 miles to walk to reach Carlisle. Half an hour into the walk and the rain starts again so it was on with the wet weather gear before trudging on. Carlisle is the most northern city on England's west coast and another significant stage in my 'Around England Walk'. After reaching the city we'll then be heading in a southerly direction toward the south coast of England.

I looked at the road map last night and had cast my eyes down the west coast; it seemed such a long distance from Carlisle to Land's End that it made me wonder if I'd ever make it. I felt daunted at seeing the south coast so far away... so remote; it made me a little depressed so I vowed not to look at the complete picture again. "Just look ahead one day at a time," I said to myself, and that is what I am going to do.

I meet up with Rob about 4½ miles further on. He has stopped earlier than usual as he was a little concerned about me getting too wet. Although I have wet weather gear on, the jacket is quite light and not as effective as it should be. I feel quite damp not just because of the driving rain but also because I was sweating profusely under clothes that stifled the body's heat. I make a quick change of T-shirt then put on my heavier waterproof yachting jacket.

I walk into Carlisle's town centre an hour later and find Rob nearby in a side street. After a breakfast of sausages, bacon, baked beans and toast, I'm ready for another session. I walk out through the dreary suburbs of Carlisle and journey on for another 6½ miles before stopping near a major roundabout where the campervan is parked. Rob then drives back to the village of Thursby where he had parked earlier. It was the carpark of a local pub called The Ship Inn.

The management and staff were very hospitable and also provided us each with a free meal. Thank you, Peter and Nancy and also a special thanks to Jen.

After this we drive to Dalston where we manage to book in to a decent caravan camping site. Unfortunately, we have no phone signal or internet access. This is disappointing, but hopefully tomorrow we can rectify the problem.

Today's pedometer reading: 25.61km (15.90 miles).

Notes of Interest: Carlisle

Carlisle is known as the Border City, but it is not as far north or as close to the Scottish border as the town of Berwick-upon-Tweed on the east coast.

In its early history, Carlisle was an established Roman settlement, created primarily to serve the forts on Hadrian's Wall. During the Middle Ages, however, Carlisle became a strategically crucial military stronghold due to its proximity to the Scottish border. Carlisle Castle is a great medieval fortress that was built during the reign of William II of England and has presided over the area for over nine centuries. The castle has had a varied and sometimes bloody past having been captured and recaptured many times.

However, the modern day castle is still relatively intact and is the home of the Border Regiment and the Duke of Lancaster's Regiment Museum.

MON, 27TH JULY 2009
DALSTON

Today is a rest day. I need to catch up on my internet work, but we still have no signal with our mobile broadband and there are no internet cafes around, so there has to be another way. Last night I approached Jan (pronounced Yan) the owner of a grade II listed mini castle called Dalston Hall, to ask if he had Wi-Fi available on his premises. He said he had and we were invited to use our laptops in his lounge bar whenever we wished. Today I've taken him at his word and we're spending much of the day working in fabulous and comfortable surroundings.

Notes of Interest: Dalston Hall

*Dalston Hall was built sometime during the sixteenth century. Various extensions and interior refurbishments have taken place over the years, creating a magnificent mansion, surpassing perhaps, its former ancient grandeur. It is now a hotel with thirteen superb, individually designed bedrooms and spacious, medieval entertaining areas. It makes Dalston Hall the ideal site for that special function. If you want to know more go to their website: **www.dalstonhall.com**.*
WARNING: Some of the bedrooms are said to be haunted!

TUES, 28TH JULY 2009
DALSTON

We drive into Carlisle this morning to get some additional sign writing done for the van. The guy did it for free; said it was his donation to Cancer Research. Thank you, Craig!
Once back at the Dalston Hall Holiday Park we immediately catch up with our laundry tasks and fill our tank with water in preparation for the van's journey down the coast early tomorrow. The rest of the day we spend at Dalston Hall.

WED, 29TH JULY 2009
WIGTON – CROSBY

Today I begin my walk from the roundabout near Thursby village. Steady rain falls from heavy, leaden-grey skies confirming yesterday's weather prediction. I stay on the road to Maryport. There is no point in seeking an alternative route for past experience reminds me that off-road public pathways are often waterlogged after long periods of rain.

The road to Wigton is very walker-unfriendly bordering on hazardous and the misty rain doesn't help. On these roads there are no side verges allowing me to avoid on-coming traffic and the huge logging trucks create an additional worry. They carry a massive amount of logs and travel at high speed; getting hit by one of these would be like being hit by an express train.

From Wigton there is a 2½-foot margin on both sides and further on, a cycle track appears alongside the road right through to Aspatria where I have my next meal break. I continue on the cycle track through to Crosby village where I will be ending the day's walk. Despite the rain I have found this session quite enjoyable. I remember giving rein to my thoughts around this time and memories of the past once again begin creeping in.

Summers were always a great time for us teenagers. When I look back it seemed that every day was fine and warm, but I don't suppose it was. We'd spend day after day on Brighton beach, all of us getting as brown as berries.

I'm on the top with brother Mick below left

If our mother was working, the girls would often have to take care of the two younger ones – Fred who was then around four, and Jan, a baby of about 15 months. Sometimes, if the girls weren't available, my mother would rope me in to look after Jan. She'd allow me to take Jan down to the beach in the pram only after I promised not to leave her unattended. I'd head off to the beach with Moe and we'd take it in turns to stay by the pram while the other went for a swim.

I remember us coming back from the beach one time and me leaving Moe to look after the baby while I did a chore for my mother. He continued to walk up the street with Ted, another friend who had joined us on the beach. I can only describe Moe's version of what happened after that.

As they began to walk back down the street they started flicking their wet towels at each other. If you get the technique right and judge the distance you can inflict a lovely sting on your mate's bare torso. Moe was caught on the side of the waist with a beauty and in retaliation he quickly gave a deft flick of his own, but in doing so he had to let go of the pram for a second or two. Now our street had quite a rising gradient from the bottom to the top and Moe obviously hadn't taken into account the effect that Isaac Newton's universal law of gravity would have on the motion of an object on wheels when sitting untethered on a downward slope, but he was soon to find out!

In that moment or two of release the pram was already about 20 feet away and gathering speed. Moe apparently took off like a petrified rabbit in a desperate attempt to grab it before it crashed into something, or more likely, came off the kerb throwing Jan headlong into the street breaking every bone in her body. As he sprinted after it the pram lurched toward the kerb. Moe watched in horror as he was still a few feet away and realised he wasn't going to make it in time.

Miraculously, it spilled over the kerb into the road and although it was teetering on two wheels it remained upright. It was heading for the kerb on the other side of the road just as Moe caught up with it. Moe said he would have loved to have known the time it took him to cover those 60 yards or so before reaching the pram. He reckoned that if Jesse Owens had been racing alongside, the athlete would have finished a poor second.

Out of breath, sweating, but with a feeling of utter relief, Moe looked down at Jan; her eyes were wet with tears from being in a state of hysterical joy and all she kept saying in her babyish babble were words that sounded like, "Again Moe, again".

Rob has found a local pub called The Stag Inn. Jemma, the young lady managing the pub, is really friendly and helpful and the few patrons that are there seem very interested in our venture especially after Rob had told them where I had walked from. Some begin giving us advice on what route we should take tomorrow and soon a very heated discussion erupts among two or three of them. However, they all make us feel very much at home and donate generously to the cause.

I had intended to walk to Maryport and proceed along the coast to Workington where I'd continue making my way right down the Cumbrian coast. However, they suggest I should go inland and walk through the Lake District. It is always a good policy to listen to local advice so after chatting with Rob we decide to head inland before reaching Maryport. We have a delicious meal at The Stag Inn before leaving to find the campsite at Dearham, which we had pre-booked earlier in the day.

Today's pedometer reading: 33km (20.45 miles).

Notes of Interest: Wigton

Wigton is a charming little town set in the heart of Cumbria. The name Wigton might derive from 'Wicga' possibly the name of a Saxon chieftain of the emerging settlement. Inglewood Forest takes up a very large part of this ancient wooded area interspersed as it is with common and heathland, which was taken over by the Normans after the conquest. The forest boundaries were extended even further during the reign of Henry II creating one of England's largest hunting reserves and placing it under Forest Law. It then became unlawful to fell mature trees or hunt the forest deer.

Wigton proudly lays claim to being the birthplace of Melvyn Bragg; now Lord Bragg of Wigton. Wigton's famous son was born and reared here and one of his books, A Time to Dance *was set and filmed in Wigton and dramatised for TV.*

The location makes an excellent walking base for exploring the surrounding area especially the Caldbeck Fells or visiting Hadrian's Wall or hiking across to the beautiful Solway coast.

THURS, 30TH JULY 2009
MARYPORT – COCKERMOUTH – WHINLATTER FOREST

Light rain accompanies me as I set out from Crosby for Maryport. On reaching the outskirts of Maryport, I turn inland on the Maryport Road toward Cockermouth. I walk past the turn-off to Dearham again, near where we stayed last night and finally meet up with Rob for a meal break on the far side of the village of Dovenby.

From Cockermouth I take the road for Keswick. This is a lovely scenic route with very little traffic, although it's quite hilly in places. As I walk I come across a public footpath sign. I remember checking my route with the charts yesterday evening and I was sure that it showed a footpath to Keswick somewhere along this stretch. The sign is quite faded and I can't make out some of the lettering, but the path seems to be heading in the same direction as I am, so I divert onto it. After a while I start walking through a copse then a little later I walk alongside a stream before the path narrows and winds up steeply into a pine forest. It finally peters out at a small waterfall and I've no option but to angrily retrace my steps back to the road.

Frustrated from the delay and the extra mile or so wasted, I begin the climb up the road toward Whinlatter Forest Park visitor centre. The van is waiting at the top of the hill so I decide to end my day's walk here.

We drive into Keswick where we locate a decent caravan camping site. After showering we go into the town and have a meal at a pub called The Bank Tavern before making our way back to the campsite for the night.

Today's pedometer reading: 26.2km (16.27 miles).

Notes of Interest: Maryport

In around AD 122, the settlement was first established as the Roman fort of Alauna. Although there was probably a settlement here during prehistoric times, the first recorded date mentioned was around AD 122 when a Roman officer called Marcus Maenius Agrippa was in residence here. He commanded the Roman fort and was also believed to be a close friend of the Emperor Hadrian. The fort became a command and supply base for the coastal defences of the western extremity of Hadrian's Wall.

After the Roman withdrawal from Britain the fort was abandoned and the town once more reverted to being nothing more than a coastal village.

The town was called Ellenfoot for many years, but in 1749 an Act of Parliament was passed allowing the town to be renamed. It became Maryport, named after Humphrey Senhouse's wife, Mary.

The Senhouse family were important landowners with a major interest in Maryport's development. Their two sons, William and Joseph, had business interests in the West Indies and both were owners of many slaves.

A coal strike in December, 1874 would eventually spread to the whole area, and affect the livelihood of around 2,000 men. The three months' strike resulted in much violence especially when attempts were made to break the strike by some 'blacklegs', who were subsequently assaulted by the miners.

In the early twentieth century, Maryport would become almost a ghost town and the government had to declare the district of West Cumberland a 'Special Area'. Despite this, hardship for the area continued and by 1933, around 57% of the town's workforce was still unemployed.

FRI 31ST JULY 2009
BRAITHWAITE – KESWICK – THIRLMERE.

It's gone 7am before Rob drives me back to Whinlatter Forest Park to begin my day's walk. Continuing on the road to Keswick and the Whinlatter Pass I soon approach Braithwaite. I notice it's an ideal location for those intent on rambling as there are various footpaths and trails leading onto the Pass and other scenic areas surrounding the village. The misty rain accompanies me as I walk into Keswick. Despite the weather the place is humming with walkers; all coming and going. Some were heading to Derwent Water, others seeking public footpaths through the surrounding countryside of copses, valleys and fells.

From here I pass through Keswick to pick up the road for Windermere. I need to communicate with Rob to find out where he is, but my phone has no signal and I'm reckoning that Rob will have the same problem. Luckily he knows I am walking on the A591 toward Windermere and it isn't long before he catches sight of me.

During this part of the walk my thoughts converge for a while on long-gone boyhood days; mostly happy days, but hard days for our mother trying to survive in our rotten house in Mighell Street.

Because all the houses in the street were in a similar condition us youngsters thought our house wasn't all that bad. After all, it was certainly far cleaner than most of them and probably a little warmer as our mother always tried to have coal for the fire. But to our mother it must have been a hellish place to raise her family. With only two gas mantles to illuminate the living room and scullery and only lighted candles for the bedrooms upstairs she must have had an awful time of it, especially during the winter. I often think about how much help she would have received had she been living in today's world!

Our back yard was quite a handy place for it housed the outside loo and was storage for our firewood and rubbish bin etc. It also led out, by way of a tall door, into the back alleyway. This narrow alleyway was used for the collection of rubbish or for the delivery of coal and firewood. For us teenagers it was an ideal route for getting down into Edward Street or by turning right, it would take us up toward the derelict building site we used to play on.

As there was no running hot water in the house an old copper was used to heat water for the weekly bathing routine. We'd bring in the large tin bath that was kept in the back yard; our mother would pour in a certain amount of cold water then add hot water from the copper with the aid of a saucepan. When the water was the right temperature my sisters would bathe in it, while Mick and I would be given a shilling each to use the public wash-baths a quarter of a mile away. Later when we were all in bed, our mother would add hot water to the tin bath and bathe in it herself.

Approaching Thirlmere Lake I notice the turn-off that will take me along the westerly side of the lake but being unsure about vehicle access on this route and the unreliable mobile phone reception we decide to play it safe and stay on the main easterly route. As I walk I realise that this road is a bit hazardous, for there are stone walls on both sides almost to the road's edge making it a walker's nightmare.

I finally meet up with Rob again about 2½ miles from Grasmere. We have a meal in a nearby tavern then make our way back to a campsite that is close to where I had ended my walk. Unfortunately there are no vacancies and other caravan camping sites are also full. Bad weather is closing in once more as we search the area for somewhere to settle for the night. Fortunately someone in the tavern in Grasmere suggests we try the King's Head Hotel near Thirlmere, a place I had passed earlier in the day. It is about a seven mile drive back to where we have come from, but it's worth it. The management are sympathetic; they not only allow us to use their Wi-Fi facility in the comfort of their lounge, but also invite us to stay overnight on their premises.

Today's pedometer reading: 30.8km (19.12 miles).

Notes of Interest: Keswick / Whinlatter Forest

The town of Keswick was recorded in the thirteenth century as Kesewic. The name is believed to derive from the Old English word 'cese' (cheese), a word that might have become 'kese' due to Scandinavian influence. The word 'wic' meaning 'special place or dwelling' might also have been affected by Viking occupation at the time.

In 1276, the town was granted a charter by Edward I, allowing the town to hold a weekly market. Keswick's modern-day market is held every Saturday in the pedestrianised thoroughfare of the town centre and Moot Hall, one of the town's most important buildings, is the focal point of the busy market.

The Moot Hall is said to date back to 1571. Its early function appears to have been a Court House, but since then it has been utilised as a prison and the Town Hall. Today it is the local tourist information ofice.

Many businesses in Keswick are tourist related, helping to provide accommodation, promote local attractions and other facilities for the thousands of visitors that flock to the region each year. An annual guide to the area, including details of approved visitor accommodation sites, is published by the Keswick Tourism Association.

The town also plays host to an annual beer festival which takes place on Keswick Rugby Union Club field. The festival is run jointly by Keswick Rugby Club & Keswick Lions and is held on the first weekend in June, This exciting festival attracts thousands of people each year, a place where they can sample many real ales, ciders and lagers while listening to live jazz bands

Whinlatter – The climb up to Whinlatter was truly worth the effort. England's only true Mountain Forest rises to 790 metres above sea level and the Forest Park offers spectacular views of the Lake District and into Scotland.

SAT, 1ST AUG 2009
THIRLMERE

We awake to another dreadful day. It's teeming with rain and there's a driving wind. Once again two minds were in conflict. The stern voice of the more domineering mind was urging me to rise and get dressed, while the more sympathetic but equally insistent mind was trying to convince me that I should stay in my warm bed.

I lift the curtain and gaze once more at the weather. The weak light of dawn has not yet penetrated through the thick, leaden clouds and the murkiness does little to hide the cheerless scene outside. That brief glance was enough. On this rare occasion, I succumb to the softer option; I pull the covers over my head convincing myself that I deserve to have the day off. At 8.30am we go into the King's Head Hotel for a delightful breakfast. After breakfast we are once again invited to use their internet facilities and soon we are settled in the warm, congenial surroundings of their lounge.

We leave the hotel around 8.30 in the evening and return to a layby close to yesterday's pick-up point; its where I'll continue my walk early tomorrow morning... come rain or shine! Thank you, Lana, for your hospitality; and also the staff of the King's Head Hotel, for their efficiency and kind cooperation.

Notes of Interest: Thirlmere Water

The conifer-clad Thirlmere reservoir dam was completed in 1894. Once the dam had been built and the area flooded, the villages of Amboth and Wythburn were completely submerged. The purpose of the reservoir was to create a constant supply of water for the city of Manchester, but in its initial planning stage the project caused much consternation.

The reservoir is 4 miles long and half a mile wide and is surrounded by 2,000 acres of coniferous forest, much of it open to the public.

There are a number of fells including Raven Crag and Armboth Fell which provide spectacular views of the lake. Thirlmere is a glacial lake and has the purest water, but the water's so cold that swimming I believe is prohibited.

At the north end of the lake, the site of the dam, there is a plaque commemorating the start of the work on 22 August, 1890.

SUN, 2ND AUG 2009
GRASMERE – AMBLESIDE – HAWKSHEAD – WINDERMERE

I start out at 6.25am under an ominous looking, dark grey sky, accompanied by a cool westerly wind. I walk the 2 miles to Grasmere and continue on through Ambleside. The walk is enjoyable as there is a footpath alongside the road from Grasmere. I soon divert onto a narrow country road that joins up with the A591 some distance along. It is a lovely walk with glimpses of Grasmere Lake on my right and a backdrop of wood-fringed hills displayed to my left. Eventually I walk past Rydal Water and into the lovely town of Ambleside. I soon find my way onto the A593 where I meet up with Rob in a coach park for my first break.

Once back on the road I watch out for the turn-off that will take me to Hawkshead. This route is a delight, taking me through the occasional heavy wooded area, through copses and valleys. Moss-covered stone walls line both sides of the road, at times making it difficult to get off the narrow road to avoid approaching traffic, but apart from that it is a very enjoyable walk.

I arrive at Hawkshead an hour and a half later. Considering the dismal weather we'd been having over the last few days, I was surprised how busy the place is with walkers and sightseeing groups everywhere. Rob is waiting at Hawkshead and after a meal of pasta I set out once again, this time for the ferry near Far Sawrey that will take us over Lake Windermere. During this session of the walk I was thinking for a time about the war years and our evacuation.

The village of Lexham in Norfolk, where we had been evacuated, must have been pretty close to an air base because I remembered the home being visited by American airmen. It is quite remarkable how the mind has the ability to recall some minor detail from such distant times in the past. I can recollect sitting on this American airman's shoulders and being carried towards the jeeps that were sitting in the driveway of the mansion house where we stayed. I think I might have been the only boy out of the 25 of us being carried this way. I suppose it was because I was one of the youngest at the home, but I remember feeling pretty proud about it.

I particularly remember the smooth khaki-green jacket the man was wearing. (It would later remind me of the gaberdine material that suits and jackets were made of in my teenage years.) Even today I can see in my mind's eye the insignia displayed on the man's upper arms and the chest of the jacket; of eagles wings in gold and some words in a sort of upswept semicircle underneath. I remember being sat in the jeep ready for the drive to the airbase, but funnily enough I can't recall another thing about that outing.

Sometime after that event, how much later I cannot say, we heard the drone of a low flying aircraft. It must have been wintertime because by the time we had finished eating our evening meal it was quite dark. We were allowed to play out for another hour or so and it was then that we heard it. The staff also came outside to see what was happening because the noise of the aircraft was getting louder. Although the Dr Barnado's home was fairly close to an airbase, we were not on their flight path so planes on bombing missions to Europe would not normally fly over where we lived; therefore hearing this deep thunderous roar nearby was in itself very unusual. Suddenly we saw it pass directly overhead; I remembered seeing the wheels down and a fire coming out of one of the engines as it headed toward the distant woods. It seemed ages before we heard the explosion, then nothing but silence. I remember how quiet we all were and I also remembered wondering whether that man who had carried me on his shoulders was in that plane.

We were not allowed in the woods for about three weeks after the crash. When we were finally allowed to go in we noticed the brown silk remnants of parachutes hanging from the odd tree and one boy found a torn glove with a ring inside. I remembered being surprised about seeing the brown parachutes because I had always thought that parachutes were white.

We heard afterwards that the pilot of the plane had purposefully steered the plane away from the nearby village and toward the woods before attempting to bail out.

After crossing Lake Windermere on the ferry, I begin walking up Longtail Hill and onto the road to Kendal while Rob drives to the Windermere Caravan Club site to book us in for the coming night. I walk on for about 4 miles or more without seeing any sign of Rob.

I'm getting a little worried at this stage, as I have been expecting him to pass by me soon after leaving the ferry terminal.

I have no signal whatsoever on my phone so I finally stop at a roadside store and ask to use their landline as I think it's possible that Rob, wherever he is, might have a mobile phone signal. After a few attempts I give up, but the shop proprietor kindly offers to try phoning the number later in an effort to contact Rob and give him some indication of my whereabouts.

I walk on for another 10 minutes or so when I see Rob coming toward me from the opposite direction. Apparently he had passed me at the very time I had popped into the store to phone, (talk about Murphy's Law!), and then carried on to the next intersection before turning back. Prior to that, he had been waiting for me to pass him back near the outskirts of the town; how I had walked past without spotting the van or him seeing me remains a mystery. Anyway I decide to finish the day's walk at the top of the hill near a place called Crook. It feels good to relax in the van while Rob drives back to the lovely Windermere Caravan Club camping ground. Within half an hour we are settled in on the site with me feeling none the worse for wear.

Today's pedometer reading: 32.9km (20.43 miles).

Notes of Interest: Lake Windermere

Windermere is England's largest lake at 10½ miles long and 219 feet deep. It is believed that the name derives from the Old Norse 'Onundar Myrr'.

It's difficult to trace the origins of human habitation on these shores, but from what evidence there is it seems likely that Neolithic man had a settlement here.

It was the Industrial Revolution that heralded in a new era for Lake Windermere when its water was needed to power production essential for the growing industries such as the cotton mills of Lancashire and the North. By using cheap labour that involved young children being made to work long hours, mill owners became wealthy and soon began building luxurious holiday mansions on the shores of the lake. Many of these stately homes still exist, but most have been converted into hotels or holiday apartments.

William Wordsworth (1770 - 1850), helped popularise the area as a tourist attraction by describing the English Lake District in glowing terms.

MON, 3RD AUG 2009
WINDERMERE – KENDAL

We leave Windermere Caravan Club and head out to where I stopped my walk yesterday. Light rain is falling as I approach the junction from the Crook road and join the A591 that will take me into Kendal. After a meal break on the outskirts of the town I walk on further and meet up with Rob again at a parking lot near the town's library. We are met by Victoria, a photographer from the local newspaper, who took some shots of me walking. She says that an article about my walk was to appear in the local paper. Rob and I are eager to get online for various reasons.

We try using the library facilities, but it's not satisfactory. We then go to McDonald's to use their Wi-Fi but find it too slow and the place too noisy. But boy, you wanna see what some people can eat! By this time it was too late to continue walking, so we drive back to Windermere Caravan Club site. A little later, Rob manages to find Wi-Fi facilities at another caravan camping site nearby, so after dinner we go there and stay working on our laptops till 10.45pm.

Today's pedometer reading: 14.9km (9.25 miles).

Notes of Interest: Kendal

Kendal sits alongside the River Kent, and is regarded as the southern gateway to the Lake District. It obtained the nickname 'the auld grey town' because the town was once built largely of grey stone. It was granted its market charter in 1189, and celebrates the event each year.

During the thirteenth century the wool trade brought prosperity to the town, as it did with many other places in England. Kendal was to achieve greater economic stability when, in the fourteenth century, Flemish weavers appeared in the area. From this time on many mills were to spring up alongside the River Kent.

The town's motto 'pannus mihi panis' (wool is my bread) is said to relate to the rough, hardwearing material known as 'Kendal Green' that was worn by Kendal archers of that day.

Kendal Castle is a twelfth-century stone ruin perched high on a hill on the western edge of the town; its strategic position would have given it commanding views over the town and the surrounding countryside. In its time the castle passed through several owners, including the Crown. Later, Richard II would gift the castle to the well-known Parr family. It was Catherine Parr who became Henry VIII's sixth wife in 1543. The castle was derelict by 1571.

TUES, 4TH AUG 2009
KENDAL – BURTON-IN-KENDAL – CARNFORTH

Rob drives me back to Kendal in the early morning and by 7am I am back on the road walking. I decide to take the A65 to hopefully connect onto the canal towpath and meet Rob 7 miles further on towards Morecambe. Unfortunately, I take the A591 instead and eventually find myself on the M6. I'm thinking of retracing my steps as walking on the motorway is illegal, but I decide to take the risk and I continue on to the next junction. Big mistake David!

I am walking breezily along the emergency strip (that's a vehicle width section) for about half an hour when a Highway Patrol vehicle with flashing lights rolls up behind me. The two guys tell me what I already know and offer to escort me off the highway by driving on to the next junction. I explain that my charity walk means covering every inch of the journey on foot. They are both quite taken aback when they realise that I have been walking anti-clockwise around England and had started out from Brighton on the south coast. I give both a leaflet and ask them to look at my website sometime. One guy named Seb thinks it is quite strange meeting up with me this way, for his grandmother had just passed away from cancer the day before. I offer my commiserations on his loss as I realise from the way he spoke that he must have been very close to her.

They are both pretty decent guys and they quickly suggest that I should hop over the fence and connect onto the canal towpath that lay 20 or so feet below. Funnily enough, it was the towpath I was hoping to get onto earlier, but I had somehow missed the turn-off to it.

We say goodbye from across the fence and I climb down the bank to the canal below. I walk along the towpath for a while, but I know I have to meet Rob who is waiting now at Burton-in-Kendal. I'm soon walking on the correct road and eventually meet up with the van parked on the outskirts of the town. I have been walking for 3½ hours on this session and I'm feeling hungry and tired.

I have a meal and a bit of a rest then continue on towards Carnforth where I meet up with Rob again at the Carnforth Hotel. The people here are really friendly and Rob has told them all about the walk. Before we leave, Paul, one of the patrons, gives us some sound advice about the towpath that I intend to use in my walk toward Preston. Thanks John (Buster) for your donation, and for everyone's hospitality. We soon find Bay View Caravan Site, a lovely, friendly, spacious location with great views. We are given a site free of charge. Thank you Jill and Anna!

Today's pedometer reading: 31.2km (19.30 miles).

This is the third section of the journey.

It took 5 weeks to walk 496 pedometer miles (798km) through 8 counties before reaching **Kilkhampton**. Rob and I have a big row and he leaves me in **Lancaster**. Rob arrives back in **Preston**. While in **Liverpool** old memories of the city emerge. We experience great hospitality with Sheila in **Parkgate**. I trek over the beautiful **Hergest Ridge** near **Kington**. We arrive in **Bristol** after walking over the magnificent **Severn Bridge**. From **Bridgwater** we travel to **Ilfracombe** to stay with Emi and Pete. I meet a friendly squirrel in **Culbone Woods**.

CHAPTER 15

LANCASHIRE

WED, 5TH AUG 2009
CARNFORTH – LANCASTER

We leave Bay View Caravan Site quite late as their gates remain closed until 7am, so we both sleep in for a while.

I walk on the road toward Lancaster and meet up with Rob near the cathedral. We call in at the visitor information centre to pick up some info on camping and caravan sites, before proceeding out of Lancaster. Rob and I have a bit of a row at this stage. Actually that's a bit of an understatement.

Naturally when living together in confined spaces for months on end things can get a bit touchy, but in the past we had always managed to prevent any real argument from erupting. This time it is different; I am tired and become angry over an issue and it boils over into a full scale row resulting in Rob packing his bags and making his way back to Lancaster station on foot. I try phoning him to get him to reconsider, but he is not willing to listen. He's made his mind up to get back to Brighton on the first train out of Lancaster.

Suddenly I find myself on my own! I am now in a bit of a quandary; I am determined to carry on walking but how can I do it with the camper van to worry about? I drive to a campsite in Caton about 4 miles north of Lancaster. I am not quite due for a day off, but I'll stay here tomorrow and have a break from the agenda I have set myself as I need to relax and to think.

Today's pedometer reading: 21.2km (13.6 miles).

Note: long-distance walkers often experience emotional downturns, especially when walking for days on end and I am no exception. I think the last two weeks have been pretty hard, physically and mentally, due to the poor weather and the challenging terrain. While the physical body can withstand the demands made upon it, the mental or psychological challenges can sometimes bring pressures that result in weariness of both the body and spirit. Rob and I have been together for almost three months so naturally I begin to miss not having him around. I am pretty distressed but also angry; distressed that he is gone and angry to think he could leave me in such difficult circumstances. I suppose it's times like these that you need to force yourself to think positively and take one day at a time.

This evening I check my email messages and discover that some donations and messages of support have come through, including one from Seb, the patrol officer whom I had met on the M6 yesterday. They help raise my spirits and keep me from dwelling negatively on this long, arduous and often stressful venture I have undertaken.

Notes of Interest: Lancaster

There is little information on Lancaster until around the eleventh century, but there are signs of Roman occupation. It is also quite likely that a settlement existed beside the River Lune well before the arrival of the Romans.

The city's name was first recorded in the Domesday Book in 1086 as Loncastre. The Celtic word for the local river was 'Lune' and to the Saxons a 'ceaster' was the name given to a group of buildings, so I suppose it's feasible that, as time went by, this name would change to Lancaster.

Further archaeological work within the castle is really essential if only to authenticate historical events, but as it is still utilised as a prison, investigative research is compromised. However, it seems that the castle's days as a prison are numbered as I believe it's due for closure by the end of March 2011.

Lancaster Castle has a dark history; its court was responsible for countless gruesome sentences and indeed it was the site of the infamous Pendle Witch Trials in 1612. The accounts of the many public hangings, witchcraft trials, judicial aberrations including mistrials, slave trade involvement and other distasteful activities are all part of this city's less salubrious past.

It meted out more hanging sentences than any other town in England, apart from London, earning Lancaster the nickname, "the Hanging Town".

The famous Pendle Witches trial in 1612 was a consequence of the endemic and puritanical religious fervour and anti-Catholic hysteria that existed during these times. Even the King at the time, James I, was so obsessed with witchcraft that he decreed it a capital crime. It gave encouragement to the witch finders who, often with official backing, would roam the countryside arresting anyone suspected of witchcraft or those failing to observe recognised religious doctrine.

Among the populace there would be those who would make accusations of witchcraft against another, especially if by doing so they might exact some sort of vengeance on a neighbour or curry favour with the authorities.

In the Pendle Hill case two local families in the villages around Pendle Hill were arrested and taken to Lancaster for 'trial'. It seems that a girl, nine years of age and a daughter to one of the accused, appeared as a crucial witness for the prosecution. The outcome resulted in ten of the Pendle 'witches', including a woman from Yorkshire, being condemned and hanged for their 'crime'.

This period of religious fervour, superstition and intolerance would link Lancaster with one of the most sickening judicial periods in Lancastrian and English history. In its heyday, the "Hanging Town" would have seen thousands of people turning out to watch the many public executions.

During that period there were many more 'fortunate' souls who managed to escape the gallows only to be sentenced to transportation to one of the many penal colonies.

THURS, 6TH AUG 2009
LANCASTER

Today dawned bright and clear. I stayed in bed till after 7am. I lazed around most of the morning before deciding to attach the magnetic stick-on signs that I'd had since Carlisle, to the van. After that I relax while watching TV although much of the time I was actually planning in my head how to cope with driving the van while continuing with the walk. Once I had it clear in my mind what to do I was itching to get going again. I will drive the camper van the 30-odd miles down to Preston, park it somewhere, and then get a train back to Lancaster to start my walk back toward Preston by way of the Lancashire canal towpath.

FRI, 7TH AUG 2009
LANCASTER – GARSTANG

At around 9am I leave the caravan site at Caton and drive to Preston. At Preston station I manage to get the vehicle parked in the Network Rail security yard for the couple of days that I'll be away. This was kindly arranged by Joe Taylor (thank you, Joe!). I find an Argos store in the shopping mall and purchase a larger backpack.

After packing all requirements including sandwiches, a cooked pizza and bananas, I make for the station. I catch the 11.40 to Lancaster and 20 minutes later I am walking through the city toward the Lancaster Canal. This is my first introduction to walking on the towpaths that run alongside the canal systems of England and what a delightful experience it is.

The towpaths are naturally on flat terrain, quite a change from the hills I have been on throughout much of Cumbria and Northumberland. The twists and turns of the meandering waterway makes the towpath walk even more interesting as the idyllic scene ahead is constantly changing. Through delightful copses to open fields, alongside clusters of beautifully decorated narrow boats or through riverside villages, the walk provides me with a constantly moving vista of the beautiful Lancashire countryside.

Just as pleasurable is meeting the friendly people on the canal; individuals who obviously have a great appreciation for the serene and perennial world that's synonymous with the picturesque waterways of England. I pass a group of people who are sitting down on camping chairs by the side of the canal. They invite me to stop and join them for a beer. Being hot and thirsty I willingly take up their offer. Barry, one of the four, shows me around his canal boat moored close by. The exterior is stunning and the interior is surprisingly spacious and luxurious. Reluctantly I part company with the group for I need to get going as I still have some distance to go to reach Garstang. At 6.15pm I walk into the town and soon locate the Royal Oak pub where a room has already been booked for me by Barry's friend.

It's such a relief to take off my backpack and relax for a while before experiencing the sheer bliss of standing under a refreshing shower. Feeling revived once more I make my way down the stairs to investigate the food situation. After a great meal of haddock, chips and mushy peas and a pint of local ale, I wend my way back upstairs to my room and am in bed watching TV by 9pm.

Today's pedometer reading: 23.3km (14.46 miles).

Notes of Interest: Garstang

The town of (what is now) Garstang has an ancient history according to Neolithic and Bronze Age relics and artefacts found in the area. The name Garstang may have originated from the Saxon word 'Gaerstung' meaning common land or meadowland although the Domesday Book describes it as 'Cherestanc'.

In the eleventh century, however, other titles are evident such as Gayerstang, Gayrstang and by 1292 it appeared to be known as Gayrestang.

There used to be stocks in the market place, but I believe that the last one of these was destroyed in 1939 while lying in a loft. They would hold miscreants for an allotted period depending on their crime and passers-by could throw tomatoes or rotten eggs etc at them. They could be put to good use today, but boy, can you imagine the protests from 'Human Rights' groups!

Garstang declared itself to be "the world's first Fairtrade Town" in November 2001, and looked to influence other towns and cities to adopt a similar philosophy.

Recently planning approval had been given to building one of the UK's largest wind turbines in the town. Its purpose: to provide power for the local award winning Garstang factory to produce its famous cheese.

SAT, 8TH AUG 2009
GARSTANG – PRESTON

After a full English breakfast, I leave the Royal Oak in Garstang ready to tackle the second half of my walk to Preston. The weather is fine and clear promising a warm, sunny day.

Once on the towpath I soon get into a rhythmic stride passing attractive narrow boats moored up at the bank with one or two already moving sedately through the tranquil waters of the canal. There are surprisingly few walkers on the towpath considering it's the height of the season. Those that I meet expound the delights of their surroundings but many suggest that I shouldn't use too many superlatives in my description of the area. 'Let's keep it a secret' is the consensus of opinion from the locals and regular visitors.

In the past, whenever I had given any thought to Lancashire, Gracie Fields, cotton mills and dour landscapes would spring to mind; but now, after just a couple of days my impression of the county is altogether different.

When passing through Lancaster the other day, I picked up some leaflets from the Information Centre, one of which was on the history of the Lancaster Castle. Many people were tried and sentenced at the Lancaster Assizes purely over their religious beliefs. Today during my walk I begin thinking about that particular leaflet and muse over those times and the people caught up in the religious trials of that era.

I wonder about the many innocent people that must have been put to death simply for their religious views or for being wrongly accused of witchcraft. My thoughts then jump back to a different age, to those who would have suffered the same fate under the rule of the Roman Empire or during the Holy War of the Crusades, mostly in the name of religion. I thought about the countless number of innocent people who would have perished during the Spanish Inquisition or the religious fervour of Medieval England with the bouts of Anti-Catholicism and Anti-Protestantism that existed throughout those troublesome centuries.

It then set me thinking about the twentieth century and about the six million or more people exterminated, simply for being Jewish; and in that same century the ethnic cleansing of entire populations in Europe and elsewhere. There was genocide on the African continent and conflict in Ireland still raged. Spilling into the new century are the indiscriminate killings by radical suicide bombers underpinned by an extreme and distorted interpretation of their religious doctrine. I begin to wonder if things would really improve during this twenty-first century. Personally, I find it difficult to believe in the existence of God simply because I seem to come up against so many inconsistencies.

As I walk some of these old questions begin to form in my mind, issues that have been with me since my religious grounding as a kid at the Dr Barnado's home. I remember the preacher saying that on the last day of creation God made man in his own image and in his likeness. Therefore, as a youngster, I always pictured a man in a long white gown with a flowing white beard, like a stern Father Christmas, sitting on this great big throne looking down on us from above. I always imagined him as being white.

Of course the reason we think of him as being white and male is because Jesus is said to be the Son of God; those who believe this in its literal sense will have no cause to doubt God's appearance or gender.

More questions began to form in my mind as I walked. It is said that we humans are just one of 'God's Creatures' on Earth. So do all God's creatures go to heaven or is that holy sanctum reserved for our species alone? Does this God preside over just the planet Earth or does his domain extend over our galaxy or all the galaxies of the universe? It's a question that I've sometimes put to religious people over the years and the answer is always more or less the same: "God presides over the entire universe" they say. If he has dominion over the universe how can he also keep a benevolent eye on the welfare of the human animal that lives on an infinitesimal pinpoint of a planet somewhere out there among the cosmic mass? Of course, if he is this all-seeing creator, this entity who has masterminded everything since the birth of creation, then I suppose anything is possible.

During our evacuation days, I remembered how we children were bombarded with a tirade of meaningless anecdotes from the pulpit. Among them was the one where we were led to believe that if we had sinned but truly sought repentance we would be forgiven; yet, simultaneously, we were threatened with everlasting torment in hell if we did things which, by today's thinking, would be regarded either as natural or at worst, trivial.

Therefore, does this mean that you could be the most evil person, one who has caused untold suffering and distress to many, yet if you are repentant and seek true forgiveness on your deathbed, your sins will be absolved and you will be allowed to enter the 'Kingdom of

Heaven'? Yet someone who has been far less sinful, but who has not 'sucked up' to his God at the last minute, is doomed to hell fire and damnation?

We Barnado's kids were also told of the importance of baptism; that if a child hadn't been baptised he or she would not be accepted into the Kingdom of Heaven. This unchristened child, we were told, would not go to hell either but would, after death, remain in some sort of limbo for eternity. I faintly recall that those in the home who were christened would actually have pity for those who were not.

As I walked I remember thinking that most holy books must have emerged at a time when the populace was mainly confused, ignorant and widely superstitious. Any catastrophic events such as earthquakes, fires, floods, famine etc, would have been instantly regarded as a sign from the gods. I thought how easy it would have been for the wise men, the priests, the devout ones of that ancient period to concoct stories to instil fear and respect from the masses in order to gain and maintain control.

I often wondered why a religious person is, by definition, always regarded as a 'good' person. I suspect that there is probably no real difference between a 'good' religious individual and a 'good' atheist. When you think about it you could argue that the religious person has to be good in order to please his God, whereas the atheist is good because it's in his very nature to be so!

I suppose it's all the bigotry, the hatred, the hypocrisy surrounding religious doctrine that makes me view it all with scepticism and mistrust. At one time during the walk my mind veered off at a tangent (which it often does!). I remember thinking that if there was such a thing as the Devil, it would have been that sly little bugger who created religion in the first place. When you really give it some thought, what better way to set man against man...to set nation against nation; and what better way to get good men to do evil things in the name of their God!

I enjoy a shandy at a pub near Newsham before leaving the towpath in favour of a shorter route by road that will take me into the city of Preston.

Today's pedometer reading: 28km (17.38 miles).

Notes of Interest: Preston

There were probably scattered settlements along the banks of the River Ribble long before the birth of Christ. Over the centuries they would help create the city of Preston.

After the Dark Ages, the town came under the control of monks and consequently became known as 'Priest's Tun'. In 1322 Robert the Bruce set fire to the town and during the Civil War Preston became a major battlefield

During the fourteenth century the plague arrived, causing greater misery for the populace. Some references say that about 3,000 people within the boundary of Preston died from the dreaded plague and in the greater area 13,000 people succumbed to the deadly disease.

The Industrial Revolution brought Preston to the forefront of nineteenth-century, steam-powered, industrial development. Soon there was full employment, mainly within the cotton manufacturing industry. Toll roads and bridges appeared; the Lancaster Canal became a busy industrial highway and later came the railway system. Eventually, gas lighting (of which Preston was a pioneer) began to light up the streets at night.

However, conditions within industry were appalling. The commercial success of the many cotton-spinning and manufacturing establishments depended on cheap labour and by the mid-1800s the exploitation of young children was widespread. Children as young as eight were forced into working more than 12 hours a day.

To house the workers, ranks of poorly built terraced housing began spreading out across adjacent land; it would bring about an era of dreadful living and working conditions. Disease became a constant companion to their miserable existence and produced the highest infant mortality rate in the kingdom. Thousands poured into the city for work, turning the old quarters into overcrowded slums. The filthy conditions caused by pollution, inefficient water supplies and an almost non-existent sewerage system, coupled with the high child mortality rate would create civil unrest and social problems for years to come.

During the same century the town made great progress in the industrial world; public transport, innovative entrepreneurial ideas, new inventions and even sporting achievements would all make their mark in the city's future.

In 1842, Preston experienced a number of significant events; there was the cotton depression and the shooting of five strikers in Lune Street. The following year, from October 1853 to May 1854 came the 'Great Preston Lock-out' when almost a third of the working population were made unemployed.

More recent times, however, have seen Preston rise to greater prosperity.

SUN, 9TH AUG 2009
PRESTON

This morning I have a plan in mind! I had checked the navigator map last night and have now decided that I will drive the campervan down to Ormskirk, about 15 miles down the A59 on the way to Liverpool. I will leave the van parked somewhere secure and then catch the train back to Preston to start my walk back down to Ormskirk.

I wasn't sure if or when my son, Robert was going to return, but I was determined not to let it stop me from continuing the walk south. However, at Preston station my well-laid plans went awry for I was told that there was no train service to Ormskirk on Sunday. Ah well, it will have to be tomorrow then!

I make the most of being in Preston for the day. I visit a Wetherspoon establishment where they offer free Wi-Fi. I indulge in a cheap but wholesome breakfast, after which I spend much of the day updating on my laptop between cups of black coffee and biscuits. I am still parked up in the Network Rail security yard at the back of Preston railway station. I relax there for a while before going to a nearby pub for an evening meal. After the meal I indulge in a small whisky before heading back to the van for a relatively early night.

MON, 10TH AUG 2009
PRESTON

I awake to a dismal morning. Persistent rain drives against the window of the campervan. However, the good news is that Rob is on his way back from Brighton. I decide to abort my trip to Ormskirk because the bad weather conditions might result in me missing the train back to Preston to meet Rob on his arrival. Instead, I phone my son to say that I'll be waiting to meet him at Preston station. I return to Wetherspoon's for brekka and try using their Wi-Fi again only to find it's currently unavailable due to a technical fault. I decide to go to the Station Hotel and use their Wi-Fi, and where I also have a drawn-out lunch while waiting for Rob to arrive from Brighton.

It's good to see Rob again and we are soon making our way out of Preston to a caravan club site 3 miles away in Whitestake. We are met at the site by Barbara, who makes us very welcome. We are soon settled in for the evening and I prepare myself for a long walk tomorrow. Thanks for your donation, Barbara, and for the use of your lovely caravan site.

TUES, 11TH AUG 2009
PRESTON – BURSCOUGH – ORMSKIRK

Rob drives me back to Preston railway station to start the day's walk. Weather conditions are ideal for walking; heavy cloud-cover and cool with little wind. I consider going onto the canal towpath for a while but decide against it as I realise that faster progress can be made by using the cycle path running alongside the A59.

I catch up with Rob 7 miles out from Preston near a little town called Much Hoole. After a break I continue on to Burscough where Robert is preparing another pasta meal. Rob and I chat to some of the locals to get information on campsites in the area. Ten minutes later I am on my way again walking toward Liverpool.

The flat terrain and broad fields of the surrounding countryside is a refreshing change to the ruggedness and hill walking of Cumbria's Lake District and a cycle path runs all the way through to Ormskirk making the walk even more enjoyable.

On this part of the walk my thoughts turn once again to my teenage years in Brighton. This particular memory triggered probably by the whisky I'd had in Preston the evening before. You see I rarely drink whisky; it's not that I don't enjoy it, it's just that it seems to dehydrate me to such an extent that I end up needing to drink water throughout the night. Yet I remember detesting even the smell of whisky for many years after the time I had got drunk on the stuff.

Moe and I had been to the cinema in Brighton and as we were walking back I bumped into a Scotsman who was about to enter a nearby pub. I can't recall his name, but he had been a bricklayer on the building site that I had worked on after first leaving school. He immediately offered to buy Moe and myself a drink on the strength of a bonus he'd received that day.

Moe, I remember, ordered a beer while I (being stupid) said I'd have whatever the Scotsman was having, so I ended up with a whisky in my hand!

It was the first whisky I'd ever had and I recall that it tasted pretty awful; but the second tasted better and after the third I began downing 'em like a seasoned whisky drinker. It wasn't until I left the pub and hit the fresh air that I realised things were not quite as they should be. I was not feeling good!

At the Steine I said goodbye to Moe who walked back up to Mighell Street, while I caught the bus out to Moulsecombe as our mother had recently acquired a council house there.

I sat on the top deck of the bus with this queasy feeling in my stomach and feeling very sorry for myself. In those days smoking was allowed on the upper deck and on this particular day everybody seemed to be up there, all pufing away as if it was their last day on earth (I didn't think I was going to make it that far) and it seemed that all the smoke was wafting in my direction! I remember feeling terrible and about to throw up, so I quickly got off the bus. I had jumped off two stops earlier so I was hoping the walk home might make me feel better. Being totally absorbed in my own sorry predicament I had completely forgotten that two of my attractive female cousins and my aunt were visiting that weekend from London.

I stumbled inside the house, went into the living room and sat on a vacant armchair amidst a hazy semblance of familiar faces and voices. I remember hearing my mother say, "Are you alright David?"

The next second I threw up all over the carpet and then must have partially blacked out. I came to my senses feeling people fumbling around with my clothing and heard someone saying, "Is he always like this Freda?"

I must have passed out again because all I remember after that was people struggling to get me up the stairs to my bedroom. The next thing I knew I was being turned on my side and the bedcovers pulled over me. I heard a detached voice say something like: "It's best if he's lying on his side, if he's on his back he'll drown in his own vomit." As I sank back into an uneasy slumber I'm sure I heard the sound of females giggling just before the door to my bedroom closed. I think I ended up in bed for about two days afterwards recovering from a massive hangover with little sympathy from my mother. My fall from grace was not all bad as it gave my female cousins a lot of enjoyment, for it became their habit to recount the event with considerable embellishment and much merriment over the years.

An hour or so later I stride into Ormskirk where I finish my walk for the day. We find a caravan site known as Abbey Farm and John Perkins, the owner, allows us to stay free of charge. Thank you, John! Today's pedometer reading: 29.9km (18.56 miles).

Notes of Interest: Ormskirk

The name 'Ormskirk' is said to be Old Norse in origin and might have derived from the name 'Ormres kirkja'. 'Ormr' is supposed to mean serpent or dragon, and 'kirkja' being the Old Norse word for church.

There is a thought that Ormr might have been a Viking chief who settled in the area, but this premise has no substance as there is no archaeological or recorded evidence to support this.

In 1286 the town's monks were given a Royal Charter by Edward I of England, to hold a market and the custom has prevailed for over seven hundred years. During that period market day was always held on a Thursday, but nowadays I believe it is held on Saturday also.

CHAPTER 16
MERSEYSIDE

WED, 12TH AUG 2009
ORMSKIRK – LIVERPOOL – SEACOMBE

We leave Abbey farm as soon as the barrier is raised. Overcast skies and cool weather conditions are the order of the day as I begin walking from Ormskirk at 7.15am. Three hours later I meet up with Rob at the Switch Island Retail Park. We decide to have breakfast in the Baker's Dozen, a pub/restaurant close by. We meet a very pregnant young lady called Jenny who is managing the establishment.

She seems very interested in what we are doing and shows our leaflet to her manager, Phil. He offers us breakfast on the house along with the coffees we had already ordered. Both Rob and I think it's the best breakfast we've had since the start of our journey – not that we've had that many outside the van. Thanks Phil! Thanks also to Jenny for making us feel so welcome. Look forward to hearing about your new arrival, Jenny, especially as it will probably be around the time we finish the walk on 10th Oct, 2009... hopefully!

I walk into Liverpool on the waterfront route. We decide that Rob will drive through the Mersey Tunnel while I go across on the ferry to the Seacombe terminal where Rob will be waiting for me.

I arrive at the terminal only to find I have missed the 3.15pm ferry and will need to wait 75 minutes for the next one. I might tell you that I hate waiting around for anything; consequently I hate queuing with a passion. I walk up to Lime St railway station – just to have a nostalgic look at it again – then I pop into an old pub (I think it was The Crown) for a quick shandy before heading back to the ferry terminal.

Arriving back at the terminal, I find there's still 20 minutes to wait so I buy myself a cool lemonade and sit down on a bench. I begin to think about the last time I was in Liverpool... It meant going back in time; almost six decades, in fact, when a nervous, callow youth, who had just turned 16 years of age, journeyed up from Brighton to join SS Alcinous of the Blue Funnel Line on her maiden voyage out of Liverpool.

I had been home less than a month from the Outward Bound Sea School at Aberdovey, North Wales, when I was given notice to join the ship. I was apprehensive about going because there had been this talk about how hard the 'Scousers' were on Southerners. I still remember walking up the gang plank amidst the hubbub of noise and activity that was indicative of a vessel being readied for sea, wondering what life was going to be like for me over the next 3½ months.

The Alcinous had been built in Newcastle and was completed and ready for her first voyage in April 1952. She was a conventional cargo ship licensed to carry twelve passengers and was joining a fleet of Blue Funnel vessels that plied their trade mainly to the Far East. All of Alfred Holt's Blue Funnel ships were given Homeric names due to Holt's deep appreciation for Homer's Odyssey.

About two days later we cast off from our berth in semi-darkness and made our way out into the Irish Sea ready to catch the early morning tide. I knew our route and the ports of call, as the ship's schedule was posted up in the main galley. The far-off places with exotic sounding names excited me; yet at the back of my mind was a worry of what might lie ahead, especially with the Liverpudlian crew that I had yet to meet.

The trip over the Mersey is quite a nostalgic event as I had ferried over to Birkenhead a number of times in those far-off days. That was due to being billeted out with a crew member's Liverpool family in Birkenhead while working shoreside on the Alcinous when she was in drydock. I had found the Liverpudlians were some of the most friendliest and hospitable people you'd ever wish to meet.

It was an enjoyable and relaxing trip, but all too soon I am disembarking at the Seacombe Ferry Terminal where Rob is waiting patiently for me.

I decide not to walk further as it is getting rather late so I join Rob in the Seacombe Tavern for a shandy. We chat with the proprietor for a while, but I am eager to leave and meet up with Lesley and Roger, the parents of Jo, my grandson's girlfriend. Lesley's mother Sheila offers Rob and me a bed for the night so we leave the Tavern and drive to Park Gate on the Wirral.

It is a welcome change to be in a lovely house and being waited on by Sheila. After a great meal we relax in the lounge chatting over a glass of red wine until I find myself nodding off in the chair. I take my leave and go upstairs to the bedroom that Sheila had prepared for us. I must have fallen asleep as soon as my head hit the pillow.

Today's pedometer reading: 30.1km (18.69 miles).

Notes of Interest: Liverpool

A settlement might have existed on the banks of the Mersey long before the first century AD, its people dependent on the river for washing, fishing and easy access to the sea. From these humble origins Liverpool has grown into the unique, cultural city we see today.

It is thought that the settlement became known as 'Liuerpul', meaning a muddy water creek or pool. References to other names exist such as 'Elverpul, which might have evolved when eels found in the Mersey were a major food source.

The settlement grew into a thriving fishing village and then in 1200 AD a charter was issued by King John that would help stimulate growth; yet despite this, Liverpool's population in the sixteenth century was still no more than a few hundred.

In the eighteenth century, however, Liverpool began to grow and in 1715 the city had the first wet dock in the country. The slave trade would also help the town prosper for there was considerable financial gain in the handling and shipping of these unfortunate people. The slave trade also became the stimulus of rapid growth for Liverpool's black community.

The Great Famine in Ireland was to create social unrest in that country and from the 1840s huge numbers of Irish migrants began arriving into Liverpool increasing the city's burgeoning population.

By the nineteenth century, a good percentage of the world's trade was being handled through the Liverpool docks and from then on, the city made rapid growth ensuring its development into the twentieth century when it would eventually become the great metropolis that we see today.

The crucial importance of Liverpool, with its port facilities, was highlighted when Merseyside became the target of systematic bombing raids during World War II. One such raid in May 1941 was so intense that operations at the docks came to a standstill for almost a week.

At the close of the war, it is estimated that 2,500 people had been killed, 11,000 properties were totally destroyed and almost half the homes in the metropolitan area were said to have sustained damage.

But Liverpool's post-war tattered suburbs would become the breeding ground of young entertainers such as The Beatles, Gerry Marsden and Cilla Black, personalities that would make their mark, both on the world's stage and on the culture of their home city of Liverpool.

While crossing the Mersey today, I thought of Gerry Marsden's great Liverpool ballad, 'Ferry Cross the Mersey', although I suppose for many Liverpudlians, especially the Liverpool football supporters, 'You'll Never Walk Alone' may be the most popular song of the city. This Rodgers & Hammerstein number has remained the anthem of the crowds at 'The Kop' for almost four decades and is even inscribed on the club gates.

Apparently, from what I've read, John Lennon, one of the founding members of the Beatles, was born in Liverpool on 9th October 1940 during an air-raid.

THURS, 13TH AUG 2009
SEACOMBE – WEST KIRBY – PARK GATE.

I'm awake at 7.30am. I dress hurriedly and go downstairs where Sheila is busy preparing breakfast. It's after 9am when Rob and I drive away from Sheila's home. We make our way back to Seacombe Terminal to begin my day's walk. From Seacombe I continue on toward Liscard, where I stop to buy an Ordnance Survey Explorer map for the Cheshire region. On my way through Liscard, a lady on a bike stops to chat about my walk and then makes a £10.00 donation. Thanks Sally!

A little later I divert off the road to call into a large B&Q store to buy a much needed rubber tip for my walking stick. The tapping sound of the stick as I moved along kept reminding me of Blind Pugh in Treasure Island! Back on the A551 I pass through Leasowe with the Leasowe Golf course on my right and meet up with Rob near Moreton. After feeding on rolls with cold sausage filling prepared by Sheila, I continue on the coastal route with its great views over Liverpool Bay and the Irish Sea. At West Kirby I meet up with Roger and his beautiful black Labrador, Bella, at Marine Lake. We walk along on the lovely Wirral Way for a few miles before meeting up with Rob and the campervan near Gayton.

It is almost 5pm and I decide to call it a day. We all meet up at the Red Lion in Parkgate for a relaxing drink or two. It is here that Neal, a complete stranger, makes a donation of £20.00. Thanks Neal!

Back at Sheila's home, another lovely meal is prepared, but after the meal and a couple of glasses of red wine I am again feeling shattered and ready for bed.

Today's pedometer reading: 30km (18.63 miles).

Notes of Interest: Parkgate

Parkgate on the River Dee was, in the eighteenth century, a thriving port and a major embarkation point for Ireland. Owing to the build-up of silt, which has created a large sandbank impeding navigation in that area of the river, it no longer has this facility.

Apparently the name originated when the port had to be re-sited due to silting problems. It was established further downstream near the gate of Neston's hunting park. Hence the settlement of Parkgate emerged.

It is said that in the 1700s Lady Hamilton, a local Neston girl and mistress of Lord Nelson, would bathe here, in the belief that it might cure a skin complaint.

Today the area draws many visitors for there are a number of attractions to keep the visitor well-nourished and entertained. Parkgate is situated on the bank of the River Dee Estuary, about half a mile westward of the village of Neston where it commands a magnificent view of the Welsh coast.

FRI, 14TH AUG 2009
GAYTON – THE WIRRAL WAY

I go downstairs about 6.30am to write up my diary while everyone else is still in bed. Sheila soon appears and begins preparing breakfast. After breakfast Rob drives Roger, his dog Bella and me, back to Gayton to start our walk. It's great having company on such an enjoyable and picturesque route. It isn't long, however, before Roger leaves with Bella to make his way back to Parkgate while I continue on the Wirral Way toward Chester.

I manage to rendezvous with Rob at a lay-by near Craxton Wood and after a meal break I carry on walking toward Chester. There is a cycle/walking track running alongside the road making this walk quite pleasurable. I meet up with Rob again about 2½ miles from Chester where we decide to finish for the day. We find a camping caravan site about 500 metres further back along the road and soon we have a power connection and are able to relax for the rest of the day.

Today's pedometer reading: 19.3km (11.98 miles).

Notes of Interest: The Wirral Way

The Wirral Way is a sealed public pathway, which was once a railway track. It is 12 miles long and goes from West Kirby to Hooton in mid-Wirral and is situated within the Wirral Country Park where superb views abound especially over the Dee Estuary.

Wirral Country Park is worth a visit as often a huge variety of birds can be seen nesting in the dense foliage and feeding on the berries in winter. Then there's the panoramic view over the Dee Estuary and the distant Welsh shore where on clear days even the outline of Moel Famau in the Clwydian Hills can be seen.

The glistening mudflats of the estuary reflect the ever-changing light, especially in autumn when the dramatic, red sunsets offer great delight to any traveller lucky enough to pass by this way.

CHAPTER 17
CHESHIRE

SAT, 15TH AUG 2009
CHESTER – BROXTON

We leave the caravan camping site at 6.25am as soon as the gate opens. Then it's just a short drive to my starting point near the turn-off to the Mollington Grange Golf Club. Walking through Chester, I soon divert off to pick up the Shropshire Union Canal's towpath walk that will take me some distance before having to join the A41. Once again I find the towpath to be an immensely enjoyable walk and I understand now why many people regularly walk the towpaths of England during their holidays.

I reluctantly leave the towpath at Christelton and travel through some lovely parkland areas before meeting up with Rob a mile and a half further on at Waverton. After a meal break I continue walking toward Broxton where I have my second stop for the day. It is around this time that my thoughts once again harp back to those early merchant navy days when I joined the SS Alcinous for the Far East.

By the time we arrived at Gibraltar I had become familiar with my duties and, more importantly, I was feeling comfortable with most of the crew. I had become friendly with a deck boy called Jim Penney. Jim was about my age and we were the youngest of the crew.

I remember a steward I was working with taking me to one side after I had taken issue with him over something or other. His name was Pete McKay but known as Mac by the crew. He told me that the best way I could get the respect of the crew was to get on with my work without mouthing off. He added that, at my age, it would be to my advantage if I were to listen rather than talk. For some reason his words hit home and from then on I did exactly what he'd advised.

I particularly remember the head chef. He was a big, self-opinionated, no-nonsense character who was treated with respectful caution by all and sundry; even the captain trod lightly in his presence. Unfortunately I cannot remember his name, but I can picture him clearly as he stood over the large chopping counter or the stove with his chef's white hat flopped over his forehead and a cigarette constantly hanging from his mouth. I discovered during the trip that he had been with Alfred Holt for over 25 years and was regarded as the best chef in the line. He was fair but pretty tough on his kitchen staff, although he would back them to the hilt if they were ever criticised by others. His meals were great, but I often wondered how much cigarette ash I'd consumed over the 3½ month voyage!

I remember sitting out on the poop deck one evening after my duties were over and listening to the talk going on between the deck crew and the engineering and catering crews. Most were Liverpudlians and the banter was usually humorous and incisive, but on this particular evening an argument developed between Mac and one of the greasers from the engine room.

The greaser sounded quite drunk and appeared to pick constantly on Mac during the evening. Unfortunately I had to leave around this time to help serve late refreshments, including coffee and tea, to the passengers.

The following morning news began to circulate about a fight that took place on the aft deck that night. It was Jim Penney who filled me in with the details. Apparently, the discourse between Mac and the big greaser got so bad that a fight developed. Jim Penney said it was frightening the way Mac dealt with the greaser. Apparently the fight was over in minutes with the greaser lying flat on the deck with various injuries including a broken nose from a Liverpool kiss. When the chef heard about it he was delighted. Mac was one of the catering crew and a favourite with the chef, so that morning the steward was treated to a slap-up breakfast. It was noticeable that the deck crew had renewed respect for Mac after the fight.

I remembered going through the Suez Canal. It was such a profound experience, especially during the evening when I could relax against the ship rails and gaze at the changing terrain of desert and sand dunes. On one occasion I remember seeing some Arabs, dressed all in black, suddenly appear over the sand hills. They sat there on camels watching our ship as it glided by. I wondered about them; where they had come from; where they were going to spend the night; if they had wives and children.

Too soon we were out of the canal and into the Gulf of Aden heading for the Yemeni town of Aden.

I carry on for a third session, but after an hour I decide to finish the walk at Grindley Brook about 2½ miles from Whitchurch. Today's pedometer reading: 30.4km (18.87 miles).

Notes of Interest: Chester

Chester lies on the River Dee in Cheshire, England, close to the border with Wales and was founded during the early years of Roman occupation. It became a sizeable Roman fortress or 'castrum' during the reign of the Emperor Vespasian and became known as 'Deva'. It would soon develop into a major settlement in Rome's new Britannia.

When the Romans retreated from Britain at the turn of the fifth century the civilian settlements, along with Roman veterans and their wives and children, would have remained and made use of the fortress and its defences as protection from outside attack, otherwise the city might well have fallen prey to marauding tribes.

It was later taken over by Saxon invaders who improved fortifications and subsequently gave Chester its name. The town was one of the last to capitulate during the Norman Conquest of England, and when it did William of Normandy (the Conqueror) began constructing a castle in order to demonstrate the might of the Normans.

Chester was granted city status in 1541, but its expansion and development really began with the Industrial Revolution.

CHAPTER 18
SHROPSHIRE

SUN, 16TH AUG 2009
WHITCHURCH – WEM

It's 6.45am when I start the day's walk from the Eggleston Arms junction under overcast skies. A cool westerly wind accompanies me as I begin walking toward Whitchurch. Many cyclists competing in a 12-hour time trial event speed by. I decide to stay on the road as there is a good walking track most of the way. It soon peters out, however, leaving just a narrow margin to walk on. I catch up with Rob who's parked in a lay-by. After a good meal of porridge I continue on toward Shrewsbury.

I'm walking out of the Whitchurch suburbs when Rob phones me to say that there is a police road block near Prees Green and that he has had to backtrack and detour to Wem, a little town about 9 miles further on. I advise Rob to stay there and possibly shop for essential grocery items and I will carry on walking through the road block. I walk past a mile or more of stationary cars and approach the road block in time to see two damaged vehicles being hoisted onto a tow truck.

After another three hours of walking I pass through Wem expecting to see Rob parked up somewhere. I am pretty weary and eager to rest, but I walk on for a while longer before phoning Rob. I find he's waiting 2 miles further on. He returns to pick me up and then tells me that we are only 7 miles from Shrewsbury. We drive back to Wem as there's a good caravan camping site there. The staff are friendly and helpful and invite us to use their camping facilities free of charge. My thanks to the Shingler family, to Naomi and Don and the rest of the staff.

Today's pedometer reading: 32km (19.87 miles).

Notes of Interest: Whitchurch

Whitchurch was thought to be a settlement founded by the Romans during the first century AD, although it is quite likely that a settlement of sorts existed there long before their arrival. It seems that the Romans named it Mediolanum, meaning 'the place in the middle of the plain'. Situated on a low hill, Mediolanum was an ideal location on the main Roman route, between Chester (Deva) and Wroxeter (Viroconium).

Its current name has evolved from 'White Church' which refers to a church from Norman times made from white stone. Whitchurch is located in Shropshire close to the Welsh border and is reputed to be the oldest continuously inhabited town in the county.

It was granted 'town' status in 1284, and obtained a charter in the fourteenth century allowing it to hold a weekly market. I believe that even today a vibrant market is held there every Friday.

MON, 17TH AUG 2009
WEM

Ah, a day off at last. We have a 2½ hour lie-in this morning –great! It's another cool and overcast day. I love these conditions when walking, but on our only day off in the week you'd think he'd turn on the sun for us, wouldn't you!

We drive into Wem as the library has internet facilities. We have limited online time as others are pre-booked and waiting. I update my progress map and answer email messages but run out of time to update my diary. With sections from 8 days' worth of diary entries ready and waiting to be copied and pasted onto my webpage I'm getting a little peeved. We soon have no alternative but to return to the Lower Lacon caravan camping site and relax for the rest of the day.

I must take this opportunity to highlight the importance of my son, Robert's part in this venture. Without his commitment this 'Around England Walk' would have been extremely difficult, if not impossible to achieve. He has to drop me at my starting point each morning and be waiting at pre-arranged locations with prepared meals at the ready.

On top of all this he has to get up with me at around 5.30am every morning, 6 days a week. When I discussed the possibility of him assisting me in the venture I told him it would be a holiday! He'll never trust me again! So the successful outcome of this walk will be due equally to his support and my effort.

TUES, 18TH AUG 2009
SHREWSBURY – WESTBURY

We leave Lower Lacon camping site at 6.15am. Again the weather is cool with heavy cloud cover. Ideal walking weather! We miss our way getting back to my starting point but finally manage to locate it some 20 minutes later. I reach Rob some 7 miles on, in the outer suburbs of Shrewsbury where I have my first break for the day.

I'm finding it difficult to locate the road to Montgomery, the place where I'll connect up with the Offa's Dyke Path. Eventually I find the correct route and soon I'm walking toward my destination, the Welsh border. I often find country roads hazardous to walk on. Main roads usually have wide margins outside the single white line that marks the outer perimeter of the carriageway, giving a walker or cyclist a greater degree of safety. Country roads, by comparison, are often narrow and winding, and sometimes with no perimeter margins whatsoever. You can often find yourself actually walking on the road and vulnerable to the fast approaching traffic. That's how it is on this road to Montgomery. Although part of my concentration is focused on the hazards of oncoming traffic, I can't help but enjoy gazing over trimmed boxthorn hedges to the wide patchwork panorama of the Shropshire countryside.

I discard my MP3 player as I need to keep alert to the traffic, but now the road is improving to such a degree that it allows me to relax a bit. I decide not to listen to music but instead I let my thoughts wander wherever they want to go. I cast my mind back through the ages once more.

I think it was during the period between arriving back home from the Outward Bound Sea School in Wales and being called up to embark on my first ship out of Liverpool that I went to see a stage hypnotist with two chums, Moe and a guy called Dennis. I remember Moe and I waiting near the clock tower for Dennis to come down from the railway station where he worked. He had been working overtime so hadn't been able to go home and change out of his work boots.

We went to this cinema (I can't recall the name) that also doubled as a stage venue. On this occasion an Indian hypnotist named Mirza was performing. It was the first time I had ever seen a hypnotist and was eager to find out more about their act. There was a well-known hypnotist around at the time; his name, I think, was Ralph Slater. He was known as 'the lightening hypnotist' and I remember our mother, who had seen his show, telling us how entertaining he was.

Mirza came out on stage. He certainly looked Indian; he had a chocolate-coloured face and was wearing a black turban. He definitely spoke like an Indian, but there was also a rumour going around that he was actually a cockney from Stepney.

Anyway, despite the rumour, we were soon enthralled by his initial demonstrations. He then asked for volunteers to go up on the stage. He wanted six males and six females. Dennis, who had been sitting quietly throughout the show, now stood up and made his way to the stage. Moe and I just couldn't believe it! Dennis was usually quite hesitant about doing anything that represented even the slightest risk of harm or possible ridicule to him. He would never go scrumping or even roller skating with us on the promenade.

I could picture the scene as if it were yesterday. There were twelve ordinary, wooden dining chairs arranged in a sort of shallow concave fashion facing the audience, with a gap in the middle separating the women from the men. When the twelve were seated Mirza stood in the gap and explained to the audience what he was about to do; he then proceeded to put each of them under hypnosis; those that couldn't be hypnotised were replaced with other volunteers. Once they were all under he began to demonstrate his amazing powers of suggestion. The one incident that will stay etched in my memory forever was when Mirza began telling the group that their feet were beginning to itch. He then went on to say something like, "Your feet are itching so much that you desperately want to take off your shoes and get at your feet to scratch them".

With that, nearly all of them began to hurriedly take off their shoes. Dennis tried to do the same, but he had trouble with the laces on his old railway boots that appeared to be tied with knots and it took about 5 minutes of fumbling before he managed to kick them off. The audience had already started tittering at poor old Dennis who seemed quite oblivious to them. It was when they saw his feet that the tittering exploded into hysterical mirth for he had the largest holes in his socks you could ever imagine. His feet were also as black as black, as if he'd been walking through charcoal dust for a week. He didn't scratch like all the others; he just sat there looking down at his feet and wiggling three exposed toes on each foot, setting Moe and me off, along with the audience, into unbridled fits of laughter. Mirza obviously hadn't expected such a reaction from the audience so after a while, and to the man's credit, he tried to bring Dennis out of his trance by saying the pre-arranged words to the group. The others in the group immediately responded to the words from the hypnotist and started to sheepishly don their footwear...but not Dennis.

He still sat there, gazing down at his dirty wiggling toes, each wiggle in unison with the toes on the other foot, amid howls of laughter from the audience.

By now Mirza was getting a bit anxious as he obviously wanted to continue with other parts of his act. The trouble was that everyone, including the group on the stage, were laughing so much that the noise prevented him from bringing Dennis out of his hypnotic trance. The hypnotist finally managed to bring a modicum of control to the audience and then spoke quietly in Dennis's ear. Almost immediately Dennis looked up from his toes and looked around in some astonishment and mortification at being the centre of attention. He quickly put on his boots and sat there getting redder and redder by the second.

At the end of the show Mirza gave a little speech about never wanting to cause embarrassment or distress to any of his subjects and went on to apologise for the incident with Dennis.

However, I reckon most of the audience would have gone away with wet handkerchiefs and sore ribs, thinking the same as Moe and myself that it was the best and most hilarious entertainment they'd had in years. We tried to console Dennis on the way home and I remember saying something like, he should feel good about giving hundreds of people a few minutes of joy and happiness. However, this set Moe off into further shrieks of hysterical laughter that in turn set me off as well. We didn't see much of Dennis for a while after that.

I meet up with Rob again at a lay-by 6 miles on near Yockleton village. After a short meal break I walk on for a third session, finishing my day's walk at Westbury village. After the walk we drive to a recommended caravan site about 3 kilometres away. We manage to get a hook-up at this delightful caravan camping site and Chris, the lady owner, allows us to stay free of charge. Thanks, Chris! Unfortunately, we still can't get internet connection so we drive down to The Lion pub in Westbury, where Bob the proprietor allows us to use his Wi-Fi facility. Thanks, Bob! Also thanks to Pete for helping out with my computer problems.

Today's pedometer reading: 30.8km (19.12 miles).

Notes of Interest: Shrewsbury

The town of Shrewsbury was known as 'Scrobbesbyrig' during the Anglo-Saxon era. The closest interpretation appears to be 'fort in the scrub-land', although the Welsh seemed to have referred to the town since the Middle Ages as 'Amwythig', meaning 'fortified place'.

Over the years the name took on subtle changes finally evolving into 'Schrosberie' before being identified by its modern title of Shrewsbury.

Shrewsbury became established around AD 800, although there probably was a settlement on the site well before that. The town flourished during the late Middle Ages with the wool trade becoming key to its ongoing development.

Owing to its strategic position Shrewsbury has witnessed many conflicts, especially between the Welsh and English. In 778 it became part of King Offa of Mercia's empire.

William the Conqueror had further troubles with the Welsh invaders but finally managed to repel them during his reign. In 1074 William gifted the town to Roger de Montgomery who had organised the building of Shrewsbury Castle and was later bestowed with the title of Earl.

Shrewsbury, the place where Charles Darwin was born and raised, has become a thriving twenty-first century town with a rich medieval history.

CHAPTER 19

WALES-SHROPSHIRE BORDER

WED, 19TH AUG 2009
MONTGOMERY – MELLINGTON

I start my walk at 6.40am from The Lion car park in Westbury. I wonder if this walk will ever end; I sometimes think it never will! "Keep going Dave, one day at a time," I say to myself as I've said so many times in the past, but even more so lately. I continue on my way toward Montgomery and once again the road becomes a walker's nightmare. Rob is parked up a couple of miles past Marton village where I have my first meal break of the day. Soon I am back on the road, and about two hours later I walk up a steep hill into the town centre of Montgomery where Rob is waiting in the van.

After the break I go to a nearby shop to purchase an Ordnance Survey Explorer map, and another on the southern section of Offa's Dyke Path. After that, I take to the road again, heading for the Brompton intersection about 4 miles further on where I finish the day's walk. Luckily for us there's a vacancy at a caravan camping site less than a mile away. Its early afternoon and we are now ensconced in one of the loveliest surroundings we have experienced to date.

Once again our mobile broadband is ineffective, but the manager of the Mellington Hall Hotel invites us into their grand premises to use their Wi-Fi facilities free of charge. Thank you, Vanessa! Tomorrow I'll begin my walk southward on the Offa's Dyke path toward Chepstow and the Bristol Channel.

Today's pedometer reading: 27.8km (17.26 miles).

Notes of Interest: Montgomery

The county town of Montgomery is quite historic. It lies just 3 miles from the Welsh-English border and is handily situated along the Offa's Dyke Path. The settlement grew around a Norman castle that stood high on a bluff, although the town's origins go back even further in time, as evidenced by the Iron-Age hill fort that sits on the outskirts of the town. However, Montgomery is probably best known for its castle.

Roger de Montgomery (who would later bequeath his name to the settlement) was an important supporter of William the Conqueror and was bestowed part of the Welsh Marches by King William soon after the invasion. The construction of Montgomery Castle began in 1223 and was built to control an access route toward the River Severn.

At the beginning of the fifteenth century the town was sacked by the Welsh. In 1541, the castle came into the possession of another powerful Welsh family, the Herberts, and in 1593 Montgomery became the birth place of the famous poet, George Herbert.

The Old Bell Museum and the Robber's Grave are worth a visit and travellers will find a welcome in this attractive, bustling border town.

THURS, 20TH AUG 2009
OFFA'S DYKE PATH

We wake to a dismal and rainy day. I have half a mind not to walk today as I'm feeling quite jaded and weary again and the weather doesn't help.

It is still raining as I reluctantly venture out from the warmth of the campervan to start my day's walk along the Offa's Dyke Path. Following the distinctive National Trails' acorn sign, I start out on my walk toward Knighton. Not long into the walk I am confronted by a steep hill. It's a real killer as it seems to go on forever. Much of the terrain is rugged and consequently very hilly; it's also wet underfoot, which really tests my resolve. Feeling despondent, wet and weary I plod on for a few more miles, finally stopping at a stile to rest and eat a bacon sandwich that Rob has prepared for me.

I'm finding these steep slopes quite hard, especially going down as it's really putting pressure on my knees and this slows me up considerably. Five hours later and I am still battling with the terrain. The rain had stopped, but on this high ground the strong south-westerly wind is now impeding my progress. I'm very much behind schedule as the going has been tough, but I finally make it down to where the Offa's Dyke Path crosses the road into a farmyard area, and where my worried son is waiting nearby. I can well understand Rob's concern for our mobile phones are down through having no signal and I am about two hours overdue. I've found myself in remote areas without a mobile signal on a number of occasions throughout this walk and I've wondered what might happen should I sustain a bad injury. So far I've been lucky – let's hope my luck continues!

At the farmhouse, Rob was befriended by Tess and her mother, Irene. Both have been equally concerned about my non-arrival as my son had given them a run-down on the situation. Tess invites us into her fourteenth-century home for tea and coffee and I rest in the coolness of the large living area. Too soon we have to leave and I strike out on foot for the village of Clun.

At Clun we shop for groceries and buy the tastiest of sausages at the local butchers before visiting the White Horse to check out their Wi-Fi facility and sample their local ale. Shortly afterwards we locate a Caravan Camping Club ground, but unfortunately there's no electricity on site, so after a gas-cooked meal we both retire early to bed.

Today's pedometer reading: 28.3km (17.57 miles) (covered only 8.5 road miles).

Notes of Interest: The Offa's Dyke Path

The Offa's Dyke Path was named after King Offa who, in the eighth century, ordered the construction of the Dyke to divide his Kingdom of Mercia from rival kingdoms to the west, which is now Wales.

Offa's Dyke Path is 177 miles / 285 kilometres long and passes through no less than eight different counties. The trail crosses the English-Welsh border a number of times as it explores the tranquil Marches of the border region and passes through the Brecon Beacons National Park and onto the remarkable Hatterall Ridge.

The path goes through well-known 'Areas of Outstanding Natural Beauty' such as the Wye Valley, the Hergest Ridge and the Clwydian Hills.

This ancient man-made border passes through a variety of different landscapes, including the Black Mountains, the rugged Shropshire hills, and the Eglwyseg mountains. The Dyke path also touches the towns of Montgomery, Knighton, Kington, Hay-on-Wye, Monmouth, Abergavenny and Chepstow.

FRI, 21ST AUG 2009
CLUN – KNIGHTON – KINGTON

I leave Clun at 7.15am and head for Knighton 7 miles away. This time I decide to take the road route rather than Offa's Dyke Path as I need to make up for time lost from yesterday's walk on the trail. A blue sky and a cold bite in the air seems to promise a fine day, but about 3 miles out the rain pours down on this lone walker who had decided not to take his wet-weather gear! The road to Knighton is certainly not walker-friendly and I have to be constantly alert to approaching traffic. Coming into Knighton I meet up with Christine, a lady cyclist. She escorts me up the hill, then leads me to the parking area where she thought Rob might be waiting for me.

After a long break of about 1½ hours I return to the Offa's Dyke Path and begin my walk to Kington, 14 miles away. It was 7.15am at the start of the walk and as I come down off the Dyke Path into Kington it's now 6.15pm. I now realise that, after deducting the time taken for rest breaks, I have been walking for over nine hours. During these hours there have been periods when I've done a lot of thinking. All sorts of subjects are mulled over, but I remember in particular thinking of obesity and the problems that arise for people with this condition.

I remember looking at some of the black and white photos that my sisters and I have. Some are not very good, probably taken with a Box Brownie; nevertheless, they represent an authentic record of the childhood and teenage years of our family. An observer might notice that almost everyone in the photos, including the many bystanders in the background of the crowded beach snaps, was slim; you had to look really hard to find someone of a portly physique.

There are well-documented reasons for the leanness of the general population in those days. It was due, to a very large extent, to the food rationing of the war years. In fact, rationing didn't come to an end until the early fifties. Sugar was still rationed up to September 1953 and I believe that the end of all food rationing did not come about until July 1954. However, even after this, items such as meat, butter, margarine, lard and cheese were at times still hard to come by.

So although we were not aware of it at the time, this rationing regime would have probably provided us with the healthiest of eating habits compared to the diet of all subsequent generations.

Activity was another reason for the trim waistlines of that era for kids were far more active than the youngsters of today. In the Dr Barnado's Home during the war we were allowed out much of the time. Apart from school and church services we would be playing in the fields or in the woods climbing trees or playing footie until we were called in for supper.

It was a similar story as a young teenager in Brighton. During the day we'd either be playing in the ruins of a building up the road, down on the promenade roller skating or, if it was summer, we'd be down on the beach for much of the day. After dinner, older children would be allowed out to play in the street (the streets were pretty well devoid of cars in those days) until it got dark or until our mother called us in for bed.

Some family members by Brighton Pier - I'm in the front, second from the right

Very few people had cars; there were no TVs or computers to keep us in our chairs and precious valve radios couldn't be operated with a remote control. Alcohol was something that youngsters hardly ever indulged in (despite my whisky drinking incident!) and the places to 'hang-out' for young people were usually on the dance floor on a Saturday night, the cinema or a local cafe.

As I walked I remembered thinking how different it was back then compared to today. We now live in a totally different world with eating temptations all around us; a factor that presents so many difficulties for the overweight child, teenager or adult who wants to shed the pounds.

Before I set out on my walk I remembered seeing numerous cooking programmes constantly being shown on television. I would immediately change to another channel because I resented the fact that the hierarchy controlling the programmes we watch seem to think that we are obsessed with anything related to the cooking of food. Not a day goes past without seeing these so-called celebrity chefs showing off their skills or presiding over some cooking contest in which teary-eyed contestants melodramatically display 'life or death' emotions about the judgement of their creations! It is my humble opinion that these programmes simply encourage the 'eating without hunger' obsession that has developed within today's society.

I realise that becoming obese is not always due to overeating as glandular and thyroid malfunction can sometimes cause the condition, as can the long term use of certain steroids. But poor nutrition and little exercise is usually the cause. Much of the blame for the current obesity problems must also lie at the ever-open doors of the supermarkets; an industry that governments seem unwilling to confront.

Attractively packaged, cunningly displayed food products on supermarket shelves to lure the unwary into adding yet another unnecessary item into their already overloaded trolley cannot be controlled, but enticing the shopper into buying multiple items to obtain a reduced single-item price should, in my view, be stopped. Chocolate goodies – two packets for £3; hot-cross buns – 3 packets for £5; ready-made meals – 5 packets for £4 is just a micro-sample of the way many supermarkets are now pushing their products onto the consumer. Parents with young families may benefit, but they'd get equal benefit if the individual product reflected the same price as those shown on the multiple offer.

I wondered as I walked whether the majority of shoppers had the need or the freezer space to buy multiple packets of food items. Obviously many do, thinking that they're making a saving; but I suspect that this promotion method can only lead to further gluttony or bin disposal once the products have exceeded their 'use-by-date'.

Excessive eating and waste is immoral when you consider that at least half of the world's population, (fellow human beings who share this planet with us) are suffering from severe malnutrition.

I meet up with Rob at The White Swan where I am greeted with an enthusiastic reception from Norman and Tom. Thanks, Norman for your donation to pay for tonight's camping site costs.

Actual road miles were approximately 21½, but my pedometer told the real story of the circuitous and hilly Offa's Dyke route.

Today's pedometer reading: 45.3km (28.13 miles).

Notes of Interest: Kington

Located near the Welsh-English border, the lovely town of Kington lies in the shadow of the evocative Hergest Ridge. You'd be as enchanted as I was with the panoramic display of open countryside and the hills surrounding the town.

The most plausible explanation of how the name of Kington came into being would be to assume that it was derived from 'King's-ton', being Anglo-Saxon for 'King's Town'. Similarly, nearby Knighton would have probably been 'Knight's Town' at one point, and Preston may have originated from 'Priest's Town'.

Because Kington sits on the west side of Offa's Dyke it is likely that it was in Welsh hands prior to the eighth century, although it eventually fell to the Anglo-Saxons before finally being taken by the Normans.

Kington has developed into an attractive town; a far cry from the former settlement clustered around an imposing castle that sat high and mighty on the hill above the River Arrow.

CHAPTER 20
HEREFORDSHIRE

SAT, 22ND AUG 2009
KINGTON

Today has to be a rest day as I am still feeling the effects of yesterday's mammoth walk, so Rob and I have a lie-in watching TV. It's the first time we've had Saturday as a day off and we make the most of it by turning on the sports programmes.

There are no laundry facilities on site so we take our washing to the local laundrette. We arrive back at the camping site at lunchtime where we relax with a bottle of red wine and locally made pork pies.

I have been thinking for a while about doing at least one marathon distance during the walk. By that I mean an actual road distance rather than a pedometer recorded one. Originally I considered tackling it on a Sunday as I would have the following day to recover for we normally have Mondays off. But while walking yesterday, I thought – why not make it on the last day of the walk? (1) The terrain in West and East Sussex is relatively flat; (2) I'd have as much time as I wanted to recover; (3) Most importantly, a few of my supporters might come and join me.

Once again we cannot get online due to a poor mobile broadband signal so I'm unable to update my diary or send or receive emails. We decide not to worry about it and instead we just relax and enjoy the rest of the day.

SUN, 23RD AUG 2009
KINGTON – GLADESTRY – HAY-ON-WYE

We leave the camping ground at 6.45am. Ten minutes later I'm walking out of Kington and climbing up a very long and steep hill towards the Hergest Ridge. On reaching the top I am immediately confronted with the most captivating scene. The surrounding terrain has an immediate impact upon me for the area, aside from the panoramic views, seems to have a strange, dramatic charm of its own. Copper-coloured fern and green bracken are interspersed among expansive tracts of grass as far as the eye can see. It is one of the most beautiful places I have encountered. It also has a sort of poignant effect on me that I can't quite explain.

Walking along the wide velvety green carpet I come across a small grassy area surrounded by small trees and other foliage. There's a plaque that bears the name of a lady who's buried here. I ponder over this peaceful, sepulchral place for a while and various scenarios skip through my mind as to why she came to be lying here.

I walk on still wondering about the lady and her connections with Hergest Ridge but also taking with me some intuitive understanding of her need to make this her final resting place. Not long after I come across a motley group of horses grazing right in my path. I wander through these multi-coloured animals that vary in size from hip height to well over 7ft, expecting them to hurriedly disperse, but instead they just look up from grazing and quietly watch me as I move amongst them. I can't resist the temptation to stop and take some pictures right there and then.

There is a tall black horse that moves a bit closer towards me. I scoop up a handful of grass and hold it out to it and the horse immediately gathers it up with rubbery lips from my open hand. I carry on walking for some time before realising that the same horse is quietly following me. I try shooing it away, but it continues to shadow me for a mile or more before realising I wasn't going to pay it any further attention. The next time I look back it was just standing there in the distance gazing after me. If I had been merely rambling rather than on a mission I could easily have stayed around these wonderful animals a little longer.

Soon I am walking down through the village of Gladestry to face another long walk that will take me up to the Disgwylfa Hill, another beautiful and breathtaking scenic location. I lose my way a mile out of Newchurch village having missed the Offa's Path sign through taking the wrong fork in the path. It leads me about 2 miles away from my route and I finally end up at a church where a few people are about to enter for the Sunday service. One gentleman offers to drive me back to the place where I had taken the wrong fork. I accept his offer with gratitude.

I arrive at Hay-on-Wye just after 2pm. We eventually find a Caravan Club camping site just a mile out of the town and we soon make ourselves comfortable for the rest of the day.

Today's pedometer reading: 26.19km (16.26 miles).

Notes of Interest: The River Wye

They say that the Romans constructed a bridge of wood and stone just upstream of present day Chepstow. The source of the River Wye is in the Welsh mountains and it flows from there to several towns and villages such as Hay-on-Wye, Little Dewchurch, Ross-on-Wye, Symonds Yat and Monmouth before meeting up with the Severn estuary a little below Chepstow.

This lovely river is also valued by nature conservationists throughout the UK, and has become a 'Site of Special Scientific Interest'. It is navigable up to Monmouth and has been since the early fourteenth century. The river is relatively unpolluted and considered by many to be one of the best salmon fishing rivers in the country. It is also popular with canoeists, especially beginners, due to the relatively slow river flow in many areas.

I remember my mother telling me about Symonds Yat Rock where on a clear day it provides a spectacular vista of the place where the three counties of Herefordshire, Gloucestershire and Monmouthshire meet.

The Wye was used by commercial vessels until the 1950s when rail haulage became more practical. These days the river still attracts a wide number of pleasure craft.

CHAPTER 21
MONMOUTHSHIRE

MON, 24TH AUG 2009
CAPEL-Y-FFIN – PANDY

A fine rain accompanies me as I walk out of Hay-on-Wye at 7am. The Offa's Dyke Path leads me up on higher country toward the Hay Bluff where a gathering mist is building up over the hills. It begins to worry me for the higher I climb the thicker it gets. The rain becomes heavier and the mist is rapidly closing in, seriously affecting visibility. The Offa's Dyke Path acorn signs are quite small, and some of the older signs are faded or partially concealed by foliage. It is crucial to locate them to keep on the right track; miss one in a remote area such as the Hay Bluff and you can easily become lost, especially in a thick mist.

I walk for another half hour or so, but with the deteriorating conditions and the increasingly slippery terrain I decide to return to the road. Getting back to the road isn't easy as the fog has thickened to such an extent that retracing my steps is an ordeal in itself. I come to a fork on the hillside and I'm not sure which narrow path to take; one will be nothing more than a well-used sheep track, the other will be the correct path. There are no acorn signs to help me so I'm going to have to work it out for myself!

I deliberate for some minutes wandering a short way down each track before deciding which one to take. I choose the right-hand path and about 15 minutes later I breathe a sigh of relief when the track broadens into familiar terrain and a little while later, as the mist clears, I see the winding country road some distance ahead. An hour later I stop to eat, seeking shelter from the rain in the porch of a nearby church.

The long walk takes me through Capel-y-Ffin and past the thirteenth-century Llanthony Abbey. I stop near here at an isolated roadside pub as I need to eat again and seek temporary shelter from the persistent rain. Half an hour later, after a pint of local ale and a bowl of chips, I set out once more toward Pandy.

While walking on the Hatterall Ridge and looking over at Llanthony Priory my thoughts turn once again to religion.

I begin wondering what it must have been like during the days when this thirteenth-century priory was at the zenith of its godly influence. I imagined it being an important symbol amidst the religious fervour that engulfed a largely ignorant, gullible and superstitious populace of that era. I thought about how fortunate we are today, for there is no doubt that as our knowledge of the universe widens our scepticism and questioning of religious doctrines increase.

And yet, no matter what the scientific discoveries in the fields of archaeology, geology and geophysics might bring, there will always be those who will steadfastly believe in the biblical version of ancient events. However, whatever a person's outlook may be, it's one that should never be disparaged or discouraged as everyone has the right to follow their own religious beliefs.

Today, as I walk, my thoughts dwell for some time on the different religions that exist around the world and I begin to wonder why faith or belief in some supernatural power seems to be an essential part of the human psyche.

In Luke 17:20-21, Jesus points out to the Pharisees that the 'Kingdom of God lies within you'. Is this man Jesus implying that the 'Power of Good' lies within the human soul? Maybe the Power of God or Goodness does not lie up there in the heavens but within all of us; a golden thread that might one day make Heaven on Earth a reality? That such a possibility exists is where my faith lies.

As I walk I ponder upon the fanatical elements that spawn from religious doctrine. Whether it is Christianity, Islam, Judaism, Hinduism or the many other religions throughout the world, it is the extremists, the fundamentalists, who create the problems.

The Bible, as with the Koran, the Tanakh or any other holy book, is susceptible to interpretation; ideal for those hardliners who wish for a sectarian existence enabling them to administer complete control over their followers. Read between the lines of the Christian Bible and you could easily come up with a brand new religion. Manipulate a meaning, take it out of context and some parents can easily satisfy themselves that refusing a vital blood transfusion for their dying child is their rightful Christian duty.

The everyday Catholic, Protestant, Muslim or Jew has a charitable disposition toward other religions; I speak from direct experience, having good friends from each of these faiths. Fanatical zealots, however, are a different breed with expectations and goals that stretch far beyond the norm. Their religious beliefs are set in stone; so much so that they have to nurture their children from the cradle into believing what they believe.

Children playing together have a natural acceptance toward one another. But a child raised in a devoutly religious household soon learns to discriminate against others. An Irish child can be indoctrinated into becoming the Catholic who hates Protestants or the Protestant who hates Catholics. A child reared within the walls of a zealous Muslim home learns to regard those of other faiths as infidels and as a Shi'ite they will be taught to distrust the Sunni or the Sunni to despise the Shi'ite and both are taught to have contempt towards the Kurds.

Children emerging from any radical form of religious upbringing might easily regard those of other faiths as people to be despised, shunned and, in extreme situations, might actually find religious justification in the indiscriminate killing of others. Such is the power of radicalisation.

A Jesuit once said: "Give me the child of three and I'll show you the man." But there is a simple little song from that great musical, *South Pacific,* the lyrics of which describe it in another way:

> You've got to be taught to hate and fear
> You've got to be taught from year to year
> It's got to be drummed in your dear little ear
> You've got to be carefully taught.
> You've got to be taught to be afraid
> Of people whose eyes are oddly made
> And people whose skin is a different shade
> You've got to be carefully taught.
> You've got to be taught before it's too late,
> Before you are 6 or 7 or 8,
> to hate all the people your relatives hate
> You've got to be carefully taught.

I eventually reach Pandy at 3.15 pm. I have been walking for almost eight hours. Rob is parked up in the high street and I am so relieved to see him for we had lost phone contact for some time. We go to a lovely Caravan Club camping site that Rob has found and as soon as we we're hooked up I immediately settle back and fall asleep.
Today's pedometer reading: 32.58km (20.23 miles).

TUES, 25TH AUG 2009
PANDY – CROSS ASH – MONMOUTH

It took all my willpower to rise from my bed at 5.30am this morning. My legs still ache and a niggling groin injury is making itself felt. As I start walking I'm hoping that the weather is going to stay dry. My destination is Monmouth and I'm walking there by road rather than the Offa's Dyke Path because of the wet conditions during the past few days.

The sky darkens and once again light rain begins to fall. I catch up with Rob at Cross Ash and after a meal break I continue on toward Monmouth. The rain is now falling hard and I am wet and cold by the time I meet up again with the camper van. After another short break I reluctantly emerge from the warmth of the van and continue my journey.

On the outskirts of Monmouth I am surprised to see Rob heading towards me. I follow him as he turns into a road from the roundabout ahead of me and drives into a nearby caravan camping site. They have a space available, thank goodness! Realising I was on a charity walk they are also letting us stay free of charge. We are soon hooked up to the power and are ready to relax for the rest of the day.
Today's pedometer reading: 25.2km (15.64 miles).

Notes of Interest: Monmouth

The Monmouth Archaeological Society working on sites along Monnow Street have uncovered a wealth of information about the town's early history.

Monmouth, it is said, dates back to the Roman occupation of this area of Britain, where they built a network of forts, one of which was Blestium now known as Monmouth.

The Battle of Monmouth took place in 1233 between the rebel forces of the 3rd Earl of Pembroke and a royalist force under John of Monmouth. St Thomas' Church and Monnow Bridge were torched by the rebel victors during the battle. For their involvement in the chartist uprising of 1840, protestors John Frost, Zephaniah Williams and William Jones were sentenced at Monmouth's Shire Hall and found guilty of treason.

They would become the last people to be sentenced to be hanged, drawn and quartered. Lucky for them their sentences were later commuted to transportation to Australia, although apparently this decision created a huge outcry from the public.

Lord Nelson made two notable visits to the town and praised the people of Monmouth for their loyalty to the crown.

WED, 26TH AUG 2009
REDBROOK – TINTERN – CHEPSTOW

I leave the camping ground a little late today. I am in two minds about whether I should walk as the weather forecast is pretty awful. At 7.30am my mind's made up to go. After crossing a field and going over an old iron bridge I reach the road that will take me to Chepstow. I have my first stop near Redbrook. It's a brief stop as I am running behind my day's schedule due to the late start. At Llandogo the rain gets heavier and I am beginning to feel uncomfortably damp, not just on account of the rain but also because of sweating beneath the restrictive wet-weather gear I'm wearing.

A couple of miles further on I pass through the delightful village of Tintern. It has a charm of its own; one of those places in which I'd love to stay around longer but apart from a brief visit to a delightful second-hand book shop, I carry on. Unfortunately the day's mission does not allow for such luxuries as sightseeing, but I couldn't resist tarrying awhile to take some photographs of the impressive Tintern Abbey ruins. I continue on in the rain heading toward Chepstow feeling tired, wet and thirsty, and finally walk into the town just before 3pm.

I meet Rob at the Castle Car Park, and after visiting the nearby Information Centre we call in at the Chepstow Castle Inn for a well-earned taste of their local ale in relaxed surroundings. Phil, the proprietor, and his son are very accommodating making Rob and I feel very welcome. We are about to leave when I am suddenly presented with a fine walking stick by one of the patrons. We soon find a small but nice campsite a little way out of town.

Today's pedometer reading: 30.36km (18.85 miles).

Notes of Interest: Chepstow

It is thought that the earliest inhabitants of the area were those of the Mesolithic age which would have been around 5000 BC. Archaeological investigations suggest that this settled habitation continued through to the end of the Roman occupation of Britain in AD 400. Of course it is likely that the settlement was there through the Dark Ages, but there are no records to confirm this.

Chepstow sits about 3 miles from the Severn Bridge, the crossing point over to Bristol. In Norman times Chepstow, it is said, was known as Estrighoiel, derived from the Welsh word 'ystraigyl' meaning a bend in the river. It wouldn't become known as Chepstow until around the fourteenth century. Apparently the word Chepstow derives from the old English 'ceap' or 'chepe stowe' suggesting a 'market place'.

Chepstow Castle might be one of the oldest surviving stone fortifications in Britain. The town was recognised by the Normans as being the ideal site for a castle due mainly to its strategic position on the River Wye and its ideal defensive situation.

According to the Domesday Book, the castle's construction in 1067 was monitored by the Duke's favourite castle builder, William FitzOsbern. The castle appears to have been speedily constructed and the probable reason for that might have been due to William the Conqueror's urgent need for an effective defensive structure against the constant threat from the west. From the fourteenth century, conflict between England and Wales was to end and the Welsh border castles gradually lost their importance.

THURS, 27TH AUG 2009
CHEPSTOW

I'm not walking today as Rob isn't feeling too well. We have a good mobile broadband signal here so I think it will be a good opportunity to update stuff on my website.

Its late afternoon now and we drive back to Chepstow to have a final look around this last Welsh border town before heading out over the Severn tomorrow. We also pop in to the Chepstow Castle Inn to say hi to Phil and his son, Rhodri. Soon after this we make for the bridge that spans the river bordering Wales and England and take a photo of each other standing with one foot in Wales and the other in England. After this we return to our camping site in Sedbury buying fish and chips on the way. We both go to bed around 10.15pm as I have a feeling that I might be on a long walk tomorrow.

CHAPTER 22
BRISTOL

FRI, 28TH AUG 2009
CHEPSTOW – SEVERN BRIDGE – BRISTOL

Arise early today, and after a good breakfast we drive back to the parking site adjacent to the castle where I finished walking the day before yesterday. The weather conditions are pretty poor as I begin walking on the route that will take me over the old Severn Bridge and into England. Driving rain and a headwind impede my progress as I approach the Wye Valley Link Road roundabout on the western flank of Chepstow town.

Half an hour later I am on the M48 pedestrian approach to the Severn Bridge. Crossing the Severn on foot is an unforgettable experience. Looking down toward the mouth of the Severn I'm confronted with breathtaking views of the Welsh coastline and to my left the Avon coast on the English mainland. Gazing up river as I walk I witness further outstanding panoramic scenes.

After the crossing I go up to the Service Park and take photos of the magnificent Severn Bridge with the Welsh coast serving as a backdrop. Soon after this I'm on my way again. The rain has eased, but the wind is increasing and I am facing a headwind that continues to slow me down.

I meet Rob at Pilning for my first break, after this I manage to get on a coastal path that leads me almost to the outskirts of Avonmouth and from there I make my way to the A4 that will take me into Bristol. The wind has become my ally for it is now at my back and pushing me toward my destination.

My thoughts today focus on my timetable and whether I will be on schedule to finish my walk on 10th October, only 6 weeks away. I also remember thinking about the discussion we had with some locals while in a country pub a couple of days ago; it was about the origin of hops. It reminded me of another time!

Our mother could never afford to take us on a proper holiday so each September we used to go to the hop fields of Kent. This was before the introduction of mechanised hop picking, when the need for mass labour at harvest time was crucial. Our family, together with some odd bits of furniture like a chest of drawers etc, would be picked up by a truck from the hop farm. The back of the truck was framed and covered with tarpaulin for shelter. Once at the fields we were allocated two hoppers' huts.

As youngsters we were always delighted to be there because, although we had to help with the picking of the hops, there were acres of open space to play in and lots of places to explore once the day was over. The long, drawn-out, warm summer evenings were ideal in getting familiar with the other kids, many of whom we'd met the year before. Most of these children were from London's East End. There was such a great number of Eastenders there; they'd come down on special trains each year and would have the same hoppers' huts they'd lived in over previous generations of hop-picking. For those families it would have been a welcome break from the smoke and grime of London; it also meant money in each and everyone's pocket.

I remember the time when my disabled sister Vivienne, had accidentally started a small fire in the hut. She had overfilled the parafin stove and the spillage ignited a nearby towel. She'd managed to put it out, but not before Fred, who would have been no more than four or five at the time, had run off to tell our mother of the news. Viv remembers shouting: "Come back Fred, the fire's out...Come back," but to no avail. This resulted in a mother's frantic quarter of a mile dash across the fields to reach the family's huts, with visions of finding the charred remains of her disabled daughter playing constantly on her mind.

When she arrived at the hut Vivienne was calmly sitting there with the charred towel tucked underneath her. Our mother was so relieved to find that her daughter was okay but also terribly angry that she had been given such an awful fright. Consequently poor old Viv got a real telling-off. When Viv spoke about it later we all realised that young Fred was really the one responsible for wreaking the havoc.

In my last year at the hop fields I was promoted to Tally Boy and would record the weigh-ins before accompanying the tractor and loaded trailer to the oast houses, where the hops would be off-loaded, sorted and dried.

Carol, Viv, Fred, Mum & Jan, hop picking in Kent

Hop picking had a big social and financial impact on our family and we always looked forward to September when we'd pack our things and head for the hop fields of Kent.

About 4 miles on I meet up with the campervan that's parked on the side of the road. Two hours later I'm walking into the leafy outskirts of Bristol. Rob has already located a campsite at the marina in Bristol and as luck would have it, considering it's the bank holiday weekend, they have a site available. We go to the Asda store and buy groceries before returning to the Baltic Wharf Caravan Club site to settle in for the evening.

Today's pedometer reading: 34.92 km (21.68 miles).

Notes of Interest: Bristol

If some recent archaeological evidence is to be believed then human activity in the Bristol area might possibly date back to the Upper Palaeolithic era around 20,000 years ago or earlier. But coming forward to a mere 1,400 years ago and we'd probably find an Anglo-Saxon settlement between the Rivers Avon and Frome, known as Brycgstow (a place of settlement by the bridge).

Around the start of the eleventh century the Normans built one of their strongest castles in the town and by the twelfth century Bristol had become a crucial port, handling much of England's trade with Ireland.

The plague ravaged the region and this terrible infectious disease would devastate the people of Bristol, affecting their recovery and the town's progress for much of the following century.

Bristol would become an important maritime centre and a convenient departure point for important sea voyages due to its strategic position. The rapid growth of the slave trade would help its economic recovery as it became involved in various aspects of this sickening eighteenth-century trade of humankind. Bristol often played a major role in the second stage shipment of these unfortunate souls and products of the slave trade such as sugar cane and rum would enter England via the Bristol port.

It also seems that slave auctions might have been regularly held in Bristol from which a small number of captives found their way into aristocratic homes around England.

At the height of the slave trade a huge number of slaving ships, designed to crowd in as many bodies as possible, were fitted-out at Bristol. Probably half a million people or more would be shipped this way, packed like sardines, before undergoing the arduous sea journey to the Americas where, if they survived, they would enter a hard life of slavery.

The city of Bristol experienced its fair share of bombing raids by the Luftwaffe during World War II, especially in one raid that became known as the 'Bristol Blitz'.

Today Bristol is one of the finest and largest cities in the South West.

CHAPTER 23
SOMERSET

SAT, 29TH AUG 2009
BRISTOL – FLAX BOURTON – WESTON-SUPER-MARE

As it's a bank holiday weekend it's going to be difficult to get a site without pre-booking so as we were lucky to have two days here in Bristol Marina it makes sense to stay here. This means that different arrangements have to be made. I decide to walk to Weston-super-Mare unescorted; leaving Rob here on the site and give him a break from driving. After the walk is finished I'll catch the bus back to Bristol...simple!

I start out by going through a gate in a fence then walking through a country path and over a rail bridge to connect to the A370. My first stop is at a roadside trailer cafe in Flax Bourton where I have a coffee and an egg and bacon sandwich. Fifteen minutes later and I'm on the road again.

Much of this walk through the North Somerset countryside is a scenic delight, especially through the beautiful wooded Broxton area and through Cleeve and Congresbury.

Around 7 miles on I stop again this time at a pub called The Angel, to have a meal of potato wedges and salad. I walk into Weston-super-Mare at 1.45pm and at 2.15pm I am on the bus making my way back to Bristol. I arrive back at the campsite at 3.15pm, and after a shower and pasta meal I feel fully recovered from my 20-plus mile walk.

Today's pedometer reading: 36.3km (22.50 miles).

Notes of Interest: Weston-super-Mare

From archaeological evidence it seems that a small settlement has occupied the area since the Iron Age.

The name Weston, similar to Preston, Kington and others, is made up of two Old English/Saxon words 'west tun' meaning west settlement. The last part of the name describes the town's location in Medieval Latin. From what I have gathered 'super', spelt with a small s means on or above, and 'mare' in the Latin tongue means sea.

Weston-super-Mare's oldest structure is Worlebury hill fort on Worlebury Hill, and this apparently dates back to the Iron Age. During past excavations of the hill fort ancient human remains were uncovered, some of which showed evidence of violent death.

The Bristol Channel has a large tidal range, so much so that on low tide the sea uncovers areas of unpleasant thick mud. Unfortunately it resulted in the town's colloquial title, 'Weston-super-Mud'.

As with many seaside towns, the Victorian era brought about a boom in Weston's seaside holiday trade, strengthening its growth and prosperity. The boom was mainly created by the arrival of the railway system in 1841 for it made travel so much easier. Thereafter, a multitude of visitors began flocking in to Weston from all over the west including the Midlands.

During the Second World War the town was unfortunately on the route for enemy bombers targeting Bristol. It is likely that the Luftwaffe dropped many of its bombs over the town, either thinking it to be Bristol or to rid their excess load before returning to Germany.

The first bombs fell on Weston in June 1940, but in January 1941 and in June 1942 the worst bombing raids were to occur and large areas of the town were destroyed.

Birnbeck Pier, built in 1867 is, I believe, still lying derelict although it has recently been sold for an undisclosed sum.

The Grand Pier, after a multi-million revamp, was destroyed by fire on the 28th July 2008. Construction began on a new pier and pavilion in 2009, and the pier was reopened at a cost of £39 million on 23rd October, 2010.

SUN, 30TH AUG 2009
WESTON-SUPER-MARE – HIGHBRIDGE – BRIDGWATER

Rob and I leave the Baltic Wharf Caravan Club site at 6.50am and drive down to Weston-super-Mare. We find the bus stop outside the petrol station where I had finished walking yesterday and I immediately begin heading toward Bridgwater, my next destination.

I walk past the Weston General Hospital and soon I'm striding among the broad fields of North Somerset.

Only two hours out and it begins raining again and the westerly wind is quite gusty, making the walk unpleasant. The tall hedgerows and foliage on both sides of the road conceal much of the passing countryside, but this time it's a blessing as by walking close to the windward side I manage to shelter from much of the driving rain.

I catch up with Rob near East Brent for a meal break, a change of T-shirt and a leg stretch before carrying on once more, heading southward. The rain has almost stopped, but now I'm walking on this stretch of the A38 where there are hardly any walking verges. The traffic hazard forces me to climb through hedges and walk on the fields alongside the road.

My second stop is near Highbridge where I have my usual cold pasta dish and a cup of coffee. I make it a brief stop as I am hoping to make it to Minehead before stopping for the day. I change into a pair of dry walkers and plod on to Bridgwater. On this session of the walk my thoughts turn again to my early years.

The only way our mother could get Mick and me out of the Dr Barnado's home once the war had ended was to convince them that she had adequate living accommodation and was financially able to feed two extra mouths. The reason behind such stipulations was that there had been cases where children had gone back to their homes only to be taken back into care weeks or months later because of neglect and poor treatment. My mother had often spoken to me about it saying that there were some mothers who, after tasting a life of freedom for a number of years had no real interest in being shackled by a strange child or children who had suddenly landed back on their doorstep. It was these 'unwanted kids' who often ended up back in care.

For our mother it meant leaving London, where she had been working, because suitable property was hard to come by there due to the extensive wartime destruction of urban areas. Any that were in relatively good condition were quickly snapped up by the wealthier folk which helped to drive rental prices higher. Many people now sought to live on the south coast, especially in larger places like Hastings, Eastbourne, Bournemouth and Brighton and this growing demand made reasonably priced rental properties hard to come by. It took our mother another few months of searching before finally locating a property big enough which she could afford and a further three months before the authorities would allow us to go home.

The house was in Mighell Street and it was to be our home for the next five years. It wasn't what you'd call the most comfortable of homes, but it had the required number of bedrooms to accommodate the family, which was to include my brother and me. Our mother had also found regular part-time work and that, along with the small widow's pension, was enough to secure our release from the home.

The house was old, cold and draughty, (a plaque on the first house in the street was dated 1822); however, to Mick and I it was home and one stop from heaven. I don't remember this, but my mother told me that when we first arrived home we would call her 'Miss'. She was heartbroken over this, but she went on to say that it didn't take either of us long to merge into our new life with gusto and that we were soon addressing her as 'Mum'.

Moe in Mighell St after recovering from Polio

At Bridgwater I turn off on to the A39 toward Minehead. I expect to see the van at any moment, but after walking on for another hour without sighting it I decide to phone Rob to find out where he is. It turns out that he's taken another route and has been waiting in a parking spot about 3 miles out of Bridgwater. A phone call soon clarifies the situation and within 10 minutes Rob is driving up the hill toward me.

At least the extra distance isn't wasted as it means I'm almost 3 miles further on toward Minehead. I think about continuing on for a while, but the thought of walking for another hour or so does not appeal.

During the week we had a call from Pete and Emi to say they were staying at a Holiday Park in Ilfracombe and they invited us to join them. It's a proposition too good to miss as it means Rob and I can have a refreshing break for one night and escape the claustrophobic existence of campervan life.

We waste no time in continuing on to Ilfracombe but on the way we encounter the 1 in 4 gradient Porlock Hill. This hill is a test for most vehicles, but for a heavy camper van with front wheel drive it's a formidable undertaking. We finally make the summit, with the temperature gauge rising at an alarming rate – in tandem with a rapid rise in our stress levels! The climb is a real concern to us and we quickly realise that we will need to find a detour when walking this section later in the week. Porlock Hill is not just a challenge to the van; its steep, narrow and winding nature makes it quite hazardous for anyone attempting it on foot.

The rain has become heavier again as we approach the John Fowler Holiday Park where Pete and Emi are staying and where they have arranged a free apartment for us. It's really good to see them and after a great meal we go into the large entertainment area and distribute our Cancer Research leaflets to everyone at the tables. There must be at least three to four hundred people here and later, on request, I go up on the stage to talk about the venture.

Today's pedometer reading: 37.9km (23.50 miles).

Notes of Interest: Ilfracombe

The settlement that would one day become Ilfracombe was (according to historians) recorded in the Domesday Book as Alfreinscoma; its translation being: 'Valley of the sons of Alfred'. It appears that the settlement might have existed since the Iron Age or even earlier.

On the predominant hill of Hillsborough (formerly Hele's Barrow) Iron Age Celts are said to have established a hill fort where lovely Ilfracombe can be seen, nestled between the National Park of Exmoor to the East and the golden coast with the surfing beaches to the West.

The natural layout of Ilfracombe harbour makes it a welcome sight for sailors seeking a safe port in a stormy Bristol Channel; even more welcome would be seeing the light beacon from St Nicholas's Chapel, presumably the oldest working lighthouse in the UK. It is situated on Lantern Hill and has been there as a beacon for over 650 years.

In the 1820s four tunnels were carved out by Welsh miners to provide easier access to the beaches and to the pair of tidal pools; a development that proved immediately popular with Victorian bathers. The pools were segregated and this would have allowed for a relaxation in the dress code where previously the female would have had to adhere to covering up the whole body. The men, it seems, could now swim naked in their own pool. The tunnels are still being used today so just look for the 'Tunnels Beaches' signpost.

It is said that Joan and Jackie Collins attended school in the town as evacuees during the war.

MON, 31ST AUG 2009
ILFRACOMBE

It's our day off and we're sleeping in... Ah luxury! Pete and Emi are scheduled to vacate their premises by 10am as they need to get back to Brighton for work the following day so after a great breakfast we say our goodbyes and watch them as they drive out of the car park. I'm feeling a little nostalgic seeing them go, knowing that they will be back in Brighton in around six hours whereas it's going to take us another six weeks.

We're allowed to make use of the apartment for the rest of the day at the courtesy of the John Fowler Holiday Park. After a shower Rob and I spend the next few hours updating websites, answering emails and so on. Around 5pm we go into Ilfracombe for fuel, then head north for Bridgwater. We decide to divert onto a more circuitous route to avoid the steep Porlock Hill and then take the road that leads to Williton. The journey takes longer than expected, and we finally locate a camping site in the village of Roadwater. The site is on a farm, and the ground is not that level, but at least we have electricity and toilet facilities.

TUES, 1ST SEPT 2009
WILLITON – BRIDGWATER

Today was to end up being different from the norm. Yesterday I discovered that the tax disc on the van had expired so I plan to visit a post ofice and get it renewed. Trouble is it means going into Bridgwater and waiting around till 9am when the post ofice opens and afterwards getting Rob to drop me off at the parking area where I had finished my walk the day before.

Last night's campsite was close to Williton, the village where I had intended to end today's walk so it seems more practical to walk from Williton to Bridgwater then get to the post ofice in the afternoon when the 17-mile walk was over. I could start my walk early from Williton rather than starting late from Bridgwater where I'll have to wait for three hours for the post ofice to open. It's going to feel a bit weird walking in the opposite direction, but it's certainly the most practical solution and I'll still be covering the correct course on my walk around England.

My first meal break is in the Plough Inn car park in the village of Holford. I'm on my second walking session of the day when I meet Jo and Graham who have just parked their campervan in a lay-by. I stop to chat for a while as they are a friendly couple and seem interested in my venture. They live in Prague and are touring the length of Britain. Jo brings me a cuppa from a nearby catering van and Graham takes a couple of photos before we part company. I finish the day at the same parking spot where I had completed my walk on Sunday.

After renewing the van's tax disc we drive back to Williton and then turn off toward the coast. We soon find a lovely caravan site near Watchet, and we're allowed to use their facilities free of charge. Thanks to the friendly staff of the Warren Bay Holiday Villas.

Today's pedometer reading: 27.72km (17.2 miles).

Notes of Interest: Bridgwater

The town of Bridgwater was, according to some historians, originally a settlement called Brigg meaning quay. In the Domesday Book, however, the town is recorded as Brugie or Brugia.

In the Monmouth Rebellion of 1685, James Scott, the Duke of Monmouth, displayed aggression towards the king claiming his right to the throne. Apparently the people of Bridgwater concurred and openly declared the duke as their king. The rebellion was crushed and resulted in nine people being hanged, drawn and quartered for treason. James Scott, it seems, was later beheaded in the Tower of London. A hundred years later Bridgwater became the first town in Britain to petition for the ban on slavery.

Three men, three women and one child were killed when the first bombs fell on Bridgwater on 24 August, 1940 and in preparations for the invasion of Europe, American troops came into the town.

In 1943-4 an Italian prisoner of war camp was established at Colley Lane.

WED, 2ND SEPT 2009
WILLITON – MINEHEAD – PORLOCK

By the time we leave Watchet and return to Williton to start the day's walk it's close to 8.30am.

On planning my route yesterday evening I decided to take the West Somerset Coastal Path. The route will take me back to Watchet where I will turn south to connect with the coastal path. The weather is cool and the skies overcast, ideal for walking, but the forecasters have warned of more bad weather approaching from the Atlantic.

The coastal path running alongside the beautiful Exmoor National Park is a delight, but the journey takes longer than expected due to the terrain. Robert comes to meet me as I walk past the Minehead and West Somerset Golf Course. By the time I reach the van I've been walking for almost three hours. It's during this period that I remember thinking about the social security benefits available in this country and about the people who take unfair advantage of the system. I suppose what triggered this line of thought was what happened when Rob and I were eating a meal while parked in a supermarket car park the other day.

I was watching vehicles driving into a section of disabled parking bays that were close by. It didn't dawn on me straight away, but I soon began to notice something odd. I remember nudging Rob and making some comment about it and then we both sat watching for about an hour or so. During that time we saw around 25 vehicles come and go from these disability bays. The occupants of at least 20 of those cars appeared to have no disabilities whatsoever. Most of them jumped out and disappeared inside the store faster than you could say 'Pretend you're lame; disability's the game!'.

Rob would pop out of the van now and then to check to see if new arrivals were displaying disability stickers; all but two of them were. It made me wonder about how these obviously able-bodied people had managed to satisfy their doctors that they were deserving of a disability status. But then it occurred to me that maybe they had possibly borrowed the vehicle from a parent or grandparent. But whatever the reason, it just didn't seem right or fair that this sort of thing should be allowed to happen.

I thought to myself about how different things are today compared to yesteryear. When I left school you were automatically expected to get a job; it was the norm and any kid who was unemployed was looked upon as being a little odd. I don't think unemployment benefit existed in those days or, for that matter, incapacity or disability benefits. This would have made life pretty hard for some individuals, but on the whole people worked and enjoyed what the far less materialistic world had to offer.

Today it seems that the pendulum has swung completely the other way. Successive generations have seen a growing culture of dependency, where able-bodied people can now be looked after by the state. We live in a society where incapacity or disability benefits can be easily obtained by physically-able people, with all costs met once again by the poor old taxpayer. Many of these claims, I feel, are duplicitous to say the least.

As I walk I begin wondering about the number of cars that must be out there, being driven around (and replaced with a new one every three years) by undeserving cases, all from the taxes of those unfortunate people who work to earn their daily bread. It is said that striving is the mother of progress; that all our achievements in science, medicine, music, social reforms and so on are due to our willingness to strive – and at times to struggle – in our effort to reach a particular goal.

Unfortunately, we now have an ever growing element within our society that believes there is no need to strive; that one can live a comfortable existence without the need for effort. It's a culture that has been with us now for a long time; in fact, if we look back we'll probably discover families out there that have not worked (strived) for almost two generations.

The worry is that, due to the ever-increasing number of people prepared to live this way, our political leaders feel they have to cater to them in order not to lose their votes. Even TV programmes are geared to the interests of this growing sector in order to maintain high viewing ratings.

They say that people get the society they deserve. And we, the silent majority, just sit, observe and disapprove of such social decline, yet do nothing positive to prevent it.

The rain has not materialised so I'm going to carry on towards Porlock. I walk along the curved promenade of Minehead and out onto the South West Coast Path. Half an hour into the walk I meet up with a couple of hikers, Andrew and Rob, who are into their first day of a three-day walk to Combe Martin.

Not far out of Minehead a long steep hill causes temperatures to rise and heart rates to quicken. Soon after, the rain comes down and we hurriedly put on our wet weather gear. The three of us then carry on toward Porlock. On the way down a long, steep incline, we meet a couple trudging up toward us. We chat in the rain for a while as they seem interested in my walking venture then, after giving last minute advice to each other on what lay ahead, we part company. I watch as Ann and John labour up the steep rocky path that Ann had aptly named 'Heart Attack Hill'.

It's still pouring with rain when the three of us arrive in Porlock so we are all soaking wet as we say our goodbyes. Rob and Andrew are off to a B&B in Porlock Weir, whereas I am only 100 metres away from the Porlock Caravan Park where Rob has already parked up.

Today's pedometer reading: 31.41km (19.50 miles).

Notes of Interest: Porlock

It is widely thought that around 9-10,000 years ago, our planet had seen the end of the last glacial period; a time when ice caps had melted and sea levels, along with air temperature, had risen.

A warm, wet climate might have been the prevailing weather pattern at that time and a Mesolithic settlement would have probably existed where Porlock sits today. They might easily have had a comfortable living thanks to the climate, spending their time gathering plants and fishing in the flat, thickly wooded surroundings of their domain. They would have also hunted extensively, if the bones of wild cattle discovered near their habitat are anything to go by.

Before the end of the ice age, however, many of today's beach areas such as Porlock, might easily have been a considerable distance inland.

On display at the Visitor Centre are the bones of an Aurochs discovered on Porlock beach in 1999. The last known animal of this species is believed to have died in Poland in 1627.

If you're walking on the South West Coast Path you might stay overnight at Porlock (as I did) before continuing on the next strenuous section to Lynton.

There is a new, well-signposted toll road that bypasses the 1 in 4 gradient on Porlock Hill. It's a very scenic route so I would strongly advise motorists to take it!

Services are still held at the twelfth-century Culbone Church, reputed to be the smallest church in England. It is a 2-mile (3.2 km) walk from Porlock Weir and about 3½ miles (5.6 km) from Porlock itself.

THURS, 3RD SEPT 2009
PORLOCK

Today is another day off. That's two days off in a week. I could easily get used to this idle life! However, I must maintain my walking schedule otherwise we'll have problems reaching Brighton on the planned date. We had originally intended to arrive back at Brighton Pier on 9th October; that would have made it exactly five months from 10th of May, the day we started out. The problem with that arrival date is that it's a Friday. We had already received indications from some of our Brighton supporters that they are preparing to meet us at Worthing on that final day if it happened to fall at the weekend, so it makes sense to have Saturday 10th October as the last day of the walk.

My phone has died. It's an essential tool for arranging where to meet up with Rob so walking without it is not an option. It has succumbed due to the damp conditions it has been exposed to over the last few weeks. Yesterday's downpour must have been the final straw as rivulets of rain had been trickling into the pocket of my waterproof for much of the day and it's the pocket that holds my mobile phone. Luckily I had arranged where to meet up with Rob before it turned itself off for eternity.

The phone would be even more crucial on the coastal path for the atrocious weather has made the going heavy, slippery and somewhat dangerous in places. In the event of an accident it's essential to have the means to make contact with Rob or the local emergency services. We drive back to Minehead, the most likely place to pick up another mobile phone. We try Tesco and then a couple of stores around town, but there's nothing in their limited range that really suits. In the end I go back to Tesco and buy the most appropriate model I can find.

Back in Porlock we take advantage of the free Wi-Fi connection that the Porlock Caravan Park has given us and I manage to update my diary and progress map and also answer back-dated emails. Late in the afternoon we acquire some literature on the coastal path route from the local information centre and this evening I study it carefully. I'm quite concerned as the terrain looks pretty rugged and I know the wet weather we've been having will have adversely affected the ground conditions. Ah well, no good worrying. Tomorrow is another day!

CHAPTER 24
DEVON

FRI, 4TH SEPT 2009
PORLOCK – CULBONE – LYNMOUTH – LYNTON

We leave Porlock at 7.40am and I'm soon on the path to Porlock Weir. From the Worthy toll house I proceed toward Culbone. Culbone Church is the smallest church in England and I'm told it still holds regular services. It appears in the Domesday Book and apparently in the *Guinness Book of Records*. It's certainly worth taking a picture of this unusual building so I go to the pouch where I keep my camera handy, but to my dismay the pouch is empty. I remember now downloading photos onto my computer and obviously had forgotten to put the camera back in the pouch. I could have kicked myself, but my tired legs were not up to it!

I loved the walk through Culbone Woods, although it was marred somewhat by the cold, wet conditions and muddy footpaths in places. It appears that these woods were once home to a leper colony and that their main commercial activity to keep themselves alive was charcoal burning.

As I've already mentioned in previous extracts, there's something about walking through a forest or a wooded area on your own that creates a sort of peaceful awareness within you. You catch the movement of creatures more readily and the sound of birdsong seems more acute, yet the peculiar stillness remains. If you have ever walked out on virgin snow, especially in the evening or at dawn, you will get some idea of the atmosphere I'm attempting to describe.

Walking through the woods I notice a young grey squirrel coming toward me along the track. I expect it to dart away at any moment, but it just keeps approaching. I stop walking and watch the creature as it comes within two feet of where I'm standing; it looks up at me for at least five seconds or more, then turns and casually bounds up onto the lowest branch of a nearby tree. I couldn't understand this unusual behaviour for every squirrel I had seen during my walk had quickly scarpered on catching sight of me. Maybe this one had previously been associated with a family or the public in some way and was expecting me to throw it some peanuts or something. Whatever the reason, it would have been a great moment to capture on film.

Coming out of the woods the route becomes quite rugged at times, constantly dipping steeply down into watery gullies before rising up again. I stop on two occasions to rest and eat. Today thoughts, as usual, have come and gone, but memories of my early days in Brighton linger for a while.

In the late forties/early fifties rationing was still in force, but other legacies from the war years were evident in the demeanour of some of the characters that were around back then. There was a small middle-aged lady who would walk quite rapidly along a street, then suddenly, without warning would scuttle backwards even faster. I remember one of my friends saying that on one occasion he'd seen her waiting to cross a busy street; he offered to escort her over as she seemed quite confused, only to receive a whack from her stick for his pains. It was rumoured that she had been buried for days in the cellar of her house after it had been bombed during the war.

Then there was this guy we knew as Eric who would always be sitting on a bench on the promenade. We kids thought of him as being a homeless person, and also an alcoholic as he always seemed to have a bottle of some kind or other nearby and his head continually nodded erratically in a sideways motion. The strange thing was, if you walked up to him without him seeing you until the last moment, he would give you a startled, terrified look, grab his bottle and quickly dart off to another bench. As youngsters we were quite amused at these antics, but I later heard that he had been in the invasion force in France and had become shell-shocked due to prolonged duress under enemy fire.

There were other interesting characters around in those days, such as a tall guy who was called the Gentleman Totter. A totter was a person who collected old clothes, rags or other unwanted items. Every time you saw him with his cart he seemed to be dressed up in a different outfit; not just any old outfit but usually a dark elegant dress suit with a top hat and everything. It was generally known that his clothing comprised of whatever he'd managed to pick up over previous days. Judging by his apparel we all came to the conclusion that there must have been a lot of ex-funeral directors living in the neighbourhood!

There was also an active little lady called Ma Kelly, the winkle lady. She would go down onto the rocks every low tide to pick the winkles then walk up the streets with her barrow selling her wares by measuring out pint or half-pint quantities of winkles from glass jugs. Her big son would sometimes accompany her and he would bring along a large laboratory jar containing what appeared to be some sort of strange exotic creature – until he proudly pronounced that it was his very own preserved appendix!

Even some of our close neighbours were weird. There was one woman who lived close by who I thought had a face that was a dead ringer of a Rhesus Monkey. She would be seen sitting on her front doorstep most times of the day, constantly smoking a fag. She had a family of at least four kids, and we often used to wonder how she cared for them. Back in those days, when borrowing a cup of sugar, milk or tea was a daily occurrence, a visiting neighbour to our house was never a surprise. Trouble was that most times the borrowing was only an excuse for a neighbour to moan about their domestic situation, as if our mother didn't have enough worries of her own.

When we arrived back from Dr Barnado's there was an older lady living in our house; her name was Polly Atkins. She was known to be a White Russian – whatever that means! She certainly spoke with a foreign accent, but she seemed anything but white! Our mother also thought that Polly Atkins wasn't her true name. Boarding her was a way of supplementing the family income, but she was only with us for a matter of months as our mother realised she needed the extra room for her extended family now that we were home.

Sometimes on a Sunday morning we'd hear the sound of tambourines, drums and wind instruments as the Salvation Army (the Sallies) marched up our street. They'd stop a little way up the road – where most of the boozy fathers lived – and begin belting out songs like 'I'm Aitch-A-Pee-Pee-Wy (H.A.P.P.Y)'. I'm sure the Sallies did it to cause discomfort to the 'sinners' in the street because every time they began to sing, windows would fly up and verbal abuse would fly down. But it didn't ever deter those stalwarts in uniform from playing, for the cacophony of sound and singing remained a regular Sunday morning occurrence. During the festive season they would often start out much earlier on a Sunday morning and would begin with 'God Rest Ye Merry Gentlemen', a carol that would create an even greater abusive response often mixed with humorous comments. It must have had some positive effects though because at least one man we know of later gave up the drink and joined the Sallies!

Unfortunately, the street we lived in is no longer there for at least three quarters of it was pulled down to make way for the American Express building.

After five hours of walking I start climbing up to the high, windswept hills of Countisbury. The wind has increased to such an extent that it's getting difficult, at times, to move forward. As I come over the brow, the dramatic scene of a dark, grey-green sea and white bands of surf rolling in on the curved shoreline is displayed far below me; and there nestling in among the trees is Lynmouth. Once again, I regret not having my camera.

Finally, in the company of three lady hikers who I had met up with near the town, I walk down into Lynmouth and liaise with Rob who's sitting at a table with a couple who are obviously also walkers as they have their walking poles lodged between them.

My son has a pint of the local ale ready for me, which I tackle with relish. We sit for a while chatting about the day. Rob has already told the couple about my charity walk and where I have come from this morning. They find it hard to believe that I have walked that distance in a single day, especially via the coastal path, and were duly moved to offer us both another drink. I politely decline as I still have some hard climbing ahead of me.

After a 15-minute rest I decide to tackle the long, steep, zigzagged road alongside the unique water-powered funicular railway that leads up to Lynton. Rob has already obtained a site at the Lynton Camping and Caravan ground and we plan to meet up there. I'm quite relieved when I finally start walking towards the campervan that I've spotted parked on a site near the river. I arrive with the van already powered up and immediately head for the showers before settling down to enjoy the rest of the afternoon and evening. It's been a long, tiring day.

Today's pedometer reading: 28.9km (17.9 miles).

Notes of Interest: Lynmouth and Lynton

I suppose the most memorable event in Lynmouth's recent history would be the effects of the storm that hit the township on the 15th and 16th August, 1952. Even during the first two weeks of that month six inches of rain had fallen on Exmoor plateau; the ground underfoot had become saturated and unable to absorb the huge deluge that was about to descend on the area. From early morning the rain fell in torrents; the 9 inches (229mm) of rain on that single day caused floodwater to cascade down the northern escarpment of the moor where it merged into Lynmouth's twin rivers. The thousands of tons of water and the gathering debris caused a dam to rapidly build up in the upper West Lyn valley. Eventually the dam burst sending a huge wave of water and debris down the river; in its path was the village of Lynmouth. Within a few short, terrifying hours over 100 buildings were destroyed or seriously damaged, 28 bridges were demolished and 38 vehicles washed out to sea. Thirty-four people were to lose their lives and another 420 would be made homeless.

The Lynton/Lynmouth Cliff Railway, a water-operated funicular railway joining the twin towns of Lynton and Lynmouth was opened in 1890. This unique system operates on a water-fed counterbalance system, so as one car descends the other ascends. This unit comprises of two cars, each capable of transporting 40 passengers, joined by a continuous cable running around a pulley at each end of the incline, with the speed controlled by a brakeman travelling on each car.

While researching the 1952 flood I came across another memorable event that's worth a mention. On the 12th January 1899 a three-masted ship, the Forrest Hall, carrying 13 crew and five apprentices, was hit by a severe gale and floundering off Porlock Weir. She had already lost her steering gear and was dragging her anchor when the alarm was finally raised for the Louisa, the Lynmouth lifeboat, to go out and assist.

The terrible weather conditions made the launching of the life boat impossible. The coxswain of Louisa, Jack Crocombe, decided to take the boat by road to Porlock's sheltered harbour around the coast, and launch it from there. It was an audacious and formidable plan, for the lifeboat and its cartage weighed about 10 tons and so transporting up the steep hilly sections would be a daunting task.

It took approximately 20 horses and 100 men to start hauling the boat up the 1 in 4 gradient Countisbury Hill. Men were then sent ahead with picks and shovels to widen the road. Fifteen miles (24km) of rugged Exmoor terrain had to be traversed, but the critical stage was the descent down the steep and dangerous Porlock Hill. With horses and men pulling back on ropes to slow its progress and after demolishing part of a garden wall and felling a large tree, the lifeboat finally reached Porlock Weir at 6.30 in the morning.

Despite being cold, wet, hungry and exhausted, the crew successfully launched the vessel and after rowing for over an hour, courageously battling against heavy seas, they finally reached the stricken ship. They rescued all 13 men and five apprentices without suffering a single casualty; unfortunately four of the horses used for hauling died from exhaustion.

SAT, 5TH SEPT 2009
LYNTON - VALLEY OF THE ROCKS – COMBE MARTIN

I leave the Lynton camping site at 8am and proceed up the hill to reach the turn-off that will take me on the coastal path to Combe Martin. Lynmouth is a real gem of a place and I would love to spend more time here. It has a chequered history and was almost totally destroyed in the floods of 1952.

I take the route to the Valley of the Rocks. The surfaced track is wide and easy to walk on and the sea views are spectacular. I soon merge into the delightful woodland around Woody Bay. This scenic walk is not as enjoyable as it should be as the ground underfoot is often boggy and muddy making the going slow and slippery at times. The path rejoins the road again and I now have to choose between diverting back onto the coastal path or continuing the walk to Combe Martin by road. I know from my literature that the coastal path ahead will be too tricky and hazardous and also time-consuming so common sense prevails and I opt for the road.

From the maps I realise that the Heddon Valley is going to be a formidable walk even by road, but I am still not prepared for the long winding steepness down to the valley. Soon I'm climbing up the steep, twisting hill toward Trentishoe. Trekking through these coastal reaches of Exmoor's National Park is another unforgettable experience. The ruggedness of the coastal cliffs on my right and the extensive panoramic vista that meets my inland gaze keeps me enthralled throughout this section of the journey.

Eventually, after six hours of walking and the Atlantic's shifting breeze still toying with my tired body, I reach Combe Martin. As I approach the town centre, I'm surprised to see Rob driving out of the town, but as soon as he sees me he waves then turns around to pick me up near the town centre. Rob had been on his way to check out a caravan camping site when he saw me so we drive there together. Fortunately, it's not too far from Combe Martin and we're soon settled in for the evening.

Today's pedometer reading: 27.7km (17.2 miles).

Notes of Interest: Combe Martin

The pretty village of Combe Martin lies in a sheltered valley on the western fringe of the Exmoor National Park and is located among some of the most panoramic coastal scenery within North Devon's 'Area of Outstanding Natural Beauty'.

The name apparently derives from 'cumb' meaning 'wooded valley' and the afix from the name of FitzMartin, a Norman family who inherited the manor from one of the supporters of William the Conqueror. (It seems that old William managed to ensconce many of his cohorts into important places throughout England!)

The main street of Combe Martin, which winds along the valley, is said to be the longest main street of any village in the country. It is thought that in the 1¼ mile-long stretch there were once nine pubs all on the same side of the road, allowing drunken customers to do a pub crawl without ever having to cross over and risk being knocked down by a car.

An unusual feature of the village is the 'Pack of Cards' pub, built around 1700 by George Ley and financed, it is said, by his gambling successes. When first built it had 52 windows, 13 rooms and 4 floors, a sequence that matched a traditional pack of cards.

Just to the east of Combe Martin Bay are the Hangman cliffs. At 820ft, the Great Hangman is the highest cliff in southern Britain.

Combe Martin's Wildlife and Dinosaur Park contains a varied assortment of animals within the park and also includes the 'Domain of the Dinosaurs' attraction. In the enclosure are the scary life-size models of the mighty Tyrannosaurus.Rex, the Dilophosaurus and the Velociraptor among others.

SUN, 6TH SEPT 2009
COMBE MARTIN – WATERMOUTH – HELE – MUDDIFORD

I start walking through the elongated town of Combe Martin a little after 8am. On reaching the miniature seafront I turn left and join up with the South West Coast Path to Ilfracombe.

There are lovely views on this scenic trail, especially when leaving Watermouth, but the ground underfoot is still wet and boggy in places, making the walk slow going. I come off the coast path at Hele and decide to stay on the main road as I will soon need to divert on to the road that leads to Barnstaple. Due to weak phone signals Rob and I have difficulties contacting each other.

Unable to check on my progress Rob drives toward Barnstaple to get a signal. We finally make contact and eventually meet up for the first meal break. This session has taken me 3½ hours to complete. After the break I start out again, this time heading for the village of Muddiford.

I meet up with Rob and we go into the Muddiford Inn and Restaurant for a sample of their ale, as I have decided to end the day's walk here. Relaxing in these convivial surroundings at the end of another tiring day is just great. We check their menu and to give Rob a break from cooking we decide to eat there. The meal is delightful with a generous mixture of vegetables, roast potatoes and roast pork cooked to perfection. After the meal we relax for a while before heading off to the caravan camping ground that Rob managed to book us in to. It's a lovely campsite not too far from Barnstaple and we're soon settled in. The owner generously allows us to stay free of charge as his donation to Cancer Research UK.

Today's pedometer reading: 24.5km (13.2 miles).

Note: road mileage from point A to point B can differ considerably to miles walked on a coastal path route, depending on the winding nature of a particular section. For instance the distance from Combe Martin to Muddiford by road is only around 8 miles, whereas my pedometer recorded a figure 5½ miles in excess of that!

Notes of Interest: The Tarka Trail

The Tarka Trail covers around 180 miles in a looping route through North and mid-Devon. It's a popular pedestrian and cycle trail that goes from the rugged Atlantic Coast, running alongside the Rivers Taw and Torridge, (the two rivers of Tarka the Otter *fame) before reaching the lovely Devon Countryside and the northern slopes of Dartmoor.*

The trail takes the traveller through landscape that has changed little from those described by Henry Williamson in his classic 1927 novel Tarka the Otter. *It passes through towns such as Lynmouth, Torrington and Ilfracombe and often merges with the South West Coast Path, the Dartmoor Way and the Two Moors Way.*

The picturesque route continues through the Torridge to Torrington section, a sealed disused railway line ideal for both cyclists and walkers. It joins the South West Coast Path along the North Devon Coast, reaching Lynmouth before winding up Countisbury Hill to pass through Lorna Doone Country; a route with superb views across Exmoor's National Park.

MON, 7TH SEPT 2009
MUDDIFORD – BICKINGTON – BIDEFORD

We drive back to Muddiford village. The weather conditions were again dismal, with overcast skies and a light misty rain. I've decided to take the minor road route to Barnstaple as visibility is poor and the A39 into Barnstaple is bound to get busy coming into the rush hour. Once over the bridge I catch up with Rob in Bickington in the outer suburbs of Barnstaple and after a meal break I divert onto the Tarka Trail that leads me through to Bideford.

The Tarka Trail is a delightful route for walkers and cyclists alike. It embraces around 500 acres of spectacular North Devon coastal and country landscape. Much of the trail runs through secluded havens, ideal habitat for a variety of bird and animal life from the swift kestrel to the playful otter. In fact, it is said that the landscape has hardly changed since the twenties when Henry Williamson wrote his classic novel. From my brief time on the trail, I can well believe it.

From Torrington the trail takes me inland and I need to keep to the coast as much as possible, especially on this part of the walk. In the lovely town of Bideford we go to the tourist information centre to pick up some literature on the South West Coast Path, for tomorrow I will be heading coastward and away from the Tarka Trail. However, one day I would like to return and walk the entire trail; that would really be something!

I meet up with Rob just past the Westward Ho! roundabout and I decide to end the walk here as it's almost 2pm. We have difficulty in finding a suitable camping location so finally we drive back to Instow on the Tarka Trail where we manage to book into an attractive Caravan Club site.

Today's pedometer reading: 26.2km (16.2 miles).

Notes of Interest: Bideford

The original Old English name for this attractive seaside harbour town used to be Biddeford.

In the sixteenth century Bideford became quite an important port and maritime activity was buoyant, so much so that naval press gangs roamed the haunts of seamen, pressing the unwary into a hard, unforgiving term at sea. It was also rumoured that Sir Walter Raleigh brought the first shipment of tobacco to Bideford port; whether that's true or not is difficult to establish. Nevertheless several Bideford roads and a hill bear his name.

The thirteenth century Long Bridge, with the unusual feature of 24 different sized arches, spans the River Torridge. A New Year's Eve tradition, I believe, is to start walking or running across the Long Bridge as the St Mary's Church begins to chime the midnight hour and complete the crossing before the chiming stops.

Charles Kingsley, the author of Westward Ho! made his home in this area of North Devon. The name is quite unique as it's the only town in the country that contains an actual exclamation mark in its title!

Bideford has the dubious honour of being host to the last executions for witchcraft in England. In 1682, three women from the town: Temperance Lloyd, Mary Trembles and Susanna Edwards, were tried at the Exeter Castle Assizes. All three pleaded not guilty to the crime of witchcraft, yet despite their desperate pleas of innocence, they were hanged just outside the city at Heavitree.

TUES, 8TH SEPT 2009
WESTWARD HO! – BUCK'S CROSS – KILKHAMPTON

We leave Pyewell Farm caravan site at 6.30am and drive back to the Westward Ho! roundabout to start the day's walk. The skies again are heavy with cloud and fine, misty rain hangs in the air. I'm wondering whether to stay on the A39 or return to the South West Coast Path. This section of the coastal path is pretty strenuous and time-consuming and the recent wet weather will have made parts of the path quite slippery, thereby increasing the risk of injury, especially on steeper ground.

The estimated walking time from Westward Ho! to Hartland Quay on the coastal path is 11 hours so I'm glad to be walking on the road, for it should only take me around three hours to cover the same distance. Much of the journey this morning, however, means walking on the road's edge although on occasions there is a grass fringe wide enough to walk on. Walking on the road edge is okay when the road is straight, but when it winds and dips the fast oncoming traffic can make it quite scary at times. I have my first break at Buck's Cross before continuing on for another 7 miles for my second meal break, in an off-road parking area just past the West Country Inn.

After resting up for half an hour I walk on to Kilkhampton as I'm feeling good and find the cool weather ideal for walking. It will also get me closer to the Caravan Camping location that we had booked earlier in the day. For some reason my thoughts today dwell mainly on my sea-going days on board the SS Alcinous.

After coming through the Suez Canal I remember balmy days before reaching the Gulf of Aden, and then anchoring off Aden itself. The ship had hardly come to rest when some of the Arab boys (I think they were known to us as Pukka Wallahs) would climb aboard while others would be calling out from their dhows which would be loaded to the gunwales with produce of every kind. Of course, these weren't really 'boys' – it was just a rather demeaning term used for the Arab boat people in those days.

From there we continued to experience light winds through the Arabian Sea and Indian Ocean before arriving on the Malayan coast where we stopped at Port Swettenham, (not called that today) Penang and Singapore. We went on from there to Japan, stopping at Nagoya and Yokohama and another port, the name of which slips my mind. It was in Yokohama that I had my first experience with Japanese girls. I was with Jim Penney and a young officer apprentice whose name I can't recall. We went into a small bar off the main port road; it was a dimly lit place run by the usual Mama-san and Papa-san. The place was empty apart from three lovely looking Japanese girls sitting at the other end of the bar that the Mama-san said were her daughters. Anyway we got chatting to the girls and buying them drinks until some hours later they invited us to go home with them. Even then as a raw sixteen year old, I thought it strange that the Mama and Papa-san would allow their three 'daughters' to go off on their own at two o'clock in the morning with three young, randy foreigners!

I remember us being lead through a tangle of alleyways before stopping at what appeared to be a conglomeration of small, dimly lit, thatched huts. One of the girls opened up the door, drew back a rattan curtain and we found ourselves in this large room with what looked like rattan clad walls and three red-silk covered mattresses on a rattan-covered floor. We three nodded and winked at each other, for we had already paid a certain amount of yen to the girls, and were all thinking that this was going to be our night.

It was obvious from the start that the girls recognised us as being inexperienced in the ways of grown men and they took full advantage of it. We had already paired off before leaving the bar and it wasn't long before we were lying in a bed with our chosen girl beside us. They were happy for us to kiss and cuddle, but their behaviour changed when we started getting too horny. They would resist our advances and begin to jabber to each other in their mother tongue, with one or the other interjecting now and then with bouts of uproarious laughter. As I lay there, I remember thinking that we three were probably...no definitely... the objects of their amusement.

Every now and then the three of them would rise from the floor beds and while still jabbering away, make this sort of weak tea which they would offer to us. This sort of behaviour went on all through the short night. The following morning the girls led us back to the Port Road before kissing us goodbye. None of us had been successful in having sex with the girls. I'm sure that if we had been in separate rooms we would have made out to each other that we'd 'had it off,' just to save face; but being together in the same room kept us all honest. As we walked back to the ship we made a pact that we would not tell anyone about our experiences that night. We all knew that if the crew found out, we'd become the butt of their wicked humour for the rest of the voyage.

After finishing the walk we drove to the caravan site and were soon hooked up to power and able to relax for a while. Later I fired up my laptop and updated my diary entries and progress map.

Today's pedometer reading: 36.7km (22.7 miles).

Notes of Interest: Kilkhampton

The village of Kilkhampton in north east Cornwall was mentioned in the Domesday Book as 'Chilchetone'. The hamlet was recorded as having: 26 villagers and 23 smallholders and their livestock amounted to 50 cattle, 600 sheep, 40 goats and 20 pigs; ownership of which would incur an annual levy value of £18. It would also show that within the 'Chilchetone' boundary there were 30 acres of meadow, 20 sq. furlongs of pasture, considerable woodland and enough land for 40 ploughs. Recording all land-holding, property and livestock in the Domesday Book enabled Duke William to monitor and impose full taxes on his people

The magnificent Norman south doorway and the lofty eight-bell tower give some insight into the ancient past of Kilkhampton Church. This building is reputed to be around 450 years old although there are some historians who believe that some parts of the church originate much further back in time.

Kilkhampton Church is one of many churches dedicated to St James the Great, a saint who, it is said, would spiritually protect people on their pilgrimage to Santiago de Compostela.

The 'Camino de Santiago' has become popular with walkers throughout the world. Each route ends at the tomb of St James in Santiago de Compostela, north-west Spain.

This is the final section of the walk.

It takes another 4 weeks and 3 days to walk from **Kilkhampton** to the **Brighton Pier**. I travel through five counties and cover around 490 pedometer miles (788.5km). Some of the most stunning views were to be seen from the **South West Coast Path** including parts of the **Jurassic Coast**.

I miss my route to St Just after leaving **Connor Downs**. I finally arrive at **Land's End** – a significant stage of my walk! We divert from **Helston** to enjoy an evening with relatives at **The Lizard**.

At last the final stage! I walk a marathon 26.4 mile with Emi to reach **Brighton Pier** before walking on to my ultimate destination – **Brighton Marina**.

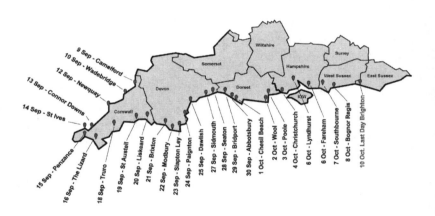

CHAPTER 25
CORNWALL

WED, 9TH SEPT 2009
KILKHAMPTON – CAMELFORD

Today I begin walking a little before 7am. The day dawns cold but clear, heralding what I hope will turn out to be a fine day. I am soon on my way out of Kilkhampton watching the campervan disappear into the distance. I begin walking briskly along the A39 toward Camelford, today's destination.

Parts of this section are a delight to walk along, especially through the wooded areas of Bush and Stratton. I liaise with Rob who's parked up a few miles further on and after a stretch and two bowls of porridge I'm out on the road again.

The road's quite hilly on this section, but it feels good getting the heart rate up and the body temperature to rise. I'm walking in the sunshine again, a refreshing change from the damp, dismal weather I've experienced almost since Carlisle. I catch up with Rob in a lay-by and after a meal of tuna and pasta I continue on toward Camelford, arriving in the town a little before 2pm. Surprisingly, I'm still feeling good despite walking more than 20 miles. Today I had another one of those periods where every sight and sound became almost surreal. Robert has located a great caravan camping site not too far away and it isn't long before we roll in to the Jenny Wells Caravan Site where we are generously invited to use their facilities free of charge. Thank you, Jenny Wells!

Today's pedometer reading: 34.9km (21.6 miles).

Notes of Interest: Camelford

The name of Camelford might possibly derive from a combination of the ancient Celtic word 'cam' meaning 'crooked stream', and the English word 'ford', although this explanation is not accepted by everyone. However, the nearby river might lend weight to the theory.

There are those who still believe that Camelford was once the famed 'Camelot', but most historians refute any such claim. However, some do believe that a real warrior king died in a bloody battle just outside Camelford at Slaughter Bridge. Could this have been Arthur? Whatever one's opinion, it's all conjecture, for the real truth is forever lost in the mists of the past.

An incident in July 1988 was to bring Camelford into national prominence when 20 tons of aluminium sulphate was poured into the wrong tank at the nearby Lowermoor Water Treatment Works on Bodmin Moor. It contaminated the water supply to the town and the surrounding area.

It was claimed to be the worst incident of its kind in British history. Michael Meacher, the environment minister at the time, was to visit Camelford later, calling the incident and its aftermath "a most unbelievable scandal".

THURS, 10TH SEPT, 2009
CAMELFORD – WADEBRIDGE

We leave Camelford at 7.15am. The weather is again cool but with clear skies.

I meet up with Rob 7.5 miles further on at a Texaco fuel station. After refuelling the van we stay in their parking site for a meal break before I continue walking. Today I decide to finish my walk early as I need to spend some time getting internet connection and I want time to make contact with the media, so we stop for the day at Wadebridge. We find a lovely touring site in a delightful setting just south of the town. The Laurels Holiday Park has given us free use of their facilities by courtesy of the management. Thank you, Edna and Ray.

We immediately catch up on our laundry, fill up with water and other necessities before spending some time on the laptop and making a few phone calls. We relax in the sun for the rest of the afternoon. Later we tune in the TV to watch the ladies football international between England and Germany.

Today's pedometer reading: 20.25km (12.5 miles).

Notes of Interest: Wadebridge

It seems that Wade was the name of the initial settlement that existed near the River Camel; it was only after a bridge was built that the name changed to Wadebridge.

In earlier days crossings were made by way of a crude ford over the river. Apparently, there used to be a small chapel on each side of the river and people would pray for a safe crossing at one of the chapels before wading across at low tide; once on the other side they would give thanks to God in the other chapel. Like me wanting to kiss the ground after touching down from a long flight!

These river trips must have been quite hazardous on occasion, for it is thought that a reverend at that time became concerned at the number of deaths of both humans and animals during the crossing, and as a result he organised the building of a bridge to span the river.

The bridge was completed in 1468 and the village of Wade soon became known as Wadebridge. The bridge has been widened on two occasions in the past and more recently in 1994, it underwent further changes including the alteration of the paving stones and the creation of a cycle track along the length of the bridge.

FRI, 11TH SEPT 2009
WADEBRIDGE

Today has been a day off from walking. The Laurels Holiday Park is a great location to spend a relaxing day.

The weather is fine with a light northerly wind, so we put out the chairs and soaked up warm rays of the sun; appreciated all the more after the damp, dreary weather we've experienced walking down this west coast. In the early evening we drive back to Tesco to buy groceries and to refuel. After the evening meal we watch some TV and retire to bed around 10.30pm.

SAT, 12TH SEPT 2009
WADEBRIDGE – NEWQUAY

Rob drops me off on the outskirts of Wadebridge near the top roundabout on the A30. The weather is cool and clear, indicating the advent of a fine day. The early morning birdsong seems louder than usual, bringing much enjoyment to my walk toward Newquay. I catch up with Rob in a lay-by over 7 miles out from Wadebridge. After a leg stretch and two helpings of porridge I study the map and decide on the route I'll take to reach Newquay. Rob then drives off toward our destination. As always, thoughts come and go as I walk, but during this morning session memories of my mother and those dark days of the war take precedence.

I recall, on one occasion, my mother telling me that there had been a period of a few months when she had no idea where four of her children were. Due to the massive demographic and logistical problems involved with shifting huge numbers of individuals around the country in those early years of the war, the authorities often lacked the time or the wherewithal to process or record information on every person's whereabouts. Mick and I had been sent to Dr Barnado's from Stepney Causeway, and when our mother tried to find where we were, nobody seemed to have any specific details with regard to our location. Soon after this, Jean had also been evacuated elsewhere without our mother being informed and it took ages for her to unearth details of her daughter's whereabouts. Vivienne had also been sent to another hospital without our mother knowing, so it must have been a period of real anguish and a living nightmare for her.

Communication was the problem. There was no phone at the place our mother had been evacuated to and her new address was often unrecorded. Unable to reach the correct department by public pay-phone, our mother would travel to the various evacuation authorities, in Vivienne's case, her previous hospital, only to be met at times with an almost disinterested or negative response.

I arrive in Newquay 2½ hours later and eventually find Rob preparing a meal in a car park just off the main road and opposite the Barracuda Building. After the meal I leave Rob to clear up while I start my walk through the town and onto the A392. About 2 miles out I turn onto the road that will eventually connect with the A30 again.

Road walking is not very inspiring, but it's the only way to cover the ground quickly and after 4 months of walking I'm eager to get through the rest of it without injury by taking the easiest route available. If I was on the South West Coast Path it would take a considerable period of time to cover a terrain made more strenuous and precarious due to the long periods of wet weather. For instance, the distance covered over 3 days of walking on the road would, on certain sections, take 7 to 8 days on the coastal path. So with a little reservation and some reluctance I carry on walking on the open road. I catch up with the campervan again about 5 miles out of Newquay near a place with the strange sounding name of Monkey Tree Holiday Park. I decide to end the days walk here for I'm feeling hot and very, very tired.

Today's pedometer reading: 32.6km (20.2 miles).

Notes of Interest: Newquay

It seems that the Newquay area could have been occupied by late Iron Age or Bronze Age people according to archaeological discoveries. One of those discoveries was a coarse earthenware burial urn that was said to contain the remains of a Bronze Age chieftain; however, I cannot find further evidence of this to confirm its authenticity.

Then in 1996 an Iron Age neck-ring, which had gathered dust in a shed for almost a decade after being found in a Newquay garden, was finally shown to archaeologists from Cornwall County Council's Historic Environment Service. It was authenticated as a neck-ring dating to the first century AD (The early Romano-Briton period).

The natural protection from the curved headland would have probably encouraged people to settle here, and although there is no mention of the small fishing hamlet in the Domesday Book, a local house, now known as 'Treninnick Tavern' was apparently mentioned.

By the fifteenth century, the village was thought to have been known as 'Towan Blystra', 'Towan' being Cornish for sandhill or dune.

It wasn't until 1439 after funds became available that a new quay was built. The popularity of the new quay was such that the location soon became known as Newquay

The arrival of passenger trains in the nineteenth century was the catalyst for growth of the former fishing village and it wasn't long before a number of major hotels began springing up within the developing resort.

By the following century, Newquay had become renowned for its pilchards; however, pilchard fishing is no longer viable for the shoals have long since gone. Newquay is widely regarded as the surf capital of the UK and is now firmly established as a leader in this popular sport.

SUN, 13TH SEPT 2009
BLACKWATER – CAMBORNE – CONNOR DOWNS

I start walking from the lay-by at yesterday's pick-up point. It looks like it's going to be another lovely day, so I need to get as many miles under my belt before the afternoon heat begins to affect me.

I meet up with Rob about 7 miles further on in a lay-by near Blackwater. After a meal and a stretch I walk on for another few miles finally catching up with Rob again in a slip road near the turnoff to Camborne. After a break I walk on for another session but after a further 3 miles or so the heat of the day finally gets to me, and I end the day's walk at Connor Downs, about 2 miles from Hayle. Rob has already located a Caravan Club camping site so after doing some shopping at a Lidl store we travel to the lovely grounds of the Godrevy Caravan Club site where we get connected up and are able to relax for the rest of the day.

Today's pedometer reading: 33.3km (20.6 miles).

MON, 14TH SEPT 2009
CONNOR DOWNS - HAYLE – ST IVES

We leave Godrevy Park Caravan Club site a little before 7am and drive back to the lay-by where I had finished yesterday's walk. The cold temperature and clear skies give promise to another fine day as I walk into Hayle. A publicity board in the town centre advertises the fact that the industrial revolution started here in Hayle. Must check that out sometime!

Once over the bridge spanning the river Hayle I find a track that leads me around the estuary, past the West Cornwall Golf Club and into Carbis Bay. From here I stay on the coast road until I find a public footpath that takes me through a wooded area and under a bridge to suddenly emerge onto the golden beach front of St Ives. I meet up with Rob in the local Tesco car park and after a meal break I walk through this very picturesque town.

The view of the sandy beach and harbour from on top of the hill is quite something and it gives rise to yet another feeling of regret in having to move on so quickly and not having the opportunity to see more of another very attractive town. I walk out with the intention of linking up with the coastal road that will lead me to St Just, but somehow I miss the turn-off and eventually have to detour a couple of extra miles in order to reach it. I am so angry at missing the route; a blind, mentally deranged foreigner would have found it with ease! I try to call Rob to explain my delay, but find my phone has no signal; it's been the same since leaving St Ives so I reckon Rob might be getting a little worried.

I walk on for a couple or more hours savouring the delights of the Cornish countryside when a motorcyclist coming towards me suddenly stops by my side. He asks if I am the Around England Walker. I assure him of this, although my hi-vis sign-written jacket must have given him a clue. He informs me that my son, who's waiting at the Gurnard's Head Inn, is concerned about my non-arrival. Its little events like this that really lift my spirits. Here's a big guy, a complete stranger to Rob and me, who has volunteered to drive back along the coast road to find me. His willingness to go out of his way to help is typical of the attitude of many of the people we have encountered during the walk. I thank him and he turns around to zoom back to the Gurnard's Head Inn to reassure Rob that I haven't been attacked by some stranger or fallen over a cliff but am actually just an hour away from reaching the Inn.

I am relieved to finally walk into the Gurnard's Head Inn. The place is very busy for many other walkers have congregated here and mouth-watering meals are being served to the hungry. Unfortunately Colin, the guy on the motorbike, has already left so I haven't the opportunity to thank him again. After a rest up and a refreshing shandy I continue walking for another 4 miles before stopping for the day. I'm now only 2 miles from St Just.

It's been a big day! We find a lovely caravan camping site near Bottalack and are soon powered up for the evening.

Today's pedometer reading: 37.2km (23.1 miles).

Notes of Interest: St Ives

It was the arrival of an Irish Saint in the fifth century that attributed in legend to the town's origin. The name St Ives derives from this event and the name of the saint can still be seen in the church in St Ives.

During the Prayer Book rebellion of 1549, a treacherous act was thought to have taken place. It happened that the town's portreeve (port warden), John Payne, was invited out to lunch by the English

Provost Marshal who was visiting St Ives. The official requested that John Payne should arrange to have the gallows erected during the course of the lunch. After the meal John Payne and the Provost Marshal walked down to the gallows whereupon the portreeve was immediately compelled to mount the platform. John Payne was hanged there and then, without the benefit of a trial. His crime was being a 'busy rebel' of the Prayer Book rebellion.

Pilchard fishing was crucial to the St Ives economy and it became one of the most important fishing ports on the north coast. The greatest number of pilchards ever taken in one seine was in 1868, when 5,600 hogsheads (over 15 million fish) were caught.

During the advent of the railway in 1877 there came a new industry; the Victorian holidaymakers. The railway which winds along the cliffs and bays has now become a tourist attraction in itself.

In 1939, Barbara Hepworth and other artists began to settle in St Ives, attracted by its quaint and unique beauty. The Barbara Hepworth Museum and her sculpture garden can be found at the Tate St Ives and it was her wish that her work should remain on public display in perpetuity.

TUES, 15TH SEPT 2009
PENDEEN - ST JUST – LAND'S END – PENZANCE

I start walking from Pendeen at 7am. Soon I am strolling through the lovely town of St Just and heading out toward another significant stage of my walk... Land's End! Less than two hours later I finally reach England's most westerly point. I've been longing for this day! I knew that once I'd reached Land's End the only thing to stop me completing the walk will be a broken leg... or the world coming to an end!

We stay in Land's End long enough to have a few photos taken before starting my walk back out on the A30, then onto the road for Penzance. A few miles on I stop for another break before setting off to walk through Newlyn and onto the lovely seafront promenade of Penzance. I'm now truly on the south coast. At last I'm really on the way home! It's a great feeling. Throughout my journey I would often remind myself about how lucky I was to be physically capable of doing this walk. I'd think of those with physical impairment or those struck down with some illness leaving them unable to run, ride a bike or even to walk. This thinking triggers thoughts about my sister, Vivienne.

Viv hadn't been born with gammy legs; the auto-immune disease was probably just lying there, ready to pounce as it did when she was around 20 months old. It was originally diagnosed as being tuberculosis and it wasn't until she was around twelve or thirteen that they discovered that she actually had rheumatoid arthritis in both knees. In fact, according to the medical notes, it was recognised as Still's Disease or juvenile idiopathic arthritis (JIA), the most common form of persistent arthritis in children. The end result of years of treatment in various hospitals and sanatoriums throughout England is that she has been left with one permanently stiff leg and very little movement in the other. Viv never complains though and seldom mentions those days but will talk quite freely when asked.

Carol sitting with Vivienne on her hospital bed

I remember her describing her hospital life on Hayling Island, Hampshire; she must have been around twelve then because I accompanied my mother on one of her visits when I was around fourteen. Viv told me that she was regarded as being an 'old timer' by the staff due to the number of years they knew she'd spent in hospitals around the country.

She admits that she was a bit of a troublemaker in those days and would encourage the other kids in the ward to play up. Sometimes when she got too naughty the staff would wheel her bed out onto a nearby groyne overlooking the sea. My sister said that she didn't regard it as punishment as they would only put her out there on relatively good weather days and would leave her there until the other children in the ward had settled down or were asleep.

Viv said she just loved lying there listening to the sound of the sea and occasionally they would forget to bring her in and she'd lie gazing up at the stars until a distraught nurse would remember her and bring her back into the ward.

As I walked I remembered Vivienne telling me something of interest about one of the hospitals she was in; she couldn't recall which hospital it was as she was quite young at the time, but she thinks it may have been Stanmore Hospital in Middlesex. They used to give the kids 'tow rag' to wipe their bottoms after they'd been to the toilet. After Vivienne explained what a tow rag was I was quite intrigued as I'd never heard of it before this, so I did some research on the subject. Tow is created from hemp, a soft, durable fibre from plants of the Cannabis (marijuana) genus. Hemp was used in the manufacture of rope during the age of sailing ships. During that era fibre from the hemp could be teased out to form a sort of rag; this was called tow and it was often used to staunch wounds by naval surgeons and then thrown away.

Although paper was available in those days it was relatively expensive and prone to disintegrating due to dampness over long periods at sea, so tow rag was used by sailors to wipe themselves after toileting. However, it still had to be used sparingly so sailors would have to wash the tow rag out with sea water and keep it for further use. As much of our modern-day colloquialisms stem from our seafaring past it is likely that this is where the derogatory term 'tow rag' originally came from, although many also believe that the insult refers to being like a tramp or vagrant who was often seen with a rag wrapped around his feet – hence the words 'toe rag'.

After learning all this I was quite amazed to think that patients at the hospital were made to use tow rag in the 1940s!

I stroll along the promenade toward the marina where I find the campervan in the large car park close to the Penzance Sailing Club. We soon locate a caravan site near Marazion where the proprietor kindly gives us the site free of charge. A special 'Thank You' to the Wheal Rodney Holiday Park!
Today's pedometer reading: 34km (21.1 miles).

Notes of Interest: Penzance

The name Penzance probably derives from the Cornish words 'Penn Sans', meaning holy headland. It is believed the name comes from the ancient chapel of St Anthony's that was built upon the western headland, but this theory has little substance.

The plague was to hit Penzance in the summer of 1578 when recorded deaths were estimated to be about 10% of the village population at that time; 70 years later the plague returned to the village once again.

Its position at the far south-west corner of England made it vulnerable to frequent raiding attacks by foreign fleets during the past centuries.

The threat from the Spanish Armada of 1588 had all but disappeared when a Spanish force, under Don Carlos de Amesquita, is supposed to have landed troops in Cornwall. The Spanish raided Penzance and other Cornish settlements and proceeded to burn them down after seizing vital supplies. It is said that after the raids the Spanish held a mass before sailing away into the blue.

On 1 November 1755, a tsunami struck the Cornish coast caused by the Lisbon earthquake over 1,000 miles away. After an extremely low tide, the sea came in at a frightening speed, with waves building up to eight feet above normal, before ebbing away again. However, little damage was recorded.

In 1849, a government-led report recorded that there were 121 gas lamps used to light the town at night from October to March each year, although they remained unlit during a full moon. Fresh water was supplied to the village by six public pumps and as there was no sewage system, a refuse cart was used to collect the waste.

The railway system finally went through to Cornwall making travel easier for tourists wanting to take advantage of the mild climate of Penzance.

The town was in its heyday in the mid-nineteenth century and was noted for having a more temperate climate than most other resorts around England.

WED, 16TH SEPT 2009
PENZANCE – HELSTON – LIZARD POINT

We leave the Wheal Rodney camping site early as we have to drive back to the Penzance Marina parking grounds to begin my day's walk. At 7.10am I'm back on the road and walking out of Penzance in the direction of Helston. We are both looking forward to getting to Helston because after the day's walk we'll drive down from there to Lizard Point, the most southern point in England to see my brother, sister and cousin, who are staying there for a few days. It will be great being back with my relatives who are expecting us. We'll no doubt enjoy a great evening with the comforting knowledge that both of us can lie-in the following morning as we'll be having the day off.

As I walk out of Penzance I realise I should call in to see a guy called Gary, a friend of Pam and Bob's, but it's really too early in the morning to pay a visit so I carry on walking. Rob has stopped about 6½ miles further on in a church car park. (Not like Rob, for it's usually pub premises he aims for!) After the meal break I continue on the A394 reaching the outskirts of Helston two hours later.

I intend to carry on into Helston until I reach the road to Lizard Point, but on the way down the hill I notice the Lidl store and decide to end my day's walk here. I call Rob on the phone to join me at the Lidl car park and we go into the store to buy supplies to take down to my brother's place. Less than an hour later we drive into Lizard Point, where we receive a great welcome from Fred, Jean and Chrissie. It's great to relax after a lovely meal and we enjoy a lively evening together. We finally get to bed around 1pm.

Today's pedometer reading: 41.39km (25.87 miles).

Notes of Interest: Lizard Point

Lizard Point is the most southerly point on mainland Great Britain at 49°57' N. with the exception of the Scilly isles. The 'Lizard' title might be a corruption of the Cornish name 'Lys Ardh', meaning 'high court', but there is no substantive data to back this up.

There has been a lighthouse at Lizard Point since 1751; it's been a saviour to any shipping navigating this treacherous coastline, for it was once regarded as the 'Graveyard of Ships', a place where hazards like the 'Man 'o War' rocks were waiting to claim a victim.

It is thought that the very first sighting of the Spanish Armada was here at Lizard Point when at 3pm on 29th July 1588 the formidable invasion fleet of 120 ships appeared over the horizon.

One of the greatest rescue operations carried out by the RNLI was about to unfold on 17th March 1907, when the 12,000-tonne liner SS Suevic hit the Maenheere Reef near Lizard Point.

Despite dense fog and the terrible weather conditions, the RNLI volunteers battled turbulent seas as they manned their oars and defied the perils for over 16 weary hours to rescue 456 passengers including many young children and babies.

THURS, 17TH SEPT 2009
LIZARD POINT

This morning we have a lie in before having a leisurely breakfast with the family. We catch up with some washing then laze around for the rest of the morning.

After lunch Fred takes us out for a drive to a picturesque village near Helford. Unfortunately his Sat-Nav leads us on a sightseeing tour around remote country lanes to get there. We stop at a lovely old local pub for a drink then make our way back to Lizard Point. Later we help Fred paint his fence, although it was really just him and Rob doing most of the work with me giving some unwanted advice every now and then! After dinner we chat and watch TV for a while, but for some reason I feel desperately tired and retire to bed about 9pm.

FRI, 18TH SEPT 2009
HELSTON – CARNON DOWNS –TRURO

Rob and I are up at 6.30am. After breakfast we leave our 'rellies' to sleep on while we drive out of Lizard Point and back to Lidl's car park in Helston. It's well after 8am before I begin walking out of the town toward Truro. I catch up with Rob about 7 miles further on in a slip road just past Longdowns village. I stop for my usual break before continuing on the road to Truro. We had a good time at Lizard Point with Jean, my sister, my brother Fred and cousin Chrissie; Rob also enjoyed the break, especially being with relatives he hadn't seen for a number of years. It got me thinking about the discussion we'd had last night about our proposed trip to France next year to sprinkle our mother's ashes on our father's grave.

Our father

Our father is buried in a military graveyard in Le Grand-Luce, a village about 27 kilometres south-east of Le Mans. I went there about 14 years ago with my elder brother. The graveyard was in immaculate condition compared to the adjoining communal cemetery, which appeared at that time to be quite unkempt. I remember walking slowly along the recently mowed, neatly trimmed lawn strips that divided each row of whitewashed headstones while we searched for our father's grave. There was a monotonous similarity to the epitaphs that adorned the headstones and it soon became clear that many of the men buried here were aged between 18 and 25.

When we located our father's grave the headstone pronounced his age of death as being 35, the oldest throughout the cemetery. In the spring of 2012 we plan to hire a minivan and hopefully, with all the family siblings, travel to the graveyard at Le Grand-Luce to do what our mother would have wished and have her ashes scattered onto her husband's grave. I would imagine that the graveside visit will be a sombre time for us, but aside from that solemn task we'll make it a holiday occasion – I'm sure it's what our parents would have wanted. With a full contingent of family members including a cousin or two and maybe one or two grown grandchildren, it should turn into a memorable occasion.

A few miles on I pass Carnon Downs and its large caravan park before reaching another pretty village with the strange name of Playing Place. I have my second break here before walking on for another 3 miles to reach Truro. After drawing some money out of a cash machine in the town we drive up a hill and relax for a while in the beer garden of a quaint pub. It's not long before we are driving back to Carnon Downs' caravan touring grounds where we are given a free site for the night. Thank you Carnon Downs!

Today's pedometer reading: 30.96km (19.22 miles).

Notes of Interest: Truro

The origin of Truro's name is questionable. The most plausible is that it derives from the Cornish 'tri-veru' meaning three rivers, but recognised authorities tend to question this notion although no alternative explanation exists.

The earliest recorded archaeological signs of permanent settlement in the Truro area seem to suggest that it originated from Norman times, but it's more than likely that a hamlet of sorts existed here hundreds of years before.

Truro was an important port from around the start of the fourteenth century. It also found prosperity from the fishing industry. However, as with many other villages and towns throughout Britain, the Black Death arrived and the fear of the dreaded disease caused a mass exodus from the town. The subsequent trade recession left the town in an impoverished and neglected state.

Truro is believed to have prospered greatly during the eighteenth and nineteenth centuries, and with a flourishing mining industry the town soon became the most popular location for wealthy mine owners and others. *Truro was eventually thought of as the sophisticated centre for the county's aristocratic society.*

The Great Western Railway arrived and with it came access to many parts of England, including a direct line to London. It wasn't long before Truro had its very own cathedral and a year later it was granted city status by Queen Victoria.

Truro continued to prosper throughout the twentieth century despite the decline of the mining industry, but, like many other towns and cities it faces an uncertain future.

SAT, 19TH SEPT 2009
TRURO – ST AUSTELL

We manage to get away early from the Carnon Downs camping site and drive back to Truro town centre. I start walking out of Truro at 7.12am. The weather is ideal as it is quite cool with overcast skies.

I make good time on the road with my feet synchronising to the rhythmic beat of the music from my MP3 player. The road is generally 'walker friendly' with recently mowed grass verges to walk on. I am enjoying the Cornish countryside with its broad, freshly ploughed fields lying like brown carpets amidst the variegated green patchwork of newly sprouting crops such as young barley. I travel through a delightful wooded area on my approach into Grampound before heading out of the village and into the countryside once more. The van is parked in a slip road a little way past Grampound. I check my pedometer and realise that I have walked over 8 miles in 2¼ hours. After the break I was soon on my way again.

On the outskirts of St Austell I decide to stay on the main road rather than go into the town centre. It isn't long before I locate Rob who's waiting for me in a Tesco car park. He has already found and booked a decent caravan touring site that's 2 miles further on and by 2pm we're settled in for the rest of the day.

Today's pedometer reading: 26 km. (16.1 miles).

Notes of Interest: St Austell

St Austell is one of the biggest towns in Cornwall and its early prosperity derived from the mining industry. However, in the eighteenth century massive deposits of kaolin (white clay) were discovered by a chemist from Devon. (I've read that the word 'kaolin' originates from the village of Gaoling in Jiangxi province, China.) It was to herald in a new and prosperous future for the town in the extraction of china clay from the deposits.

The successful industry created more job opportunities, resulting in an expanding population that in turn attracted more shops and businesses to open up in the area

The clay industry has now been in decline for some time due to cheaper alternative sources available worldwide, but another development has made St Austell an important tourist location: it's the Eden Project.

The Eden Project: The main purpose behind Eden is to remind us of how dependent we are on the natural world. The project is located in a reclaimed kaolinite pit, that is about 5 kilometres (3 miles) from St Austell, and it is here that you will find the world's largest greenhouse.

Two enclosures consisting of adjoining domes embrace huge artificial biomes where you will find plants that are collected from all around the world, including houseplant species.

The first dome emulates the warm, damp conditions of the tropics whereas the second dome has more of a Mediterranean climate. The massive domes have been created by using hundreds of hexagonal and pentagonal, plastic cells that are inflated and supported by a network of steel frames. The project took 2½ years to build and was opened to the public on 17th March 2001.

SUN, 20TH SEPT 2009
ST AUSTELL – LOSTWITHIEL – LISKEARD

I start walking out from the Tesco parking lot at 7am. As I stride out of St Austell the climate is cool and overcast, ideal for walking today.

I regret not having visited the Eden Project as it's a something I have always wanted to see. Trouble is I'm too tired to go sightseeing after walking all day and I'm always too eager to get an early start in the morning. But perhaps one day I'll get back here.

About 3 miles out from St Austell I'm confronted with a long hill. Although it's still quite cool it doesn't take long for my body temperature to rise and my heart rate to increase as I tackle the gradient.

I meet up with Rob about 8 miles further on in a little town called Lostwithiel. After the break I carry on for another 6 miles stopping for an additional short break near East Taphouse. I quickly resume walking and eventually arrive in the town of Liskeard where I finish walking for the day.

After joining up with Rob, we go into a pub to watch the big match between Manchester United and Manchester City. Afterwards we search for some time for a suitable caravan site and finally manage to find the Tencreek Farm location. We are soon set up and very grateful to be given the site free of charge.

A week or so before starting my walk I had read a book about Krakatoa or Krakatau to the Indonesians. Why it should have emerged into my thinking today I have no idea; but then many thoughts come and go at random during a day's walking session. I decide I will enter something about this particular occurrence in today's diary entry as I reckon it's a good read. However, as much of my knowledge on the specifics of the event is sketchy I decide this evening to do some research on the subject.

Krakatoa is located in the Sunda Straits between the islands of Java and Sumatra off the south western coast of Indonesia. In May in 1883 a series of eruptions began which would continue for around three months, culminating, on August 27th, in a colossal explosion that blew the island apart. It became one of the largest eruptions in recorded history. The enormity of the explosion was so great that they say it was heard over 3,000km (1,860 miles) away in Western Australia.

The tsunamis that followed were believed to have been over 30 metres (100ft) high in places and of the reported 36,000 deaths recorded at that time, 33,000 or more would have died as a result of the tsunamis. There are some sources who believe the death toll could well have been much higher for there was no definitive knowledge as to the fate of those living in the many villages scattered around the area.

The blast from the final devastating explosion radiated out from Krakatoa with incredible velocity around the globe, to be recorded on barographs all over the world. Barometric pressure recordings continued to be registered for a number of days; it would show that the reverberations of the shockwave from that final cataclysmic explosion would have travelled around the globe six or seven times.

Krakatoa Island exploded with the force of 100 to 150 megatons and ejected approximately 21km3 (5.0 cu mi) of rock, ash and pumice.

Even bigger was the Mount Tambora eruption in 1815. The facts and figures relating to this event are sketchy as media attention was almost non-existent in those days. Nevertheless, it is estimated that around 10,000 people died from the immediate blast and more than 60,000 were killed from the subsequent tsunamis along with the ensuing effects from the volcanic fallout resulting in suffocation or starvation. The Mount Tambora eruption ejected an estimated 100 to 160 km³ (24 to 38 cubic miles) of debris.

The only significant modern-day volcanic eruption that springs to mind is that of Mount St Helens, a volcano located in Skamania County, Washington, USA.

The catastrophic eruption occurred on May 18, 1980, at 8.32am. It was to become the most destructive volcanic event in the history of the United States. The 24-megaton blast caused the destruction of 250 homes, 47 bridges, 15 miles (24km) of railways and 185 miles (298 km) of highway and the deaths of 57 people.

Yet the Mt St Helens eruption that ejected 2.9km³ of debris was tiny compared to Krakatoa that ejected an estimated 21km³ of debris; and yet by comparison, even the Krakatoa eruption was small compared to the Mount Tambora eruption of 1815 that ejected an estimated 160km³.

If we go back further in time, to around 71,000 to 75,000 years ago, an eruption occurred that would make all later events seem miniscule by comparison.

Recognised as one of the Earth's largest known eruptions, the Toba super-eruption occurred at Lake Toba, Sumatra, Indonesia, producing an estimated 2,800km³ (671 cubic miles) of ejected material which included the pyroclastic flow.

This is widely accepted as being the largest explosive eruption anywhere on Earth, probably since the history of mankind and it was to bring about a massive climatic change throughout the world.

It is believed that 800km³ of the total amount of ejected material might have fallen as ash and the ensuing pyroclastic flows of the eruption are said to have destroyed a vast area of land. It is thought that the tephra layer (fragmental material ejected explosively from a volcano such as ash and other deposits) were hundreds of metres deep around the main vent.

Although the eruption took place in Indonesia, the fallout of ejected material was deposited over the entire South Asian continent. Much of the tephra layer was around 6 inches deep although one site in central India, the Toba layer was estimated to have a depth of over 3m (10ft). This massive fallout would have probably decimated India's populations to a large extent.

It is thought that around 10,000 million metric tons of sulphuric acid might have been ejected into the atmosphere resulting in long-lasting, deadly fallout of acid rain.

The Mount Toba eruption is said to have started an estimated six-year-long volcanic winter and 1000-year-long instant Ice Age with temperatures colder than during the last glacial period. Such a sudden calamity would have eliminated a major proportion of the human population of that time. Genetic evidence suggests that human population fell to about 10,000 adults between 50-100,000 years ago and this might well have been from the consequences of the eruption.

What I find interesting is that many experts believe that a population bottleneck might have occurred at that time due to the extremely hostile weather conditions.

The Toba aftermath became a watershed with regard to human genealogy and various scientific observations have emerged following the finding of human remains, tools and such like in undisturbed tephra layer from the Toba eruption.

One theory is that the Toba aftermath might have resulted in abrupt adaptations being forced onto the surviving population thereby causing a rapid evolutionary process; a development beginning around 70,000 years ago rather than a natural evolutionary process spanning a million years or more.

In other words, to adapt to the harsher conditions the remaining human population would have needed to become more resilient, more inter-reactive, more innovative and more alert than ever before; qualities that would have produced a stronger and faster genetic drift within the human species.

You could say that the human race might have been even dumber than it is today if the Toba eruption hadn't happened.

Interesting eh! However, the bad news is that an eruption of that magnitude might well occur again one day.

Today's pedometer reading: 29.8km (18.5 miles).

Notes of Interest: Liskeard

The ancient market town of Liskeard is in south-east Cornwall. To the south, in easy reaching distance, is the lovely Cornish coast, while to the north is the vast expanse known as Bodmin Moor. The origin of the name Liskeard is quite obscure but 'Lis' is said to derive from the word 'court' and 'keard' might have been spelt 'kerret', possibly the name of a chief or leader of the settlement. Yet according to the Domesday Book the name of the town was originally 'Liscarret'.

Although the mining industry is said to have played an important role in the town's past development, it is the tourist industry that has become significant in Liskeard's modern economy. On the edge of Bodmin Moor there is a Holy Well enclosed within a granite baptistery. Its original use, it is said, was to treat the insane by tossing them up and down until their sanity returned.

I bet their success rate wasn't too impressive!

MON, 21ST SEPT 2009
LISKEARD – TORPOINT – BRIXTON

I walk out of Liskeard around 7am. The A38 has little early morning traffic but it soon becomes uncomfortably busy. I take a public footpath to get off the road. The path continues alongside the A38 for some time but then veers away. I climb over a stile into an open field where a large herd of cows eye me with little interest as I thread my way among them. With wet shoes and socks due to heavy early morning dew on the long grass I make my way back to the main road.

About 7 miles on from Liskeard I turn onto the road that leads down to Torpoint and the river ferry. It's mid-afternoon before Rob and I meet up in Torpoint and after a meal break we decide to cross over on the ferry today as we are finding it difficult to find a decent caravan camping site on this side of the river. It will also give me a better walking start tomorrow.

Once over the river we drive through to Brixton where we find an ideal caravan park nearby. We meet Johnny, the warden here, who gives us a warm welcome and invites us to use the Brixton Caravan Park facilities free of charge. During the evening Rob wants to visit the local pub, The Fox Hound. We go there together and I chat with the friendly patrons while supping on a small shandy. I leave pretty early as the day's walk has tired me and I need to get to bed.

Today's pedometer reading: 31.68km (19.67 miles).

Notes of Interest: Torpoint

Reaching the River Tamar from the western suburbs of Plymouth a chain ferry will take foot passengers across the mouth of the river to Torpoint. Cars can also cross by ferry from here. This little town of Torpoint is sometimes referred to as the 'gateway to Cornwall and the west'.

Torpoint eventually became a town in the early nineteenth century, although there are signs of much earlier habitation in areas near the river.

The first chain ferry started in 1832. Today there are three of these unique vessels carrying people and goods across the river.

The Torpoint Ferry crossing is one of the busiest vehicular river-crossing ferry services in the UK, with over 1½ million vehicles transported this way each year.

CHAPTER 26
SOUTH DEVON

TUES, 22ND SEPT 2009
PLYMOUTH – ELBURTON – MODBURY

We drive back to the Torpoint Ferry Terminal at 6.30am to start the day's walk. It seems to take ages to walk through Plymouth and connect with the A379 to Kingsbridge. I'm hot and tired by the time I catch sight of Rob who's parked up in Elburton. After a change of clothing, a meal and a stretch, I continue on toward Modbury, today's destination. It's during this session that my thoughts turn to my older sister, Jean.

The other evening during our stay at Lizard Point, we all began to reminisce about the past, as we often do when we are gathered together. Jean told me of the time she tried to kill me. I'm sure she was kidding, but she laughingly explained that it was true.

Apparently Jean was around 2 years old when she was playing out in the garden with me, a 2 to 3-month-old baby. Our mother had given Jean her version of the incident because my sister was too young to remember. It seems that our mother heard me screaming out in the garden and rushed out to find Jean shaking the pram violently and her baby lying there with blood on its face and bawling its head off. I think it's only Jean's version when she says that she was 'dead jealous of this new baby who was getting all the attention and so tried to do me in'. Jean has always been a gentle, loving person so I can't believe her claim that she was trying to kill me. But she will bring the story up on occasions when we are together and she insists that she really had murder on her mind and, what's more, she's always highly amused about the thought of it.

Of course, I find her version hard to believe; however, while I'm walking I remember thinking that I might have second thoughts about accepting her next invitation for an evening meal... if it means having to stay overnight!

I walk down the steep hill into Modbury around noon and finish my day's walk here. We drive out of the town to find a suitable caravan touring site. Two miles out we arrive at the Broad Park Caravan Club site and are soon hooked up for our brief overnight stay.

Today's pedometer reading: 24.48km (15.2 miles).

Notes of Interest: Modbury

It is believed that the name Modbury originates from the Saxon for meeting place (moot burgh). But there are other theories relating to the name's origin.

The Black Death took its toll and as a consequence the population of the town was greatly reduced.

Modbury was the site of two significant battles between the Royalists and Cromwell's Parliamentarians. It is thought that the first battle was in December 1642, when a contingent of Royalists saw off a small band of Parliamentarian forces. The second confrontation was in February 1643 and involved around 8,000 Parliament forces who made a determined attack the 2,000 Royalist defenders. The Royalists finally withdrew their forces into the town before making a full retreat down Runaway Lane.

The conflict at Modbury would help bring about the end for the siege of Plymouth.

By 1801, a good percentage of the population of Modbury were engaged in the wool trade, but mechanisation of the industry caused a down-turn in the town's economy. From the mid-1820s workers from Modbury and other small towns and villages would seek employment in the larger cities or turn their sights to a better life overseas.

WED, 23RD SEPT 2009
KINGSBRIDGE – TORCROSS – SLAPTON LEY

My alarm goes off at 5.30am as usual. It's darker outside these days making it harder to rise from the bed. The TV goes on and as I get up to go to the ablutions, Rob comes down quietly from his bunk and puts on the kettle. Fifteen minutes later and still bleary-eyed we watch the news in silence, while munching on some toast. We start preparing for another day on the road. Outside, the darkness of the morning shows a hint of grey light in the eastern sky as we drive down to yesterday's finishing point. The steel-grey, shadowy dawn accompanied by a misty rain greets me as I step from the van to start my day's walk. The route I'm on is quite perilous due to the winding nature of the road and the ever-thickening mist. I have to stay alert throughout, and fervently hope that the approaching motorists are doing the same.

I meet Rob at Kingsbridge 8.5 miles further on. After the usual break I continue on the A-road for a time until I find a public footpath that takes me all the way through to Stokeham where I find Rob preparing bacon and salad sandwiches. After the meal I carry on walking on a footpath to Torcross, then along the delightfully scenic causeway of Slapton Ley. I decide to finish my day's walk here as it's almost 2.30pm and I am feeling pretty shattered. We drive back to a Caravan Club site that we had driven past near Torcross and we are soon booked in and hooked up for another overnight stay.

Today's pedometer reading: 26.9km (16.8 miles).

Notes of Interest: Slapton Ley

Walking along Slapton Ley was one of the memorable periods of my journey. The 1.5 mile lake situated to my left is said to be one of the largest natural freshwater lakes in the South West of England and is part of a nature reserve. It is also a 'Site of Special Scientific Interest' that protects the rare species and their habitat within the reserve. Other creatures including badgers and otters, as well as rare flora, can be found in this wildlife haven. Unfortunately the beach which protects the Ley from the encroaching waves is continually under threat. It's a warning that this beautiful location could be lost to the ravages of nature in time to come.

Slapton Sands Tragedy: Slapton Sands brings to mind the wartime tragedy that took place there in the early hours of the 28th April, 1944. Slapton's isolated beaches of gravel, and the shallow freshwater lake together with wide grassy dune areas seemed a perfect theatre for the American forces to simulate practice exercises in readiness for the D-Day landings in Normandy in the coming weeks. Exercise Tiger was the name of the rehearsal operation and eight Landing Ship Tanks (LST's) and other naval vessels were to take part in the event.

It was an exercise that would turn into tragedy. German E-boats that were patrolling the coast around Lyme Bay observed the unusually busy night-time sea activity and soon took advantage of the situation. In the early hours of the morning they began attacking the vessels as they advanced and retreated from the beaches; by the end of the landing rehearsals, 946 American servicemen had lost their lives.

This exercise resulted in becoming one of the great tragedies of World War II with American soldiers and sailors dying needlessly due to the confusion arising from these unsuspected and unseen prolonged attacks. Unfortunately friendly fire from a ship might well have been the cause of a proportion of those casualties as live shells were directed on the beach causing more mayhem. It is said that the military hierarchy wanted to 'harden the men by exposing them to real battle conditions'.

The fiasco became one of the military's best-kept secrets until it was revealed to the world well over 40 years later.

A 32-ton Sherman tank lost in the practice landings was later recovered from the sea bed and is now displayed at Slapton Sands in memory of all the American servicemen who tragically lost their lives.

THURS, 24TH SEPT 2009
SLAPTON LEY - DARTMOUTH – PAIGNTON

The orange flare of a September dawn greets me as Rob and I part company at Slapton Ley. I start to walk on a track alongside the beach... destination Dartmouth.

The climb up from the seafront is long, winding and quite steep at times, and although the early morning temperature is much colder than previous mornings I am soon sweating. I quickly realise that I am overdressed. Rob passes me about this time and I phone to ask him to stop where convenient so that I can discard some clothing. Looking back as I climb, there are some great views of Slapton Ley and further along the cliftop there is a bird's eye view of lovely Blackpool Sands.

I stop again just out of Dartmouth for my first meal break. We then take the ferry over the River Dart before continuing the walk toward Paignton. As I walk away from the river various thoughts are pushed aside when recollections of another ferry trip begin to emerge. They are thoughts of another time and in a fraction of a second I was back on the Mersey ferry heading for Birkenhead.

After its 3½-month maiden voyage SS Alcinous was to be put into dry-dock. Teething problems had arisen and could only be attended to with the vessel out of the water. I had gone back to Brighton for a week but was contracted to be back at a given date to help other crew members with the many menial jobs that needed to be done around the ship, while contracted tradesmen attended to other tasks. I had got used to the ways of the 'Scouser' while on the ship and felt comfortable around them; but I still wasn't prepared for the hospitality and the conviviality of this Liverpudlian family from Birkenhead where I was billeted during my duty period on-shore.

They had two sons, one of whom was Mike, a crew mate classified as an EDH (Eficient Deck Hand) on the Alcinous; it was Mike who had invited me to stay with his family. There was an older brother who was working away somewhere as a bricklayer and a younger daughter of about fourteen, whose name escapes me. I was treated like one of their own and on Sunday I was happy to attend church with them because afterwards we'd go home to a wonderful roast dinner and a 'steamy pud'. I reckon I must have put on quite a few extra pounds in the short time I stayed there.

Jack, the father was a keen rugby fan and after lunch on a Saturday, he'd often take Mike and me to a match before visiting his 'local' for a pint or two. Mike was allowed to drink beer as he was of age, but I would be given a shandy and a packet of crisps. Still, I enjoyed every second in that pub as I listened to the banter and the unique humour of the Liverpudlians around me. His wife was called Bel or Beth – I can't remember which. She was a biggish woman with a lovely lyrical voice, sort of Irish I thought. She would often scold Jack for taking me into the pub, but from the twinkle in her eye and the sound of her voice, I always had the feeling that she was not being too serious about it.

Much of that time is lost in the backwater of my mind, but I do recall them saying goodbye to me at the railway station. As I was about to board the train Bel hugged me and Jack shook my hand and said, "Tarrah lad, take care o' yoursel". Not having a father of my own I remember thinking how good it must be having a 'Da' like Jack and I slightly envied Mike for it. Unfortunately contact was lost after my emigration to New Zealand, but those memories of that family remain as a constant reminder of my affection for Liverpool and its people.

I arrive at Paignton at 1.45pm and decide to stop here for the day. Rob and I meet up in the Half Moon pub where we have a great carvery meal in congenial surroundings. Later that afternoon we find the lovely Ramslade Caravan Club touring site and we are soon hooked up and resting inside the van.

I've been feeling quite tired over the last few days. I'm not sure why, as although I've racked up the mileage I feel that I'm expending no more energy than in previous weeks throughout the walk. It's more a mental fatigue I think, but whatever it is it's having a negative effect on my physical well-being. We were going to have tomorrow as a rest day, but regrettably we can't get onto the internet due to poor signal, so I've decided to walk again instead.

Today's pedometer reading: 26.7km (16.5 miles).

Notes of Interest: Paignton

Apparently Paignton is recorded in the Domesday Book of 1086 AD as a Celtic settlement. Its name probably originated from the Celtic 'Paega' and of course we know that 'ton' or 'tun' means town.

Paignton remained a small fishing hamlet, but in 1837 it was considered to be a "neat and improving village and bathing place". A seawall had also been built as a means of protecting the seafront from erosion. It is said that this Paignton foreshore property was bought from the Duchy of Cornwall about 50 years later for the princely sum of £256!

Oldway Mansion is worth a visit for it's an incredible house that was built in the 1870s for Isaac Singer, of Singer sewing machine fame. The mansion has been the venue for a number of films in the past including the 2004 movie Churchill: The Hollywood Years.

It has been said that the novelist Agatha Christie, who lived in neighbouring Torquay, would often visit Paignton to attend the Torbay Picture House. Although the cinema is now closed, it has been the location of several interesting events in the past such as being used as a temporary venue for the 1981 film The French Lieutenant's Woman, *and the town, it seems, was also the location for the 1984 film* Ordeal by Innocence.

FRI, 25TH SEPT 2009
PAIGNTON - TORBAY – TORQUAY – DAWLISH

I feel very tired again this morning. The last thing I feel like is walking. We drive back to Paignton to where I need to start my day's walk. The weather again is clear and cold so I'm hoping for another fine day. The road out of Torquay soon becomes a long, narrow, winding one and at times pretty steep. I come across another hill that seems to go on forever. I think all my troubles will be over once I reach the top, but on the way down the road narrows even more leaving me nowhere to go when traffic, especially trucks or buses, come whizzing around a bend.

At this point I decide to return to the South West Coast Path as the road was clearly too hazardous. The coastal path is quite rugged and is continually changing direction. On occasions it will divert toward the road then go off again at a tangent.

Rob has stopped at a bay about 2½ miles from Dawlish. He has been getting worried as he has been anticipating my arrival for ages and I'm now 1½ hours overdue. I'm pretty knackered by this time due to the heat and the rugged nature of the walk, but after the meal break I decide to continue my trek along the coastal path.

Eventually I return to the road and meet up with Rob on the outskirts of Dawlish. I decide to end my day's walk here as I'm feeling hot and very, very tired. In Dawlish we have some sign writing done and are then given the name of a great caravan touring site called Lady's Mile. We arrive at the site after shopping for groceries in town and we are not only given a great welcome, but our allocated site is issued free of charge.

Today's pedometer reading: 28km (17.3 miles). That same distance by road was only 13.8 miles!

Notes of Interest: Dawlish

It is believed that Dawlish took its name from a local stream with a Brythonic name, once spelt 'Deawlisc', meaning 'Devil Water' (often heavy rains running down over the red cliffs, would cause the waters to appear red). Other possible interpretations of a Celtic Welsh origin exist and I believe other names can be found in the Domesday Book.

The first settlers around Dawlish would have been predominately fishermen and salt makers who, it is thought, might have lived on higher ground but would have spent most of their time on coastal stretches pursuing their livelihood. Eventually their crude system of extracting salt from rock pools would be replaced with 'salterns' (trapped sea water pools that would dry out leaving salt residue).

The Romans had little influence on Devon for their occupation, it seems, didn't extend into the extreme western regions of England. Because of this the Celtic people and their culture remained more or less unaffected throughout the Roman period.

To the Romans, salt would have been an important commodity and the product was in demand up until their withdrawal in 400 AD. Salt-making in Dawlish petered out after this, never to revive, even under Anglo-Saxon rule.

Despite the decline of salt-making, the settlements in the Dawlish area grew, especially in the upper regions where land was fertile, with little risk of flooding

It is thought that the revered authors of their day, Charles Dickens and Jane Austen spent a good deal of time in Devon and Dawlish would also become the fictitious birthplace of Nicholas Nickleby, *Charles Dickens' classic novel of the same title.*

The town of Dawlish, like many of the seaside towns in Devon, is recognised as an attractive and popular holiday resort.

SAT, 26TH SEPT 2009
DAWLISH

We're having the day off today as we have free Wi-Fi connection so it gives us the opportunity to catch up on all the online stuff we need to do. This quiet day has also given me the opportunity to thank all those who have contacted me on occasions during my walk, whether by phone, text or email.

The Loneliness of the Long Distance Runner is a short story by Alan Sillitoe that was later made into a film. It depicts the thoughts of a young man sent to an approved (reform) school who, during his long distance running races, gives thought to his current situation and his future welfare among other things. Long distance walking has the same effect on the walker; even more so when it is done day after day for months on end. Whether it's walking on a deserted

Northumberland coastal path or through a depressing urban industrial wasteland or tramping up on remote highlands or on a country byway, the feeling of solitude is often with you. Sometimes loneliness will creep up on you during these times and then there's a hunger for contact with friends or family. When a text or phone call comes through, it's a welcome diversion from things going on in the mind and from the boredom that naturally comes from constant daily walking; but mostly all you do is think.

Well, only 14 days to go – can't wait for the finish! With the final day getting closer I need to know exactly where to start the marathon walk of 26 miles, 385 yards (42.195 km) to reach my ultimate destination, the Brighton Marina. I believe Middleton-on-Sea is the closest place, but I need to know the exact point from which to start. Anyway I'm sure I'll get it sorted in the next few days. Tomorrow should also be an interesting day because once I reach Exmouth, it will be the start of my walk along the Jurassic Coast.

Notes of Interest: The Jurassic Coast

The Jurassic Coast stretches from Orcombe Point near Exmouth in East Devon to Old Harry Rocks near Swanage in East Dorset. Its entire length of 153 kilometres (95 miles) can be walked on the South West Coast Path.

This World Heritage coastline is called the 'Jurassic Coast' because it records the best geological example of a continuous series of ancient rocks that date back through the Jurassic, Triassic and the Cretaceous periods; a time that spans 185 million years of the Earth's history.

Therefore, by walking along the Jurassic coast you are treading over a unique rock and cliff formation that spans the Mesozoic epoch; so in a walk of just a few days you might easily be travelling over 180 million years of geomorphological time.

Due to these unusual time-spanning erosion processes the Jurassic Coast is an ideal destination for school and university geology field trips as well as the scientists, palaeontologists and geologists who make regular visits to the area.

Records have it that Mary Anning, a palaeontologist, discovered the first complete Ichthyosaur fossil, while studying the fossils of the coastline around Lyme Regis.

SUN, 27TH SEPT 2009
STARCROSS – EXMOUTH – SIDMOUTH

We leave the Lady's Mile Caravan Park around 7am and make our way back to the parking site where I had ended my walk on Friday. The Lady's Mile was a great site. It seemed to have every conceivable amenity for all ages. Thanks Jake, for the free use of your site and to the staff for their helpful and friendly hospitality.

Two miles on and I'm walking through Dawlish township and heading toward Starcross. We have our first meal break here before catching the ferry over to Exmouth. From Exmouth I take the South West Coast Path that will take me to Sidmouth. It's a great walk, the weather's fine and the sea's an azure blue; it's like a mid-summer's day! It's around this time that I begin thinking about the youngsters of today and how inactive they seem to be compared to the young people of my era. It triggers thoughts of my own childhood days.

My brother and I soon became accustomed to a more liberal way of life at home after evacuation and it wasn't long before we were playing on our street (nearly always devoid of cars in those days) or on the nearby derelict building site up the road. In those days kids seemed to be always on the go.

During holidays or weekends we'd spend the days with friends around the same age and would only go home for a meal or when we were called home in the evening by a message, usually from a sibling. Our sisters had almost the same freedom and would be playing hop-scotch or group skipping with other girls in the street until mothers would call them in. As we grew older we would be allowed further afield and would spend days on the beach or roller skating on the promenades in the evening.

During weekends and holidays we'd often journey to the country where we'd pick blackberries or mushrooms, usually accompanied by our mother. The only home entertainment was the radio, listening to Jimmy Edwards as Pa Glum in *Take It from Here* or *Around the Horn* with Kenneth Williams, Bill Pertwee, plus a variety of other programmes. On other occasions we'd be standing around the piano singing all the popular tunes of the day played with enthusiasm by Dick.

On Saturday mornings we'd go to the Astoria cinema and become ♫ *The boys and girls well-known as members of the ABC* ♫ and we'd watch Flash Gordon played by Buster Crabbe being trapped by his arch enemy Ming the Merciless, and tied down along with Dale and Dr Zarcov while the death ray begins to slowly creep towards them. Usually, a mere second before it reaches them there would be a dramatic flair of music and words such as 'Will Flash Gordon and his friends survive the death rays? Watch next week to find out' would appear on the screen.

On Brighton Beach

A typical Saturday afternoon for Moe and me would be to walk down to the Steine, then up North Street to the clock tower. We'd pop into the News Theatre or walk down West Street to the Academy Cinema depending what was showing. Sometimes we'd go further down West Street and watch the Brighton Tigers Ice Hockey team at the SS Stadium (long since gone). Most of the team like Bobby Lee and Hutchins or Hutchinson the Keeper were, I seem to recall, Canadians.

Some Saturday evenings we'd put our best gear on and a group of us teenagers would go up to the Regent Ballroom (situated where Boots the Chemist has its store today) where Syd Dean and his band would be playing all the old favourites of the day. We'd stand there trying to pluck up the courage to ask a girl for a dance, knowing in all likelihood we'd be rejected due to being quite a bit younger than the girls.

I remember on one occasion feeling nervous, and with sweaty palms, going over to this attractive girl who was sitting at a table with her friends to ask her for a dance. I recall walking away feeling pretty disconsolate and peed-off about it because she had inferred that I should 'go home to my mummy as it was past my bedtime' ...the cow! I suppose the real reason for my anger was that I hadn't been able to respond with a clever answer to her smart-arse comment!

Winter evenings would see most of us boys spending our time at the Brighton Boy's Club where we'd play table tennis or compete in wrestling and boxing matches with other clubs. Although most of us teenagers were quite poor, I reckon we had a better life…and certainly a healthier one than the kids of today.

I stop at a coastal cafe in Budleigh Salterton and buy a bacon and sausage bap before carrying on towards the bridge that will take me over the river. There are some people on the bridge barbecuing food for a fund-raising event; it smells great and I can't resist buying a hamburger for extra supplement. I'm now on the second half of my walk to Sidmouth and during this session I have to tackle some steep climbs. After a couple of hours of hard slog I stop near Otterton and rest in a nearby beer garden. I buy myself a well-earned shandy and sit there gazing up at another steep climb that stands between me and Sidmouth.

Coming down from the hills I meet a few other walkers. One couple, Pat and Steve, walk with me for a time and Pat spreads the word about my mission to everyone she meets. If I'd had her around throughout my walk I'd have raised a small fortune! I finally walk down the last steep incline into Sidmouth. After meeting up with Rob we drive out to a Caravan Club site and we're soon resting comfortably on recliner chairs outside the van.

Today's pedometer reading: 29.9km (18.6 miles).

Notes of Interest: Sidmouth

In the Domesday Book, the small fishing settlement of Sidmouth is referred to as 'Sedemuda'.

The popularity for coastal resorts began during the Georgian era but gained even more favour during the Victorian period. It was a time when small coastal villages like Sidmouth would flourish.

In 1819, Sidmouth played host to Edward, Duke of Kent, and his wife and baby daughter (the future Queen Victoria). Unfortunately, less than a month later Edward died after a brief illness. The sad event took place at the Woolbrook Glen, which later became the Royal Glen Hotel, where I believe a plaque recording the royal visit is still there today.

The town sits amidst the Jurassic Coast World Heritage Site in an Area of Outstanding Natural Beauty; however, erosion remains a serious concern, especially to the residents of many of the beautiful cliftop homes in the area.

Sidmouth, with its unique charm, nestles beneath majestic red cliffs and the green hills of the glorious Sid valley. Its leisurely walks and lovely gardens are a joy to the many thousands of visitors attracted each year to the mild climate and picturesque surroundings of the area.

MON, 28TH SEPT, 2009
WESTON – BRANSCOMBE – BEER – SEATON

I walk out of Sidmouth at 7.50am. Almost immediately I'm confronted with another long and steep hill. Soon the heart rate increases and the body begins to overheat. I stop at the summit to discard my sweater and track suit pants before taking in the spectacular views; scenes that instantly make the climb worthwhile.

I'm soon walking along reddish cliffs that give signal to the dramatic Jurassic Coast. Eventually the cliftop path dips downward getting steeper as it goes. Steps soon appear, 140 of them, and they take me down to the beach. After walking no more than 50 metres along the sand more steps appear. The steps lead me back up the cliff in stages. I believe there were around 170 of 'em altogether. (Yes, I actually tried counting them!)

The ruggedness of the walk is making the going hard and slow, but after Weston Mouth the coastal path becomes easier. Eventually

I walk down toward Branscombe Mouth and notice some sort of eating place in the distance. It's a welcome sight and I'm soon feasting on a large bacon and egg bap and washing it down with a black coffee. While sitting here enjoying the break I have a call from my son, Michael, who wants to know how I'm getting on. I tell him that I'm feeling good and we chat for a while about different things but in particular about my planned arrival date back in Brighton.

Shortly after, I am ready to tackle the next steep climb that could be seen from where I was sitting. The rugged terrain takes its toll in time and effort, but the ideal weather conditions and the panoramic views are really worth the climb. I eventually walk down through the pretty town of Beer where, funnily enough, I see people sitting outside in a fairly large beer garden enjoying the great weather. I can't resist the opportunity to relax there for half an hour or so just sitting in the sun with a cool glass of lemonade.

I soon continue on for another mile and a half to Seaton. I meet up with Rob in a friendly pub where we manage to get some good local knowledge of the place and the location of a decent caravan site out of town.

Today's pedometer reading: 21.3km (13.2 miles).

Notes of Interest: Seaton

Seaton is also situated on the Jurassic Coast. It is believed that a community might well have existed here before 3,000 BC. Iron Age forts in the vicinity give an insight into its ancient history. It seems that the name of Seaton was first mentioned by Pope Eugenius in 1146; before that date the Anglo-Saxons referred to it as Fluta or Fleet.

Seaton became an important port during the Roman occupation and remained so for several centuries. The maritime facility was utilised for supplying ships and crew to Edward I in his campaign against Scotland and France.

Its use as a deep water port came to an end mainly due to the violent fourteenth-century storms that hit this coastal region, causing landslips into the estuary and shingle banks to form.

The lovely Seaton Marshes Nature Reserve stretches from the estuary at Axmouth to Colyford village and is a great attraction for birdlife throughout the year, especially during the winter months.

CHAPTER 27
DORSET

TUES, 29TH SEPT 2009
SEATON - LYME REGIS – CHIDEOCK – BRIDPORT

We leave Seaton just after 7am and I start walking eastward alongside the lovely Axe Estuary, destination Lyme Regis. I turn into what I think is Squire's Lane only to be confronted with another long, steep hill. Toward the summit I skirt around a golf course to reconnect with the South West Coast Path once more.

The route is pretty much up and down on narrow, rocky pathways and there are around 30 or 40 batches of steps leading to different levels on this 7-mile route to Lyme Regis. Unfortunately thick foliage conceals much in the way of sea views throughout this section.

I began thinking about the Jurassic ground beneath my feet and wondered what this terrain would have been like say 60 to 100 million years ago. The experts reckon that through much of the Jurassic era, the Earth would have been much warmer than today with very little ice at the polar caps; consequently the sea levels were high and the desert landscape of southern England would have been submerged beneath a tropical sea. On the other hand, if I was walking here during the Triassic period I might have been walking on hot sandy terrain or in steamy, swampy jungle undergrowth.

Finally, after a little over 2½ hours, I emerge from the bush-covered track onto a wider, leaf-strewn pathway before getting onto the road that leads down to the Lyme Regis promenade. As I walk along the promenade overlooking the tranquil Lyme Bay, I am greeted by a number of people who want to talk about the venture and I realise that Rob has been doing a great publicity job while waiting for me. This attractive seaside town, with its wide sandy foreshore, is quite captivating bathed as it is in the glorious sunshine. Rob has also organised an interview with a reporter from a local paper. After the interview we call in to the information centre for a map and information on the next coastal section to Bridport. Soon after this I take to the road again. I look back at Lyme Regis and feel a desire to revisit this lovely regal resort at a more opportune time; a town with a long and varied history, a place of fossil finds and unusual geology.

From Lyme Regis I find that the coastal pathway is partially closed with diversion advice; a problem not mentioned at the information centre. Consequently, it means having to walk on the road for much of the 11-mile section. I have a meal break near Chideock before carrying on past Bridport to Morrison's petrol station where Rob has fuelled up. I finish walking for the day at Morrison's car park.

Today's pedometer reading: 30.78km (19.1 miles).

Notes of Interest: Bridport

The modern market town of Bridport was originally a thriving fishing port. Its name may have derived from Bridian a title given to one of a number of 'Burhs' or 'defended places' although Bridian (or Brydian) appeared to be a little further east that the Bridport of today.

Bridport was already making hemp rope when around 1213 King John ordered that there should be 'made at Bridport by night and day, as many ropes for ships both large and small as they could'. From then on it became the main producer of ropes for many years. The term 'To be stabbed by a Bridport dagger' was often used in those days; it meant to be hanged at the gallows!

It is thought that in 1651 Charles II might have stayed in the town whilst hiding from Cromwell's army.

The town lies at the western end of Chesil Beach at the confluence of the River Brit.

The port of the town is now land-locked, but the harbour at West Bay is still busy during the summer season.

Bridport is regarded as an alternative 'Gateway Town' for the World Heritage Site of the Jurassic Coast.

WED, 30TH SEPT 2009
BURTON BRADSTOCK – ABBOTSBURY

It's early morning as I leave Morrison's parking area and begin walking toward Abbotsbury. Passing the Bridport and West Dorset Golf

Course I stay on a B-road for a couple of miles and then at Burton Bradstock I begin travelling on the coastal path route. Although the sun is shining, the temperature is not overly hot and the relatively easy terrain is making this scenic section of the walk really enjoyable. As always, thoughts meander through my mind. Sometimes a sight, a smell or a noise would trigger a thought, while at other times a thought or a memory would surface for no apparent reason.

Today I remember thinking about my cousin Chrissie who was at Lizard Point when we visited a couple of weeks ago. She knew about our old house in Mighell St, Brighton; in fact, she remembered more about that old house than I did! She reminisced that evening about the times she stayed with us whenever her mother, our Aunt Glad, came down from London. Aunt Glad and our mother were sisters and were very close and Aunt Glad would come down quite often during the school holidays. Chrissie lived in London's Edgware Road where the family had an allocated police flat due to her father being in the London Metropolitan Police.

I remembered Chrissie as a red-headed, freckled-faced 9 or 10 year old, who loved nothing more than coming down to the seaside town of Brighton to be with her many interesting cousins. Chrissie didn't give thought to the poor state of the building; as far as she was concerned, she was living in a big house and sleeping in a small room on the top floor with a couple of her female cousins. It was a far cry from the restrictive conditions that existed in the family's contemporary flat in London. Here in Brighton she had the freedom to trundle off to the beach or play in the street or play hide and seek in the derelict ruins at the back of the upper houses, always with the protective company of her cousins.

She remembered the times when I would come up to their room at the top of the stairs with a lighted candle under my contorted, grimacing face and them all screaming in delighted terror or when I would sit on their bed and read them frightening ghost stories. She talked about things that I had quite forgotten, like the old piano that sat by the wall near the door and the old washing machine our mother used for washing the family clothes and linen. It suddenly came back to me and I could visualise our mother sticking the washing into this tub and putting down the lid. The lid must have engaged with wooden paddles for there was a lever on the top of the lid that had to be moved to and fro by hand until the washing was clean.

The memory became even more distinct when recollecting our mother's habit of trying to get one of her children (sometimes me) to relieve her of that energy-sapping, mind-numbing duty of working that lever to wash the clothes. As I remember, none of us were keen to help her out and would only do it under pressure, a fact that reveals how selfish children can be! The clothes then had to be rinsed by hand before putting them through the mangle.

Chrissie even thought that going to the outside loo in the backyard, sitting on the wooden plank and wiping her bottom with squares of newspaper attached to a string dangling from the wall was an experience too good to be missed. And as for our alley where she could run down to Edward Street with her cousins or scoot up to the old ruins to play, well that was sheer bliss for this little ginger-headed girl from London. I suppose it's all in the 'eye of the beholder'!

I meet up with Rob three hours later at the Swannery, near Abbotsbury, where I have my first meal break. On my next session I join up with a guy called Mat who's also walking in my direction; his destination is Weymouth. It isn't long before we are walking alongside Chesil Beach. This well-known, 18-mile stretch of shingle beach is an important part of this Jurassic coastline and walking along its coastal path with Mat as company is most enjoyable.

Eventually we reach an army firing range where we have to detour as the red flag is flying. Rob comes along the path to meet us and leads us back to the Little Sea Haven Caravan Site, where we have been given a free pitch. We sit around for a while before taking photos of each other with Chesil Beach as the backdrop. We say goodbye to Mat who carries on walking toward Ferry Bridge, while we return to the van and connect up to the power. I then have 40 winks before firing up the laptop as I'm feeling unusually tired.

Today's pedometer reading: 30.87km (19.2 miles).

Notes of Interest: Abbotsbury

It is likely that there has been a settlement on this site for 6,000 years or more according to archaeological evidence
As with much of England, forest or dense woodland would have cloaked the surrounding area of Abbotsbury, a lot different to the open, arable land we see today.

There is good evidence that a reasonably large group of hunter/ gatherers might have lived and grazed cattle in the area. It is also possible that these Celtic people, who built the Iron Age forts and burial mounds in the area, might have belonged to a tribe known as the Durotriges, who lived in parts of Dorset, Wiltshire and Somerset. These people resisted Roman invasion in AD 43, but sadly by AD 70 they had either died out or had been brought under Roman influence.

By the middle of the seventh century the area had become part of the Saxon Kingdom of Wessex. It seems there is also evidence to suggest that the Vikings settled here about 150 years later.

Today, Abbotsbury is essentially a tourist attraction mainly due to its famous Swannery and its location to Chesil Beach. There is nothing quite like the Swannery for its about one of the only places in the world where you can view colonies of nesting Mute Swans close at hand.

The Swannery was created by Benedictine Monks who had built a monastery at Abbotsbury during the eleventh century. It is thought that the swans were raised as a source of food for their lavish banquets.

THURS, 1ST OCT 2009
CHESIL BEACH

Today is a rest day from walking. Well, not really a rest day as both Rob and I have been busy working on our laptops for one purpose or another. In the afternoon we drive over to Chesil Beach as I want to gaze over this long 17-mile stretch of unbroken beach without having to worry about my walking schedule. I don't want to walk too far so we just relax while I search around for a couple of unusual pebbles to keep as a memento of Chesil Beach. I had read that due to longshore drift the pebbles alter in size depending on where you are in relation to the shore.

Tomorrow we will have only nine more days to reach Brighton. Barring unforeseen circumstances we should be able to meet that target without too much trouble. I am still aiming at making a marathon distance walk on that last day. Hopefully one or more of my Brighton supporters might want to join me on that final 26½-mile session. I've also heard that many of my Brighton Marina supporters are joining us en route at Worthing pier. Their transport is in the form of a double-decker bus laid on by courtesy of the Brighton and Hove Bus Company.

Notes of Interest: Chesil Beach

Chesil Beach is a long pebble beach that stretches north-west from Portland to Bridport's West Bay. The name Chesil is believed to originate from the Old English 'ceosel' or 'cisel', meaning gravel or shingle.

The size of the Chesil Beach shingle varies from large pebbles toward the east (the Portland end), gradually reducing to pea-sized pebbles toward the west (the Bridport end).

There is a favourite anecdote you'll often hear from the locals about smugglers who used to come on to the beach in the protective darkness of night and how they could judge precisely where they were just by the size of the shingle.

The beach is around 17 miles long and part of it is separated from the mainland by a shallow strip of tidal water, the Fleet Lagoon.

There have been many archaeological discoveries, including fossil finds, along this interesting part of the Jurassic Coast and probably many more just waiting to be found.

Chesil Beach a UNESCO-designated World Heritage Site and both the beach and lagoon are Sites of Special Scientific Interest.

FRI, 2ND OCT 2009
WEYMOUTH – OSMINGTON – WOOL

I leave Rob at the Little Sea Caravan Park where we were camped and rejoin the coastal path that lay adjacent to the campsite.

I walk around the inner lake then onto a track that eventually comes out onto the road that leads to Portland Bill. It's around this point that I watch a couple of ships heading out to sea, probably ferry services to France or elsewhere. It set my thoughts back to other ships during my sea-faring days of the early fifties.

I decided to leave Alfred Holt's Blue Funnel Line, as Liverpool was quite a distance from my home in Brighton, and joined the Ellerman Wilson Line whose vessels sailed from ports such as Hull and some routes from out of London's Royal Albert Docks. The ship, its name I believe was Ariosto, sailed out of the port of London to Denmark and back. It was a 14-day return voyage stopping only at Arhus and Copenhagen. The short voyages meant I could spend more time at home in Brighton.

I particularly remembered a guy called Kirkland, although he was known as Kirk by most of the crew. He was an AB (Able Bodied Seaman), tall and of good physique with rugged dark features that made him stand out in a crowd. I noticed him after I had boarded the Ellerman Wilson vessel for the first time. He was hugging this woman who was holding a pram down on the quayside. As I watched he went to the pram and took out this little blonde kid and jiggled it in his arms for a while before putting it back. He then kissed and cuddled the woman once more before hurrying up onto the ship's gangway. I heard later that she was, as I had surmised, his wife.

When we got to Copenhagen the deck crew got off the vessel first, as they always did. I happened to be looking down at the quayside and saw Kirk go up to this blonde lady who was waiting nearby; he gave her a big hug and a passionate kiss before walking away with his arm around her. Everyone on the ship seemed to be aware of Kirk's behaviour and I soon learned he'd had this double relationship going for a couple of years. I remember seeing a film a few years later which depicted the same sort of scenario with the captain of a ship featuring Alec Guiness. It immediately reminded me of Kirk and I wondered whether his wife (or wives) ever discovered his infidelity.

Crossing the road, I soon encounter a wide, sealed path that leads me through to the start of the lengthy Weymouth promenade where I meet up with Rob at its eastern end. I take to the coastal path after the meal break, but after some time I realise the route is quite circuitous so I decide to return to the open road after going through Osmington.

The miles now pass by more quickly and after a little over seven hours of walking I finally stride into the village of Wool. Rob has already settled in at a caravan touring park that lay close by the road and I am more than ready to relax for the rest of the day as I have been beset by fatigue since the lunch break.

Today's pedometer reading: 32.85km (20.4 miles).

SAT, 3RD OCT 2009
WOOL – WAREHAM – POOLE

We leave the Wool Caravan Park at 7.15 and I take to the A-road that lay close by. It's going to be road walking from now on, no more coastal paths. Road walking is not as enjoyable as footpaths but greater daily mileage is achieved. It's another good day today as my friendly westerly wind is with me again, gently nudging me along. I catch up with Rob 2¼ hours later at a school car park near Wareham.

After my usual meal break routine I'm on the road again bypassing Wareham and heading for Poole. I am unable to connect up with Rob for my second break as the navigator has taken him on a different route from the one we've agreed to. We finally meet up 3½ hours later when I'm only 3 miles from Bournemouth. There are no caravan camping sites nearby so we drive back toward Poole and find an extremely lovely Caravan Park in South Lytchet.

Today's pedometer reading: 28.53km (17.71 miles). We now have only seven days to go to reach Brighton. Yahoo!

Notes of Interest: Poole

It is believed that the town's name derives from the Celtic word 'bol' and the Old English word 'pool' meaning a place near a pool or creek, although there are variations on this theory.

Human settlement in the area probably dates back to before the Iron Age although the town of Poole was probably founded in the late twelfth century. Its importance as a port would not emerge until around the eighteenth century when the expanding wool trade was reaching its peak.

It is thought that the Romans landed at Poole in the first century and took over an Iron Age settlement at Hamworthy, just west of the town centre. After the Roman withdrawal from England, Poole came under Saxon rule and into the Kingdom of Wessex.

The Anglo-Saxon town was attacked by the Vikings in 876 and some years later King Canute attempted to make his claim on England by commandeering Poole, as he needed a harbour base to operate from.

In 1017 Canute, it is said, married Aethelred's widow, Emma. One of her two sons from her first marriage was Edward, who became King of England and was known as Edward the Confessor.

During WWII, Poole Harbour became one of the main embarking locations for the D-Day landings at Normandy.

SUN, 4TH OCT 2009
BOURNEMOUTH – BOSCOMBE – CHRISTCHURCH

We depart from the lovely South Lytchet Manor caravan park at 6.40 am and drive on to yesterday's finishing point. I am soon on the road, walking through Branksome and into the outer suburbs of Bournemouth. It takes another hour to reach the town centre.

I experience another mindless session of walking through the eastern suburbs of the city; a trek that seems to take ages, but then at Boscombe I connect up with the A35 with some relief as I now realise that I'm well on the way to Southampton.

I meet Rob 8 miles on near Christchurch where I have my first meal break. After a short rest I carry on walking for another lengthy period when Rob phones in to say that he has located a Caravan Club caravan site near Brockenhurst. I decided to finish my walk near New Milton as I'm still feeling very, very weary.

Today's pedometer reading: 24.12km (14.9 miles).

Notes of Interest: Christchurch

It is thought that the town has been in existence since around 650 AD, and was originally called Twynam or 'tweon eam', which refers to place between two rivers. The name Christchurch appeared after the completion of its priory in 1094. Smuggling was rife prior to the 1800s and Christchurch was also involved in the illicit trade, due possibly to its sheltered harbour.

In 1784, an incident known as the Battle of Mudeford occurred when smugglers were caught unloading their goods on the beach by Mudeford quay. Problems began when two customs vessels and a Royal Navy Sloop entered the fray resulting in a desperate fight between the smugglers and the officials. A Naval officer was killed during the lengthy battle and most of the smugglers escaped. Eventually three of them were caught and it is believed that one of them, George Coombes, was tried and executed.

Many prominent townspeople were involved in the lucrative smuggling trade, such as John Cook, who it is said, became mayor of Christchurch on a number of occasions. Hannah Siller, who had once been the landlady of the 'Ship in Distress' was also actively involved and her notoriety resulted in a channel in the harbour being named after her: Mother Sillar's Channel.

MON, 5TH OCT 2009
SOUTHAMPTON – THE NEW FOREST – LYNDHURST

We leave the New Forest Caravan Club site at 7.20am as fine rain falls from the dark leaden sky. I walk toward Southampton and despite having donned wet-weather gear my clothes underneath soon feel uncomfortably damp.

I feel very tired today. I'm not sure that I can walk any great distance. Despite the lethargy I keep pushing on, constantly reminding myself that this mammoth walk will soon be over. I meet up with Rob in a lay-by about 2 miles from Lyndhurst. I've walked no more than 7½ miles yet I feel exhausted. I change my clothing and my socks and shoes before sitting down to a meal of porridge. I then have to literally force myself out into the rain for another walking session. I am now in the middle of the New Forest, something I have been looking forward to, but the climate together with my weariness lessens my appreciation of the woodland surroundings.

It's almost three hours before I meet up with Rob again on the outskirts of Southampton. I climb wearily into the van and immediately decide to end my day's walk here. There are no caravan sites nearby so we end up driving 12 miles back to the New Forest Centenary Club site that we had left this morning.

Today's pedometer reading: 26.5km (16.4 miles).

Notes of Interest: The New Forest

The New Forest is first referred to in the Domesday Book as Nova Foresta, which in its Latin form translates as 'new hunting ground'.

During the Roman Occupation the forest appeared to be known as the Forest of Spinaii and before the Norman Conquest it was referred to as the Great Ytene Forest. The word 'Ytene' is likely to relate to the tribe from Jutland known as the Jutes, who might have colonised the area before the Saxons.

The New Forest, as with much of England, was densely forested throughout the centuries, but cultivation gradually turned some areas into heathland. Today the New Forest is dotted with villages and towns and yet remains one of the largest ancient tracts of open heathland and forest in England.

William the Conqueror requisitioned the heathland areas and harsh punishments were given to those who broke the new 'Forest Law', especially when it came to the killing or hunting of venison. New regulations would result in many commoner families losing their livelihood and their farm holdings.

It is said that two of William's sons died in the forest; first was his second son, Prince Richard, then years later William who as King William II (Rufus), introduced mutilation as a punishment for flouting the Forest Laws. Some records show that a grandchild also met with an accident in the forest. The coincidence created gossip that the deaths were a punishment for the punitive treatment committed by William and Rufus on the people of the New Forest.

The following comments from a seventeenth-century writer give some insight into the thoughts of the people during that period: "He caused 36 Parish Churches, with all the Houses thereto belonging, to be pulled down, and the poor inhabitants left succourless of house or home. But this wicked act did not long go unpunished, for his Sons felt the smart thereof; Richard being blasted with a pestilent Air; Rufus shot through with an Arrow; and Henry his grandchild, by Robert his eldest son, as he pursued his Game, was hanged among the boughs, and so dyed". An iron-clad stone known as the Rufus Stone marks the (alleged) spot where King William II (Rufus) died.

TUES, 6TH OCT 2009
SOUTHAMPTON – SWANWICK – FAREHAM

We leave our caravan site and drive eastward to yesterday's pick-up point on the western outskirts of Southampton. It's 6.50am and the rain is still falling as I climb wearily out of the van and start walking toward Fareham. I stop at Bursledon for my first break. I am wet through and need a change of clothes before eating. While resting, we have a call from the local newspaper, the *Daily Echo* who want to do an article on the walk. We wait around for the photographer to show up and do his stuff, then I head towards the bridge that will take me over the Hamble to trudge eastward through the dreary suburbs of Swanwick and Park Gate.

I have been psychologically and physically weary of late and I can't really understand why. The terrain I have travelled on over these last few days has been relatively easy and my daily walking distance shorter than usual so I find it hard to reason why I should feel this way. As for my psychological condition, I always assumed I would be in a state of euphoria being so close to the finish, but instead I feel strangely devoid of such emotions. Today was no different from other days with regard to thoughts going through my head. I wondered if seeing the ships around Southampton port yesterday prompted me into thinking about the Captain Cook, the vessel that was to take me to New Zealand just three weeks after my seventeenth birthday.

After my third trip with Ellerman Wilson Line I decided to stay home with my mother as I had received notice that my emigration application to New Zealand had been successful and that I would be embarking on the Captain Cook on its next voyage out from Glasgow. I had about a month at home before that final day arrived. My mother was going to come with me as far as Euston Station where I would board the train for Glasgow. Moe, my mate, came with us to the Brighton station and I remember seeing him close to tears as we said our goodbyes. I was feeling pretty emotional myself as I suddenly realised I wouldn't be seeing him or my family again for at least another two years.

But the hardest thing for me was saying goodbye to my mother at Euston Station. She had been close to tears a number of times on our way up to Victoria station; on occasion, she'd try to warn me about all sorts of dangers that she perceived to be harmful or life-threatening in New Zealand. I was under the £10.00 migration scheme instigated by the Australian and New Zealand governments sometime after the end of the war to bolster their populations. You were contracted to serve two years working in a chosen industry, after that period if you decided to go home you could. I assured my tearful mother that I would be coming home at the end of the contract and then boarded the train for Glasgow.

On boarding the Captain Cook, I was allocated a 6-berth cabin with other boys around my age. We soon struck up a friendship and once we knew our way around the ship we took enjoyment out of everything the ship had to offer during that 5-week voyage. The days flew by and in no time we were making passage through the Panama Canal, stopping at Tahiti before going on to New Zealand. I clearly remember that final day when we were approaching the port of Wellington. It was about 5am and we anchored off the harbour for some reason. By mid-morning we entered the harbour and it was the most delightful scene imaginable, with the city of Wellington a perfect backdrop, its image reflected in the calm, sparkling waters of the bay.

It wasn't until mid-afternoon before coaches assembled to take the thousand or more new immigrants to various destinations around their new country. I was allocated a coach that would take a party of 30-odd people northward into Waikato and Taranaki. Many of us on the coach had got to know each other from our weeks on the ship and we soon began singing many popular songs of the day as we travelled along. The coach would stop at various towns along the way and the driver would call out names from a list he had with him. People would alight with their luggage and the coach would then proceed northward again. We'd all carry on singing, stopping only when the coach came to a standstill to deposit more passengers.

Songs were still being sung as the coach drew up in the small town of Stratford in Taranaki. The driver called out just one name – mine! It was a Sunday evening in late May 1953 when I stepped off that bus with my single suitcase. The day had got a lot darker and colder and the misty rain added to the gloom of the autumnal evening. I stood on a corner of the main road where my future employer had arranged to meet me and gazed up and down the deserted road. The overhanging facades that fronted the shops reminded me of those deserted streets of western towns I'd seen in cowboy movies. New Zealand shops, in those days, were not allowed to open on Sundays and that went for any other business; in other words nothing opened. A Kiwi smart-arse once told me that they wouldn't even do parachute jumps on a Sunday! As for the pubs, they were not only closed for business on Sundays, they also had to observe the strict six o' clock closing rule throughout the week. It was known as the 'six o' clock swill'.

Eventually a green Morris Oxford drew up alongside and a man got out of the vehicle, came over and introduced himself while shaking hands. We were soon driving out of the town and heading into the darkness of the back country. It seemed to take ages to motor through isolated villages and remote farm land before finally turning into a long driveway that led towards a large homestead. The farmer, whose name was Don, introduced me to his wife Betty and then showed me to my quarters. It was a Whare (the Maori name for a small out-house.) that consisted of a single bed, one bedside cabinet, a dining chair, a sink and a toilet. Don told me to have a wash-up and when I was ready, to come over to the house for dinner.

My platoon, 16th intake, NZ Army - I'm kneeling second from left

I remember lying on the bed when he had gone and looking out into the blackness of the night. Suddenly this wave of utter loneliness came over me. Since leaving my mother at Euston Station I had been in the company of people. On the train to Glasgow I found myself in a compartment with two interesting young people who were also embarking on the Captain Cook for New Zealand. Then for five weeks while on the ship I had enjoyed the company of many people, some I had come to know as friends. That ship-life camaraderie had continued right up to the moment before alighting from the coach; and that was less than two hours ago.

But now as I lay there the silence was overwhelming, so silent that I fancied I could hear the sound of bells ringing in my ear. I cannot ever remember feeling so utterly alone. I was in the back country of Taranaki, a place so remote that the young farmers in the area, whom I would get to know, would refer to the town of New Plymouth (population 34,000) as 'The Big Smoke'. Of course one adapts and I would settle into this new life of cows, bulls, sheep and sheep dogs, haymaking, ploughing and so on; that is, until the day I was conscripted into the NZ army at the age of 18yrs and 3 months.

Today I am feeling exceptionally tired again and longing to get the day's walk over. I journey on for another three hours before finally catching up with Rob who's parked in a slip road in Fareham. I am exhausted and very relieved to finish for the day.

From Fareham, we drive back to a place called Solent Breezes in Warsash, where Pete and Emi are staying. We spend the rest of the afternoon with them before the four of us head into the village to have an enjoyable evening meal. While we are eating Emi declares that she is going to accompany me on the walk back to Brighton on Saturday. I am really pleased knowing that I'm going to have company. I just hope that the 26-mile walk is not going to be too much for her.

After leaving the restaurant I place my debit card into a nearby ATM machine to draw out some cash when to my utter dismay it gets immediately swallowed up. There is a brief statement on the screen saying: 'Please see your bank', or words to that effect. I was so angry but what can you do! The only time I can ever remember seeing my card disappear so quickly was when I went into a fashion boutique with a girlfriend some years ago!

Today's pedometer reading: 25km (15.5 miles).

WED, 7TH OCT 2009
PORCHESTER – HAVANT – SOUTHBOURNE

Pete has cooked up a great breakfast this morning that Rob and I consume with relish before driving back to Fareham to continue the walk. Steady rain is falling as I walk through Fareham town centre. I call in at Lloyds Bank and report my debit card as lost then visit the local information centre for maps before heading out of Fareham.

I catch up with the support vehicle near Porchester where I have my first late-morning break. I reach Havant around 2.30pm before trudging on in the wet to Southbourne where I finish for the day. Rob has located a caravan camping ground close by the road, but the heavy rain has made the whole place waterlogged. With some difficulty we find a suitable site and soon we're sitting in the van listening to the beat of the rain falling on the roof.

Today's pedometer reading: 28km (17.40 miles.

CHAPTER 28

WEST SUSSEX

THURS, 8TH OCT 2009
CHICHESTER – BOGNOR REGIS

What a difference a day makes. My spirits today are high as I leave the wet surroundings of our caravan site near Southbourne and make my way eastward on the A259 toward Chichester. The weather is cold, but the clear skies promise a fine day and it isn't long before the warm rays of the sun cause me to discard some clothing.

Three hours later I catch sight of Rob standing near a lay-by looking out for me. We are now only 2¾ miles from Bognor Regis. About an hour or so later I walk through Bognor and continue on the familiar A259. The sunshine, the flat terrain and the cycle path running alongside the road provide ideal walking conditions, and all the physical and mental fatigue that's dogged me over the last few days at last begins to dissipate.

We are now getting close to where I think the marathon distance to Brighton might begin. Rob has gone on ahead to ascertain the distance to Brighton using the GPS navigator. Meanwhile I continue walking until some minutes later Rob phones to say that he's parked up in the Southdowns Hotel car park and that according to the Tom-Tom navigator, the hotel was 24.9 miles from Brighton Pier and 26.5 miles from the Brighton Marina, my final destination.

It takes me no more than another half an hour to walk into the Southdowns Hotel Car Park where Rob is waiting in the beer garden with a pint of local ale for me. As I sit there bathing in the afternoon sunshine and supping on the cool beer, a sense of euphoria at last begins to descend upon me. I start to realise the enormity of what we have both achieved. I say both because Rob has sacrificed around 6 months of his life to be my support vehicle driver, and without him this walk would not have been possible. While we sit there we talk about all sorts of things but mainly about what our plans will be once the walk is over.

Afterwards we drive back into Bognor for an evening meal in a restaurant before heading back to the Caravan Camping Club site. Once inside the van we open up a good Australian Shiraz that we'd bought that evening and proceed to celebrate into the early hours. We have no worries about tomorrow for it's going to be a rest day; a day to relax and enjoy; a time to savour the thought that the following day is going to be the very last day of this 5-month long odyssey.

Today's pedometer reading: 22.41km (13.9 miles).

FRI, 9TH OCT 2009
NEAR BOGNOR REGIS

Today is our last day off. I have updated everything on my website, answered emails and by mid-morning responded to last-minute donations. From then on we just relax for the rest of the day. I speak to Emi and Pete over the phone and we make arrangements to meet up in the car park of the Southdowns Hotel early in the morning. Toward evening I become mindful about 'carb loading', for tomorrow will be one of the longest walks I have undertaken during these five months. I have walked similar distances during the walk and on some tough stretches it would have been equivalent to walking 30 miles on a flat road so I should handle the 26½ miles okay, but nothing can be taken for granted.

That day in May when I set out on my Around England Walk seems such a long time ago and I remembered at the time feeling daunted by the task that lay ahead of me. Those five months now lay behind me and I look forward to the morrow with blissful anticipation.

CHAPTER 29
EAST SUSSEX

SAT, 10TH OCT 2009 – FINAL DAY!
BOGNOR – WORTHING – BRIGHTON PIER – BRIGHTON MARINA

It's 6.30am and the pale orange tinge in the eastern sky gives some assurance that this special day is going to be a fine one. It seems that the forecasters have got it right, thank goodness; there are many supporters planning to join us en route so good weather is crucial.

We meet Pete and Emi at the Southdowns Hotel car park in Bognor Regis estimated on Pete's trip mileage to be 26.6 miles away from Brighton Marina. At 7.05am Emi and I are on our way. Soon we are walking around Littlehampton on the A259 and heading for Worthing. The sun's warmth is already being felt and my spirits are high. We are going at a good pace so I know we are on schedule for reaching Worthing pier before 12 noon. It's around this stage that I let Emi walk in front of me, the thought being that I should go at her pace rather than Emi having to go at mine; also the scenery is a lot better!

After two hours we are walking through Goring-by-Sea and a little later we're approaching the seafront and heading for Worthing pier. We have already walked around 15 miles by the time we meet up with all our marina supporters. They had arrived at Worthing pier on a double-decker bus kindly supplied by the Brighton and Hove Bus Company.

I can't describe how great it feels to see them all. After a celebratory greeting we are soon on our way, on the final 12-mile stretch to Brighton. We stop at the Waterside Pub in Shoreham for a well-earned refreshment stop. The proprietor manages to raise around £80 in the short time we are there. Well done, Dino, and thanks!

I notice our group of supporters are thinning out. Some opt to go back on the bus, others to tarry a while in the Waterside Pub, but many have gone on ahead and are waiting for us at Brighton Pier. It continues to be a warm, sunny day and consequently there are crowds of people on the upper and lower promenades on the approach to Brighton Pier. I soon spot my 6ft 7" tall son walking toward me with my youngest granddaughter Romy, all of 2 years old, sitting on his shoulders. As soon as Romy sees me she gets down from her father and runs toward me shouting "Granddad, Granddad!". And there was I thinking she would have forgotten all about me after five months absence.

With Eloise, my 11-year-old granddaughter, holding my hand I approach Brighton Pier, my official starting point, to be interviewed by a waiting BBC television reporter. Afterwards with my small group of supporters we are filmed as we start on our final stage, the Brighton Marina

I check my pedometer. Today's road distance, at this juncture, is approximately 26.6 miles.

My youngest granddaughter is vying for my attention so it takes me a while before I finally arrive to a great 'Welcome Home' reception at the Master Marina Hotel. It feels great to be back among so many old friends and to know that I have finally reached my ultimate destination.

Later that evening I'm finding it hard to believe that the walk is actually over; that I've actually achieved what I'd set out to do five long months before. I think about the days of hard slogs and bad weather, when there had been niggling doubts as to whether or not I could make it. I remember the times when I'd climb into the campervan after a gruelling day's walk and wearily browse through the road map while Rob drove to a local caravan camping site. I'd gaze longingly at the south coast of England and wonder if I would ever get that far.

But with effort and some good fortune it's been accomplished and now I can relax, knowing that tomorrow, the next day and the next, I won't have to drag myself out of bed to start walking. I think I will sleep well tonight!

THE END

A Special Thanks!

Robert Wilson: this walk would not have been possible without the dedication of my son, Robert, who left Melbourne to become my Support Vehicle driver over these five long months. His has been a mostly thankless task, but it's been his support driving and his cooking of around 4 meals a day that has, without doubt, helped make this venture possible.

My appreciation to the following companies –

The Caravan Club: for allowing us to stay at their lovely managed caravan camping sites free of charge.

A to Z Signs – Mark Hooper: for attending to all my sign-writing needs on the support van and elsewhere; without charging me a penny!

Brighton and Hove Bus Company: for supplying a double-decker bus for the transport of supporters who met me at Worthing Pier on the last day of the walk.

The Argus: for promoting the walk and keeping track of my progress over the five-month period.

The South Coast Radio - Mr Paul Ross: for his help in promoting the walk during the first and final stages.

The Brighton Marina Berth Holders Association: for providing ongoing reports on my progress.

My acknowledgement to the following individuals –

As with most accomplishments there are usually people behind the scenes who, with their generosity of spirit, help make such exploits easier to achieve. It certainly was so in my case and therefore I would like to express my gratitude to the following people:

Peter and Emi Pollard: their enthusiastic support prior to and during the walk was invaluable. For Pete to drive all the way up to the Yorkshire coast to relieve Robert and become my support driver for a week gives just one example of the level of help they were both prepared to give me. They also liaised with us on two other occasions during the walk. And we mustn't forget Emi accompanying me on that final marathon walk to the Brighton Marina.

Carolyn Moffatt, my daughter: who along with her husband Tony, gave me physical and spiritual support during my stay in Australia.

Michael Wilson, my son: for his ongoing support throughout the walk.

Carol Galvin, my sister: who, with her husband Joe, gave me much support and encouragement during my stay in New Zealand.

John Boyce: for providing essential computer-graphic sign-work, banners and his image-enhancing work, all free of charge.

Steve Rix: for his invaluable assistance in creating the four map images within the book and his friendly advice on other matters.

Lewis Dillon: for transporting my supporters to Worthing Pier in the double-decker bus and being the support driver to and from Worthing on that final day.

Julie Dennison: for her photographic expertise and advice.

Gareth and Karen Meatyard: for the scanning and enhancement of the two wartime documents and Karen's helpful reading appraisal.

Asher Burman: for his help and cooperation while proprietor of the Master Marina.

And last but certainly not least, **Claire Spinks**, my editor, whose attention to detail has been awesome; consequently, she's had me 'toeing the line' throughout the production process.

A special thanks to all my marina friends (too numerous to mention individually) who supported me throughout the walk.

To all those in the UK, Australia and New Zealand who have supported me in aid of Cancer Research, thank you very much for sponsoring me. Your donations to the charities involved were of great help during the walk, for on those hard days when weather and terrain conspired against me, your contributions lifted my spirits and gave me the encouragement and the impetus to journey on.

Mum and family

Now that this five-month odyssey is over I can look back with appreciation on the incredible places and circumstances in which I found myself and, more importantly, on the goodwill and generosity of family, friends and acquaintances and of the kindness from the many strangers I met along the way.

To all my supporters wherever you are: Thank You!

STEP BY STEP

An '8km/5 miles a day' walking programme.

A formula based on my own walking experiences.

Contains:

- Practical & safety advice for beginners.

- Comments on ideal clothing and equipment.

- Beginner's Walking Programme.

- Intermediate Walking Programme.

- Advanced Walking Programme.

STEP BY STEP

An '8km/5 miles a day' walking programme.

It is believed that we Homo sapiens originated from a worldwide migration of Homo erectus from out of Africa nearly 2.5 million years ago. There are a variety of scientific counter-claims to this hypothesis, but nevertheless, whatever the figure, it's a hell of a long time since we started walking on two legs! Hippocrates is believed to have once remarked that "walking is man's best medicine", but even he was probably not fully aware of all the health benefits that can be derived from walking. Pursuing this most natural of all exercises can:

- Lower osteoporosis bone density loss
- Reduce the risk of heart attack
- Lessen anxiety and tension
- Burn calories
- Reduce stress on the joints
- Slim the waistline
- Lower blood pressure
- Improve stamina and energy
- Ease back pain
- Improve muscle tone

Even if we benefit from just half of the above then walking must be the safest and most efficient way to attain and maintain ultimate health and fitness.

There are two ways of walking. There is the 'normal' walking pace that everyone resorts to, whether it's shopping, playing golf or strolling along a promenade. The other is 'energy' or 'fast-pace' walking where a person walks at a much faster tempo to increase the heart rate to a required level, thereby improving their general aerobic or cardiac fitness, while at the same time burning off those unwanted calories to stimulate fat loss.

Of course, achieving the desired fitness and fat loss depends on the duration of each walk and the regularity of the exercise. Please note that I don't mention weight loss. That is because it often has no bearing on exercise and subsequent fat loss. The reason is simple: if you are exercising at the right intensity you will invariably experience muscle development while losing fat; as muscle is heavier than fat, weight loss can often be disappointingly below expectations. My motto would be: forget the scales but remember your belt or your dress!

I realise that some will find it difficult to spare the time allocated for the longer walks. If you are working long hours or commuting a fair distance to work each day, it can become a real challenge, especially when there are kids to think of, household chores to do, dinner to cook etc. The programme might be even more challenging in the winter when some of you will be leaving home in the dark and returning in the dark.

With these busy lifestyle situations, alternative exercises would need to be considered, but bear in mind that any sort of regular physical activity will burn calories, so instead you might consider:

(a) Utilising your lunch break to do a 30-min walk.

(b) Walking up stairs instead of taking a lift.

(c) Walking to the station or car park rather than catching a bus.

(d) Utilising your spare weekend time to compensate for insufficient exercise during the week.

(e) Negotiating with your partner on household duties so that both of you might benefit from the Step by Step walking programme.

Whatever your situation, let's hope that the following programme will give you the impetus to start on a life-changing routine.

First of all let me begin by listing the simple but essential items you'll need before embarking on the Step-by-Step programme and the ultimate goal of walking 8km/5m four days a week.

(1) **Footwear**: the single most important piece of equipment is the shoes, so it's worthwhile making sure that they have the following features:

- Are lightweight.
- Have all round comfort and support.
- Have a flexible cushioned sole to absorb shock.
- Provide enough room to allow complete toe movement.
- Are made from a breathable material (preferably). Wearing them in for a few weeks before you start on a serious programme is a good idea, especially if they're new.

Warning: don't get suckered into buying cheap. Something that costs under £20 is usually of inferior make-up so carefully check the thickness of the sole etc. It's worth buying quality!

(2) **Clothing**: light, loose and leisurely is how I'd describe the ideal clothing. Don't start off overdressed; better to be cool at the start. You can always have a light sweater in your pack if you need it.

Socks: preferably wool but choice of material not as crucial as that of wearing two pairs of socks. I always followed this practice and never once experienced blisters during 5 months of walking.

(3) **Drinking Water**: fast-pace walking will invariably cause you to sweat, so make sure that you always have drinking water on hand. I always carried two one-litre bottles with me. A recommended minimum daily intake of water for everyone is around 2 litres. When you are walking fast-pace you will naturally consume more.

(4) **Pedometer:** this handy piece of equipment allows you to set goals and gives you a focus on your progress. Mine combined as a watch, but by setting it to pedometer mode I could keep constant tabs on: Steps taken - Distance walked - Heart rate and so on. There are a variety of makes and models on the market including Heart-rate Monitors and GPS trackers so it pays to evaluate before purchasing.

(5) **Accessory Pack**: a light waist-pack is what I used during my five-month walk. They come in a few varieties. Mine had a twin water

bottle pouch, two smaller pockets for items such as a mobile phone, coins etc and a larger pouch for food, a light water-proof coat or whatever other paraphernalia you feel is necessary to take along. For me, I found that items were more easily accessible with a waist-pack rather than a back-pack. However, it's a personal preference and if you happen to prefer a back-pack then use it.

(6) **Lightweight Water and Wind-proof Jacket:** the type that can roll up into a compact size is ideal.

(7) **Walking Sticks:** I only had one and that was a rustic wooden type, but I found it an essential piece of kit. However, I would occasionally see walkers with twin sticks or poles especially around the Lake District. My daughter, who has recently walked part of the Camino Pilgrim Trail in Spain, told me that she found the two poles were a great help. I believe that the three main advantages to using walking poles are:

(1) They can help maintain balance on uneven terrain.
(2) They help work your upper body as well as your legs.
(3) They eliminate the hand-swelling condition than many people experience on long walks.

(8) **Music:** I found that my MP3 player was invaluable, especially when walking through uninspiring landscape for long periods. They should not be used where concentration is needed, such as over rough, uneven terrain or if walking on busy roads or cycle tracks.

(9) **Hat:** it is a good idea to always wear a hat. In cold weather a significant portion of your body heat (around 30%) is lost through your head. On hot sunny days a hat gives you added protection against the sun's rays.

(10) **Mobile Phone:** I cannot stress enough about how crucial they can be when confronted with certain tricky situations while walking. Here are just a few scenarios where a mobile phone becomes a vital tool:

• You are delayed due to an injury and you need to contact someone to stop them worrying about your non-appearance.

•You are lost and need advice from someone to put you back on track.

•You have fallen and broken or sprained a leg... or worse. You need to get medical help fast. (It can happen!)

•The heavens have suddenly opened and the rain is coming down in bucket-loads. You are drenched through and need to cut short your walk and have someone pick you up at some nearby location.

Okay, we've seen what we need to get– now let's look at what we need to do:

(1) **Health Risk**: if you have concerns about possible health risks associated with this walking program, please consult your doctor.

(2) **Warm-up:** at the start of each day's walk you should begin by walking at a low intensity pace for about 5 minutes to raise body temperature in preparation for the stretching exercises.

(3) **Stretching:** these exercises help loosen muscles before you start – and again after you have completed the walking session. It is very important never to stretch 'cold' muscles. The five-minute warm-up above is vital, otherwise you risk tearing the muscle and causing injury.

Concentrate mainly on stretching the quadriceps, the hamstring, and the calf muscles. You also might find that the Achilles might sometimes need to be stretched. I also found that stretching the lower back can be beneficial.

It is beyond the scope of this book to provide detailed information on stretches beyond those I've listed below, but there are many websites out there which list the most suitable stretching exercises before walking, and crucially, how to do them properly. A basic Google search of "warm-up stretches before walking/exercise" should provide plenty of additional information to complement my own and help you on your way.

Being meticulous about my warm-up and stretching routine was probably why I remained relatively free from any leg injury during that five-month period... and for a 73-year-old man, that's saying something!

Quads Stretch
You will need to stand upright and if need be, help balance yourself by leaning against a wall or a post. Lift one leg behind you so you can grasp your foot with a hand – remain upright and push your knee gently back as far as you can. You should then feel the stretch on the quadriceps. Hold for 40 seconds then switch legs.

Calf Stretch
Start in a standing position holding onto something for support. With one leg placed in front of the other bear down and forward with your rear leg until you feel the stretch on your rear calf muscle – hold for 40 seconds then switch legs.

Hamstring
Stand by a wall or post for support and extend one leg straight out on a 30" high object in front of you (higher if you can comfortably manage it), and feel the stretch on your hamstring. You can increase the intensity of the stretch by leaning forward slightly, keeping the extended leg straight. Hold this position for 40 seconds then repeat with other leg. The hamstring stretch can also be done by sitting upright on a bench with one leg held straight in front of you. Bend forward from the waist and feel the stretch, hold for 40 seconds before readjusting position.

Achilles Stretch
From the calf stretch position, transfer the bodyweight forward bending the back knee so that the Achilles tendon can be stretched, ensuring the heel stays on the ground. Or place front of foot on raised object below you and bear down with your heel; by leaning forward you can stretch the calf muscle at the same time. Keep your heel down and hold 30 to 40 seconds.

Lower Back Stretch
Stand with your feet slightly apart before reaching down to touch your toes. You don't need to touch your feet; just push down as far as you can comfortably and let your arms hang there and feel the stretch on your lower back. As with all stretches, don't bob! Just hold the stretch. Try holding for 40 seconds, and then straighten up before repeating the exercise once more.

(4) **Walking Warm-up**: after completing the stretching exercises spend the first five minutes of your walk at a moderate pace, gradually increasing your walking rate to a faster tempo. Try to develop a rhythmic walking style that you feel comfortable with; remember that each of us has an individual style or technique that differs, however slightly, from someone else.

(5) **Cool-down**: it is also recommended that you spend a little time cooling-down after your walking session by gradually reducing the tempo to a moderately slow rate for a few minutes. The scale of aerobic intensity during your walk will determine how long you'll need to cool down for, but usually about five minutes would be sufficient.

Now you need to become familiar with your heart-rate target zone. A **heart-rate target chart** can be sourced from most fitness centres, sport shops or from the internet. To obtain full aerobic benefit from walking it is necessary to keep track of your heart beat and keep it between 60 to 85% of your maximum heart rate – this will be your target zone. (A calculation based on an individual's age.) To work out your MHR (Maximum Heart Rate) simply deduct your age from 220. For instance if you are 60 years of age, your MHR will be 160. Therefore, 60% of your MHR would be 96 and 85% of your MHR would be 136, so your target zone as a 60 year old would be between 96 BPM (heart Beats Per Minute) and 136 BPM. Below 60% gives you very little aerobic benefit and above 85% is too strenuous with only moderate aerobic benefit. In fact, only if you are in excellent physical condition should you aim to go beyond 85%.

Pulse Rate: if you don't possess a device to automatically record your heart beat, then you'll need to resort to the basics. There are a few ways of measuring your pulse rate, but I found the best way is to place two fingers on your throat just below the corner of your jaw (feel around there and you'll find it). The other method is to find the pulse on your wrist by feeling immediately under your thumb line, placing two fingers about 1inch (2cm) below your wrist joint. Simply count the beats for 10 seconds and multiply by 6, or count for 15 seconds and multiply by 4 to get your pulse rate per minute.

You should check your pulse rate periodically to ensure you are continually within your target zone. Most people need to be still in order to do this, therefore having a **reliable pulse meter** has got to be the most ideal and trouble-free method for measuring heart rate.

Monitor Your Progress: having a note book handy is advisable as you can then record the time taken for each walk. Nothing will give you greater encouragement than seeing improvements in your weekly progress. If you maintain the goals set in the programmes below you will definitely see a growing enhancement in your performance – both in completing your walks faster to seeing an ongoing reduction in your heart-rate.

Monitor Your Body's Well-being: take note of your physical reaction to this new regime. Remember that if you are relatively unfit, the Step-by-Step walking programme will place extra demands on underused muscles and joints so it pays to keep check on how they're coping. Aches after a walk are common as they usually indicate that muscles and joints are being tested. Pain, however, is not acceptable; if it persists see your doctor.

If you are starting at the Beginners Programme and can successfully accomplish the targets given for the 10-week period you will find that the other two programmes will be easier to achieve.

Your Diet: if your motive for embarking on the Step-by-Step walking programme is to lose body fat, develop a fit, toned body and enjoy a healthy lifestyle then your diet is the most important - **the most essential factor** in bringing these goals into reality.

Many fitness experts believe that to achieve a well-toned, healthy body, you need to be thinking '75% nutrition/25% exercise'. I know a person who goes to the gym and does an hour's aerobic workout at least four times a week. In addition, he walks there and back each time; a distance of around 4km. Yet he still struggles with his body fat.

The basic reason is simple mathematics: calories absorbed- minus calories burned. If you are consuming the equivalent of 2,500 calories a day in food, but are burning up say 600 calories on an exercise programme, another 900 on normal everyday activity including food digestion another 500 while sleeping, you're still 500 calories behind the 'eight ball'. With those sorts of figures, your figure isn't gonna be anything like what you're aiming for!

Personal caloric requirements vary according to gender, weight, age and activity level. To maintain an ongoing energy and weight stability level, women need about 2,000 calories a day and men need around 2,500. The energy content of stored body fat can be around 3,000 calories or more, so a 500 calorie deficit would be required each day in order to stay neutral. The solution is safe and simple – create that energy deficit you need by reducing your calorie-rich intake of food and at the same time increase your energy level to expend superfluous calories. In other words, eat healthier, less fattening food and become more active!

I eat pretty healthily myself, but I am no expert in nutrition therefore cannot give you much in the way of professional guidance on this matter. However, because of the extreme importance of nutrition and the hand-in-glove relationship it has with exercise I would recommend that you familiarise yourself on the subject by using the internet or searching for a suitable book. There's plenty of specialised material out there to guide you further.

Step by Step – Beginners Programme

If you've been fairly inactive in the past, maybe recovering from an illness or overweight, use caution or **consult your doctor** before you start.

Weeks 1 & 2 - Three x 1 mile (1.5km) walks. (Includes warm-up and cool-down). Approx time: 25 mins.

Weeks 3 & 4 - Three x 1 mile (1.5km) walks. Approx time: 25 mins.

Weeks 5 & 6 – Three x 1¼ mile (2km) walks. Approx time: 30 mins.

Weeks 7 & 8 – Three to Four x 1½ mile (2.4km) walks. Approx time: 35 mins.

Week 9 – Three to Four x 1¾ mile (2.8km) walks. Approx time: 40 mins.

Week 10 – Three to Four x 2 miles (3.2km) walks. Approx time: 45 mins.

Note: it is essential when going through this 10-week beginner's programme that you aim to reduce the above times by walking faster as your fitness improves. However, regaining fitness will differ from one individual to another, so if you feel that you might be overdoing it, then ease up. Conversely, if your heart rate is not working to its optimum level then walk at a faster pace.

Step by Step – Intermediate Programme

We are now ready to start your intermediate programme. Bypass the beginner's programme if you are confident you can safely begin at the intermediate level.

As with the beginner's advice, aim to reduce your times by walking faster as your fitness improves. However, if you begin to feel physically distressed then listen to your body and ease up. But if your heart rate is not working to its optimum level then increase your pace.

After each walk try recording relevant data in your notebook such as time taken, average heart rate and so on. This will help you gauge improvements and make any adjustments, where necessary.

Week 1 – Three to Four x 1¼ mile (2km) walks each week. Approx time: 22 mins.

Weeks 2 & 3 – Three to Four x 1½ mile (2.4km) walks each week. Approx time: 28 mins.

Weeks 4 to 6 – Three to Four x 2mile (3.2km) walks each week. Approx time: 36 mins.

Weeks 7 to 9 – Three to Four x 2½ mile (4.4km) walks each week. Approx time: 45 mins.

Week 10 – Three to Four x 3mile (4.8km) walks each week. Approx time: 52 mins.

Step by Step – Advanced Programme

You now have the **8km/5miles** a day target well within your sights!

Weeks 1 to 3 – Three to Four x 3mile (4.8km) walks each week. Approx time: 50 mins.
Weeks 4 to 6 – Three to Four x 3½ mile (5.63km) walks each week. Approx time: 57 mins.
Weeks 7 to 9 – Three to Four x 4ms (6.43km) walks each week. Approx time: 65 mins.
Week 10 & 11 –Three to Four x 4½ mile (7.24km) walks each week. Approx time: 70 mins.
Week 12 – Three to Four x 5mile (8km) walks each week. Approx time: 75 mins.

You've done it!

Note: Most of the above schedules suggest the walks being done three to four times each week. I've given this as a guide, simply to give the walker some flexibility. However, it would be of additional benefit if you can aim to achieve four walks each week.

You will probably be fit enough now to complete this 8km/5 mile distance in around 1¼ hours, (depending upon terrain). That means, by doing this walk four times each week you will be dedicating a total of **five hours a week**. Now if we reckon that most of us have an average of 10 hours sleep in a 24-hour day then 14 hours of our day are spent awake. Multiply 7 days by 14 hours and we have **98 waking hours each week**. So using a mere five hours a week to maintain a fit and healthy lifestyle shouldn't be too much of a burden... should it?

Now that you've achieved the **8Km/5 mile** a day and are walking that distance three to four days a week, why not make it a lifelong commitment. I guarantee that if you combine this activity with a reasonable diet you will experience an enjoyable and satisfying lifestyle that can only come from being fitter and healthier.

If you have enjoyed reading 'The Big Walk' why not place a review on Amazon for me. It would be greatly appreciated.